Contents

NEW DIMENSIONS IN POPULAR CULTURE

EDITED BY

Russel B. Nye

Bowling Green University Popular Press
Bowling Green, Ohio 43403

The Bowling Green University Popular Press is the publishing arm
   of the Center for the Study of Popular Culture, Ray B.
   Brown, Director.

Library of Congress Catalog Card Number: 72-88412

ISBN: 0-87972-046-8 Clothbound
       0-87972-047-6 Paperback

Printed in the United States of America.

ART CREDIT: Cover design by Caroline Baker.

PREFACE

The essays which comprise this volume are products of an English graduate seminar in Literature and Popular Culture, given at Michigan State University. They are offered here not so much as models as examples of what may occur when the traditional techniques of literary study and analysis are applied, at this level, to popular culture materials. Collectively (as the students and their instructor hope) they may make modest contributions toward an increased knowledge of the popular arts, and serve to elicit interest in similar projects among students and instructors elsewhere. The gap that exists today between society and the academy is far too obvious and far too wide to need comment here; as others have suggested, the study of popular culture— seriously, with care and understanding—may assist in throwing one small bridge, at least, across it.[1]

This seminar, English 983, was not a specially-selected class, but was restricted only in size. Since all its students had completed one to three years of graduate work in English and American literature, they were familiar with the traditional bibliographical and methodological techniques required in graduate research. The topics chosen were (with a few exceptions) deliberately related in some way to literary or historical study, dealing with genre, trends, or media to which the student's training had some relevance. In addition, of

---

[1]See the introduction to *Popular Culture and Curricula*, edited by Ray B. Browne and Ronald J. Ambrosetti, Bowling Green Popular Press, 1970.

course, a student's choice of topic was determined by his own interests and by the availability of materials. Several topics which seemed feasible, it was found, had to be rejected because the necessary materials could not be readily obtained—for example, we had no good collection of early pulp magazines, tapes of radio dramas, or detective novels. But on the other hand, the students and the University Library turned up amazing amounts of popular materials hitherto unnoticed—collections of Sunday-school books, early woman-and-home magazines, a three-thousand volume Western collection, "fan" magazines, and the like. Library personnel furnished enthusiastic assistance and often purchased materials for the seminar's use. Since each student knew what the others were doing, they helped each other considerably, exchanging ideas, tips, and sources. One who found six novels in a secondhand store would tell a fellow-student who needed them; one who had magazines in his attic would save them for another. The seminar developed, rather quickly, into a cooperative venture.

Part of the interest in the course was generated by the students' search for their own materials, and their pursuit of elusive books, magazines, and other quarry. Persistence, resourcefulness, and vigilant attendance at antique sales, secondhand stores, and flea markets paid off. The majority of students, it turned out, supplied most of their own materials—one even spent his vacation in Kansas, working with a special collection. Most, to their surprise, found far more than they could use, and either reduced their plans or focused them more precisely. Each student gave his paper to the group as an oral report of about forty minutes, followed by discussion and questions, and submitted it in final written form at the conclusion of the seminar. While some of the finished papers, unfortunately, had to be cut for inclusion in this volume, editing has been kept to a minimum.

Another source of interest lay in the fact that the students felt the excitement of working with fresh and original materials, with no intervening tradition of scholarship. There was some initial trepidation at finding a minimum of secondary sources, and thus no place to start; however, this original anxiety soon gave way to relief. Since there were few or no books and articles to begin with, students immediately felt challenged by doing something no one else had done, or in a different way. A third source of student interest, and a quite unexpected one, came when it became apparent that the seminar was beginning to develop a pattern, that various papers interlocked. While neither the time nor the number of pages allotted allowed pursuit of many of the implications the papers suggested, the study of popular culture and popular literature took on an added dimension as trends and definitions began to appear in the discussions. As several students suggested, we now needed another seminar "to explore the meaning of what we had really done."

While it would be presumptuous to claim importance for this particular experimental foray into the uses of popular culture, two things emerged from the experience with great clarity. First, since six of the papers are now in the process of becoming doctoral dissertations, it appears that the study of popular culture opens up a whole new, fresh, and exciting field for exploration and exploitation. Some members of the seminar, after its conclusion, drew up a list of thirty possible dissertation topics, using only materials available at Michigan State University or from other easily-reached sources. Second, since all of the members of the seminar were involved in teaching either literature or history in one fashion of another, it is significant that all agreed that they had found, in the study of popular culture, not only new materials but new ways they might be used in their own classrooms. The study of popular literature and the popular arts helped us all, students and instructor alike, to add an extra dimension to our understanding of *all* literature and the arts; exploring popular culture helped to give depth to our comprehension of our total society and its broad, multi-levelled culture. Here, I think, the future of the study of popular culture lies. My overwhelming impression, after teaching this course, is that we have merely opened the door a crack. I think these students, and many others like them at other institutions, will push it open wide within the next decade.

Russel B. Nye
Michigan State University

MILLIONS OF MORAL LITTLE BOOKS: SUNDAY
SCHOOL BOOKS IN THEIR POPULAR CONTEXT

George A. Schneider

This paper is the result of a study of some of the didactic, moralistic literature so widely popular in nineteenth century America, and
also of speculation about the culture from which that literature seemed
so naturally to evolve. The attempt, then, is to describe some of the
roots of this now obscure literary phenomenon as well as to describe
that literature's main characteristics.

The era of early 1800's was innately receptive to the moralistic
literature published by the Sunday school movement. Innovations in
printing allowed church-sponsored printers to pour a veritable flood
of inexpensive or free religious tracts—little books with a moral—
through the spreading frontier and into the receptive hands of a growing population, one intent upon finding its democratic way to both
literacy and salvation for the soul. An example of such literature
which will serve to illustrate its nature is *The History of Little Henry
and His Bearer*, an undated (but early nineteenth century) story
published by the American Sunday School Union. Henry, the central
figure of the story, was born in India of English parents who died while
he was an infant, leaving him in care of a woman who adopted him,
and more importantly, in the care of a faithful Indian body servant.
Henry received little attention from his foster-mother; but he was
constantly watched over by the servant. When Henry was five years
old, a young English woman came to visit India and stayed at Henry's
house. She was shocked to learn that Henry could speak no English
and had never even heard of the Savior. She immediately undertook

to teach him English so that she might lead him along the road to salvation. In the year and a half, she not only succeeded but left Henry reading the Bible and intent upon converting his bearer, or servant. Little Henry died after a lingering illness at the age of eight, exacting on his deathbed a promise of conversion from his bearer as he expired.[1]

This story is characteristic in a number of ways. It is a copy of an English original, a practice especially common among American Sunday school publishers early in the century. The story reflects the importance of learning how to read, of learning to recognize sin, of understanding everlasting punishment, of converting others, and of winning salvation through one's *own* Bible reading.

Another example is the even shorter (16 pages) book, *The History of Joseph Nichols*, published by the American Tract Society. Little Joseph Nichols on his death bed prayed fervently, and

After this he was not afraid to die, but often talked of death with pleasure. . . . On the day before his death he was asked, 'Do you think you shall die?' He calmly answered, 'Yes, I shall soon die.' It was then said, 'But mamma will be sorry if you die.' 'Yes,' said he, 'and I love mamma dearly, but I love Jesus Christ better.'[2]

Again, this is characteristic of the literature in that most of the deaths described were of children who faced death with the calm assurance that they were going to eternal happiness because of their acceptance of Jesus Christ. It was rather a joy to die.

PART I. THE NINETEENTH CENTURY CONTEXT

Through the years, judgment of the flood of such moralistic, didactic literature seems to have been almost uniformly negative— when critics paid any attention to it at all. Critics, especially educators, seem to agree that it was harmful and "abnormally slanted to a materialistic, middle class cultural pattern."[3] Elitist consensus labels it as too Calvinistic and Puritanical; liberals accuse it of being politically conservative. It is only fair, however, in viewing it as popular literature, to place it within its context and to recognize its purpose. To do so reveals how these Sunday school stories coincided in a very practical manner with the needs of the times, with the successive waves of religious revivalism that swept the period, and with the innovations in publishing and distribution that brought an avalanche of moralistic literature to the eager hands of a large segment of the population.

The contemporary religious attitude was a direct outgrowth of the Great Awakening of the previous century, whose intense religious force continued through much of the nineteenth. Increasingly, the character of evangelistic preaching changed to reflect the less learned, the less scholarly. Frequently, a preacher's only prerequisite was that he "felt the call from the Lord" to preach. It was a conspicuous manifestation of the general move towards democratization, and these fervent "instruments of the Lord" who proliferated in number and preached in every village and every crossroad, fell into the pattern of preaching fire and brimstone (in lieu of scholarly sermons) and of threatening extravagant condemnation. One such exhorter is described in these terms by his son:

Religion was a misery to be endured on earth, that a reward might be enjoyed after death. It was a matter of thrift and self-interest as much as laying away money in youth and strength for old age and helplessness, and he called upon sinners to flee the wrath to come because he had been commanded to go out and preach to all the world. He preached as loudly as he sang, and with an equally good effect.[4]

This religious fervor was most vividly expressed in the nineteenth-century camp meeting, the ultimate of religious revivalism.

Before one can judge the popular moralistic reading matter of this period, he must consider the effect that such religious emotionalism had upon the average mind. Its impact upon attitudes towards education and learning must have been great. The call was for each sinner to read his Bible, do good works, be exemplary, pray and earn salvation. The whole emphasis was upon developing an ethical code, *not* an aesthetic code. If the literature of evangelism and of the Sunday School movement lacked aesthetic quality, it was because this was not important to either writer or reader; its aim was moral, ethical. It should be judged, then, in that context, in terms of its use and not its aesthetic.

The influence of religion through revivalism, especially upon the younger mind, must also have been tremendous. Here was a largely rural society caught up in the harsh realities of frontier life and death. Its most vivid expression was its drive for eternal salvation, and, in an era and an area constantly ravaged by sickness and epidemics, death was present and real to even the smallest child. One observer described how the population fared during the winter of 1831 in the Ohio River area:

Ague and malaria victims drank whisky, lacking other ameliorants of raging ills so debilitating that if one wintered so that he could in the spring pull a leek out of the ground without falling over backward he had wintered exceedingly well.

In 1832, that same observer spent time in Detroit, Michigan, "the point from which many thousands of immigrants were spreading out into the interior of Michigan. I saw the Asiatic cholera hit Detroit like a blast from a demon cloud, slaying, disintegrating and terrorizing."[5]

Thoroughly instructed as to the deep depravity of the human heart and the transitory nature of life, those who listened to the sermons must have been motivated to weigh frequently their chances for salvation. With such concerns looming large, it is understandable how one could frequently be plunged into the depths of despair when convinced of one's doom, or raised to the heights of elation at the prospect of being saved. We can only speculate about the thoughts that passed through the mind of one frequently reminded that he was nought but a miserable, despicable sinner.

To the earlier nineteenth century, the value of literacy was generally acknowledged, for salvation depended on reading and understanding the Bible. Nevertheless, particularly in remote and sparsely settled regions, it was possible for a young person to grow up without learning how to read. Faced with the prospect of an early death and constantly aware of the need for salvation, there was the desire for literacy but not always the schools—few enough on the frontier—to provide the means. The Sunday school's flood of moral little books furnished not only a chance for literacy but also for salvation.

The Sunday school movement, acting mainly as a charitable missionary movement, provided the means whereby enormous numbers were taught to read. And as one would expect, the reading material provided was moralistic, didactic, of a kind that exactly suited the evangelical temper of the times.

The Sunday school did not spring fullblown upon the American continent, but it had its genesis in England during the previous century when the Englishman Robert Raikes established, in 1780, a Sunday school to teach the poor how to read and write, (Sunday, of course, being the only day when the students were free from work). The movement became popular in England and then spread to America.

Filling a real need as it did, the movement rapidly accelerated. Several Sunday schools joined to form the interdenominational American Sunday-School Union in 1825. The books supplied by the Sunday school movement served to further tie education together with religion—if a closer tie were possible. One can especially appreciate to what degree the movement's literature would be religiously oriented when he considers how moralistic were the texts used in the few available non-sectarian public schools. The famous McGuffey's Readers' forthright aim was to teach moral lessons, and although not every selection had a moral, the earlier editions were mainly didactic. Henry H. Vail, one of the many editors, said that the books' objectives "are the proper and indispensable texts of teaching true patriotism, integrity, honesty, industry, temperance, courage, politeness and all other moral and intellectual virtues."[6]

Although free public education was far from common in the first half of the nineteenth century, that which was available often had a distinct religious orientation. Since such was the case, it is hardly surprising that those served by the Sunday school movement received a straightforward fare of moralistic religious literature. Since schools and education were originally the creation of churches, the general public expected education to be religious and undoubtedly would have been disappointed had it not been. Moral theme and didactic tone were an integral part of the educational environment of that century's citizen.

The moral tone of nineteenth-century children's books, reinforced by successive waves of evangelism, remained fairly constant, although the tone of popular literature lightened as the century proceeded. As fiction, both in cheap bindings and magazines, flooded the country, the religious community felt impelled to provide increasingly large amounts of moralistic stories to offset the bad influences of the other. The vast amount of Sunday school literature was also a reaction to the general decline in religious fervor that became apparent after the Revolution. But this ebb in religious feeling and instruction did not last long, for many "good Christians" were fired with the missionary spirit. The strong waves of revivalism influenced many religious groups to spread the gospel by forming publishing societies whose function it was to raise money for the publication of religious story books. These books, as printing technology advanced, were available at extremely low prices or were given away. In 1814, a cylinder press was perfected which could turn out over a thousand copies each hour. This printing revolution, combined with such innovations as stereotyping, and new ways of producing inexpensive paper, made it possible for new editions to run nearly endless numbers of copies.

There were many religious societies organized to spread the faith via the printed word. The popularity of their literature owed much to the efforts of generous individuals and zealous organizations who felt they were doing God's own work in spreading the gospel to the remotest regions. These religious societies and benefactors had precedents in England and Scotland, where organizations had long been active in sending missionaries and tracts to overseas colonies. In fact, even after England and America separated, English religious societies continued to spread the gospel in America via missionaries, donations and the printed word; as late as 1843, in fact, the American Sunday-School Union reported donations from English religious societies. In general, it was considered meritorious for the wealthy to buy edifying, instructive books and leaflets for distribution to the poor. Apparently, nearly all denominations were active, the Methodists being among the earliest in this country to become publishers and distributors of religious literature.

In 1809 one Rev. Thaddeus Osgood traveled three thousand miles, passing through seven states and parts of Canada. On this trip he collected over one thousand dollars, with which he printed nearly fifty thousand tracts, distributing them during the course of his travels the next year.[7]

The concern over the spiritual welfare of the frontier population was such that nearly every sizable community in New England and the Middle States formed an organization for collecting contributions for the publication and dissemination of moral literature. Apparently, the amount of money collected and the number of books and tracts purchased or published was a source of considerable pride, because records of many such groups survive.

The proliferation, competition, cooperation, and consolidations that occurred among religious publishers would make a study in itself. Briefly, however, the great interest in such publication and distribution created much duplication of effort. Seeing wasteful duplication, religious publishers soon merged to form larger, more efficient operations. Apparently, minor differences in theology were considered less important than areas of agreement which allowed different sects to sponsor many of the same moral tracts and books. A representative example of merger occurred in 1825 when the New England Tract Society merged with the New York Religious Tract Society and forty smaller publishers and distributors. This conglomerate became the American Tract Society and dedicated itself to "the promotion of vital Godliness and sound morality" by the circulation of religious tracts.[8]

To suggest the potential of this single merger, it is instructive to look at the activity of one of the forty-two just prior to its merger. In 1824, the year before the merger, one society owned 400 engravings for ornamenting books, 1,018 stereotyped pages, sixty-nine published books, and several others in the press. Since all of this was brought to the merger by only one of the group, it can be speculated that in aggregate the merger of all forty-two must have produced a potent force in the publishing field of religious literature. In fact, the combined companies published nearly 250,000 little books during the second year after the merger; by 1849, the total was just over one million volumes a year.[9]

Another such merger of church publishing societies occurred in 1825, when the American Sunday-School Union was formed. Fourteen years after its inception, the Union claimed to have 18,000,000 copies of its moral publications in circulation.[10]

But because of theological differences, many churches did not join in with the American Tract Society and the American Sunday-School Union. Many preferred to conduct their own publishing enterprises, such as The Methodist Book Concern, The American Baptist Publication Society, The Methodist-Episcopal Church Publications, The Massachusetts Sabbath School Society. Some of these, although smaller than the American Sunday-School Union, were nevertheless very active; The Massachusetts Sabbath School Society offered 986 separate titles in 1850.[11] The demand for such didactic literature was so great that a considerable number of commercial publishers, not affiliated with any church, were soon attracted to the field. By 1850 nearly every publisher offered some titles for the Sunday school trade, and although the total amount of such literature is impossible to estimate, it must have been staggering. Of course, this domestic output was supplemented, particularly during the first half of the century, by religious books sent from England. Since nearly everyone agreed that such literature was "good for people," it was eagerly distributed by missionaries, volunteer help, and evangelists from regional depositories that were set up throughout the country. The American Sunday-School Union, for example, as early as 1826, had 720 schools and societies in seventeen states with 55,000 members. This same enthusiasm seems to have prevailed among the many other church organizations as well.

To execute the program of religious education on a nationwide scale, missionaries, chapters and branches of Sunday school societies appeared in every state and territory. In 1830, the Union "resolved to establish a Sunday school in every neighborhood in the western states that was without one"; then, in 1833, "It adopted a similar resolution with respect to the southern states." To this end, the Union employed "about 350 missionaries to traverse the country and to revitalize decaying Sunday schools or to establish new ones."[12]

During the course of the century, most denominations formed their own Sunday school societies, many of them publishing a large body of moral literature or buying it from the others. The earliest of these schools were regarded by their sponsors "not as a church institution but as a philanthropic effort to improve the moral condition of the ignorant and neglected classes outside the church."[13] Such being the case, lay teachers and organizers became the principal moving force behind the Sunday schools.

Such Godly Work was carried by the little moral books and their teachers into the remotest of frontier villages by dozens of dedicated missionaries. One, who must have been an edifying example to many others, was Stephen Paxon, who was reported to have traveled over 100,000 miles on horseback, and during a period of twenty years to have organized and supplied with moral books 1,314 Sunday schools.[14] As late as 1863, in Detroit, Michigan, there were more students enrolled in Sunday schools than in public schools. Since free public education was not available statewide until 1870, the Sunday schools provided the only source of education and libraries for untold numbers living in a largely rural society.

PART II. THE LITERATURE

The flood of moralistic little books that were so widely distributed throughout the century reflects very accurately the customs, beliefs, prejudices, and attitudes of the times. Unfortunately it is impossible to reproduce adequately in a brief paper the real soul of these books and the message imparted even by their appearance. Prefaces, quotations, and titles, while quaint and informative, do not really carry the scent of old ink, the feel of faded leaves and grotesque illustrations, the curious gilt bindings. Nor can one reproduce the touching inscriptions and crude sketches made long ago by childish hands on flyleaves and margins.

The books came in a variety of sizes and lengths. There were tiny books of only eight pages, and larger books of well over a hundred pages bound in hard, ornate covers. Most were small books, especially those for the younger children. The goal seemed to be to produce as many books as inexpensively as possible in order to make them readily available for easy transportation and wide distribution throughout the frontier.

Subject matter, like the books' size and length, varied considerably. As most of the books tended to be small for practical reasons, so did most of their content tend to be didactic. After all, the books were produced in vast quantities for primarily one purpose: to propagate Christian faith, and all that such faith implied.

The subject matter of these books included hymns, sermons, biographies, poetry, travel, nature, Indian captivities, and scriptural stories. Since all such subject matter was designed to propagate the faith, certain themes appeared and reappeared in them. Among the most prominent were those dealing with how one should behave, how one should obey authority, how one might win salvation, and especially, how one should prepare for death.

The literature, like the age, had a no-nonsense attitude. The books confined themselves mainly to tales of exact literal truth. The following preface suggests this:

Such a creature as Jack Frost never existed, any more than old Santaclaw of whom so often little children hear such foolish stories; and once a year they are encouraged to hang their stockings in the chimney at night, and when they arise in the morning, they find in them cakes, nuts, money, etc., placed there by some of the family, which they are told Old Santaclaw has come down the chimney and put in. Thus little innocents are imposed on by those who are older than they, and improper ideas take possession which are not by any means profitable.[15]

Such sobriety seemed to permeate nearly all of this tremendously large body of literature. One common manifestation was the ghoulish advice often given to little children to learn about the uncertainty of life by visiting a graveyard at twilight, there to read what "the grey mouldering stone tells of the mouldering dead." One little book of rhymes suggested that

> You are not so healthy and gay
> So young, so active, and bright,
> That death cannot snatch you away,
> Or some dreadful accident smite.
>
> Here lie both the young and the old,
> Confined in the coffin so small,
> The earth covers over them cold,
> The grave-worms devour them all.[16]

In a characteristic 16-page book entitled *The Orphan*, the story opens with the little girl singing four stanzas of a hymn lamenting an orphan's woes. It ends

> I've not a secret care of pain,
> But He that secret knows;
> Thou, Father of the fatherless,
> Pity an orphan's woes.

There is an accompanying crude woodcut print of a burying ground showing the Orphan leaning dejectedly upon a gravestone.

Although there was, by 1800, a gradual relaxation of rigid Calvinist standards, we cannot assume that the new "live and let live" spirit immediately replaced the old prescriptive moralism. Far from it. Any "lowering of religious standards" was vigorously resisted, and the religious publishing societies battled against the tide of growing un-Godliness by supplying what seems to have been a literal avalanche of moral books. Perhaps some more brief descriptions of representative examples will serve to illustrate the general moral, edifying tone.

On the theme of proper behavior, this poem describes the swift and awful punishment meted out to a youngster who committed the crime of cruelty to animals while fishing in his father's pond.[17]

> Many a little fish he caught,
> And pleased was he to look,
> To see them writhe in agony,
> And struggle on the hook.
>
> At last when having caught enough,
> And also tired himself,
> He hastened home intending there
> To put them on the shelf.
>
> But as he jumped to reach a dish,
> To put his fishes in,
> A large meat hook, that hung close by
> Did catch him by the chin.
>
> Poor Harry kicked and call'd aloud,
> And screamed and cried and roard,
> While from his wounds the crimson blood
> In dreadful torrents poured.

The books showed clearly that children had a sacred obligation to submit to the authority of their parents or guardians, to be humble, submissive, and obedient at all times. Reflecting the economic insecurities of the times, the books taught that besides obeying parental orders, a son or daughter was morally obligated to maintain the parent in old age and infirmity. The warnings were very explicit. For example, one of the books contained this hymn for students to learn:[18]

> Have we not heard what dreadful plagues
> Are threatened by the Lord,
> To him that breaks his Father's law
> Or mocks his Mother's word?
>
> What heavy guilt upon him lies!
> How cursed is his name!
> The ravens shall pick out his eyes,
> And Eagles eat the same.

In general, the books taught children that disobedience, lying, cruelty, and stealing were forbidden by a "Power" that was not to be challenged. For example, one told the sad experiences of "Little Fanny," whose criminal career began after she was denied permission to stroll in the park in order to show off her new finery. She violated her parents' wishes by stealing out with her nurse, was kidnapped from her wicked maid for the sake of her fine clothes, became a "dirty beggar," and "dwelth with vice which doubled all her pain." Eventually she became a street vendor selling fish. The girl kept the thought of her home and parents constantly in mind. The young Sunday school scholars must have been amazed to learn that all this time "her mother's watchful eye followed her close" but that out of "prudence withheld maternal love" until a longer trial had proved Fanny's virtue. After sufficient suffering, Fanny was rescued, and the reader is assured that Fanny was no longer idle, vain, or opinionated, but pious, obedient, and modest.[19]

Some voiced doubts about the effects of such harshly moral stories. But even while voicing doubts, one critic felt compelled to remark cautiously:[20]

Many of them died very young, (not that they died the sooner because they were good; but being good, they were sooner fit to die); now, you yourself may die young too, therefore pray earnestly to the Lord, for the pardon of all your sins, and beg for grace to make you fit to live, and then you will be fit to die.

The truth is that the mortality rate was such that moral scare stories had more than a little relevance to their readers.

That nineteenth century life on the American frontier was real, earnest, and dangerous made for a certain serious sternness in family life. The Sunday school literature reflected and reinforced this quality, summarized in the advice given by a father to his son: "I do not recommend upon all occasions a solemn countenance. A man may smile, but if he would be thought a man of sense, he would by no means laugh."[21] To maintain an appropriate gravity, young readers were advised to strike a happy medium: "Let thy Countenance be moderately cheerful, neither Laughing nor Frowning. Laugh not aloud, but silently smile upon occasion."[22]

Until well into the century, the grim struggle for existence on the frontier gave most of the population little time or inclination to indulge in frivolities. The seemingly common attitude of disapproval is expressed in more than one of the many little books. For example, early in the century, one of the small volumes contained this warning for young and old alike:[23]

Unless care and labor are taken to keep down the evil propensities of little children to anger, idleness, and too much play, they will grow up in evil habits; and instead of being useful members of society they will be pests and burdens; will drag out an unprofitable existence here, and must expect in the coming world, that their lot will be among the miserable.

Although the concept of innate depravity received less attention than it must have in the Colonial era, there apparently remained a strong residue of such sentiment. It was not uncommon for the little moral books to include stories such as *The Memoirs of James M'Corkle*, in which a 6 year old boy is portrayed thinking thoughts such as:[24]

. . . he often said that his heart was wicked, that he was sorry he had been so wicked, that he often prayed to God to take away his wicked heart and give him a good heart.

Some books taught that "we are all sinners"; some dealt with various aspects of good behavior, obeying parents and employers, being kind to animals, avoiding unseemly levity, observing the Sabbath, or doing kind deeds for one's fellow man. But perhaps the most prominent theme was the theme of death, of the transience of life. The frequency of this theme bulks large in Sunday school literature, just as the high mortality rate bulked large in the experience of every nineteenth century family:[25]

Child
> Tell me, Mamma, if I must die,
> One day as little baby died,
> And look so very pale and lie
> Down in the pit-hole by its side.

Mamma
> Tis true, my love, that you must die,
> The God who made you says you must
> And every one of us shall lie,
> Like the dear baby in the dust.

> These hands and feet and busy head,
> Shall waste and crumble quite away;

But though your body shall be dead,
There is a part which can't decay.

CONCLUSION

From the Calvinism of the colonial era and the Great Awakening of the eighteenth century, and from the waves of religous enthu-
siasms that swept the early nineteenth, came the forces which helped
to prepare the audience for the millions of moral little religious books
that flooded the period. The shaping forces were many. In brief,
they consisted of the traditionally close relationship between church
and education; the rapid shift of a growing population into a vast
frontier; the government's inability to provide education for minimal
literacy during the period of rapid expansion; the stern, harsh reality
of frontier life; the decline of Puritan-Calvinist religious fervor; the
rise of democratic sentiment as related to government and to religion;
the high mortality rate; the successive religious revivals that swept the
country during much of the nineteenth century; the increased importance placed upon independent Bible study and salvation (literacy
being the necessary prerequisite); and, finally, the response of the
churches to the challenges of the era by their vast publishing effort.
It was this effort, made possible by the new technology of mass publishing and distribution, that put these books into so many receptive
hands. The century needed Christianity, it believed, and it needed
literacy to comprehend the Bible and its message of salvation. The
flood of moral little books with their homely precepts and their
purposeful little stories helped to fill the era's basic need for stability
and continuity.

NOTES

[1]American Sunday-School Union, *The History of Little Henry and His
Bearer* (Philadelphia, n.d.).

[2]American Tract Society, *The History of Joseph Nichols* (New York,
n.d.), p. 15.

[3]"Readers Brought Back—Morals Intact," *The New York Times*, April 21,
1963, p. 56.

[4]E. W. Howe, "The Hell Question and Rev. John Westlock," *The American Identity* (Boston: D. C. Heath and Company, 1966), p. 706.

[5]F. N. Kerwin, "Rise and Fall of Michigan's Marvelous Medicine Man,"
Wonderland Magazine, 35:5, October 12, 1969.

6"Readers Brought Back—Morals Intact," *The New York Times*, April 21, 1963, p. 56.

7Cumming, *op. cit.*, pp. 50, 51, 52.

8American Tract Society, *Of Man and Money* (New York, n.d.), p. 20.

9Cumming, *op. cit.*, p. 60.

10*Ibid.*, p. 68.

11*Ibid.*, p. 70.

12Kiefer, *op. cit.*, p. 61.

13E. W. Rice, *The Sunday-School Movement and the American Sunday-School Union* (Philadelphia: ASSU, 1917), pp. 48-9.

14*Ibid.*, p. 237.

15Anonymous, *False Stories Corrected* (n.p., n.d.).

16Kiefer, *op. cit.*, p. 21.

17Kiefer, *op. cit.*, p. 22.

18J. G. Curtis, "Saving the Infant Class," *Scribner's Magazine*, November 19, 1929, p. 65.

19American Tract Society, *The History of Little Fanny* (New York, n.d.).

20G. Burder, *Early Piety or Memoirs of Children Eminently Serious, Interspersed with Familiar Dialogues, Prayers, Graces, and Hymns* (Baltimore, 1821).

21L. Hollowell, *A Book of Children's Literature* (New York: Farrar and Rinehart, Inc., 1939), p. 317.

22*Ibid.*, p. 319.

23Kiefer, *op. cit.*, p. 191.

24Cumming, *op. cit.*, p. 117.

25A. Taylor, *Hymns for Infant Minds* (New burgh, 1820).

NINETEENTH CENTURY GIFT BOOKS: A CURIOUS COMBINATION OF POPULAR AND ELITE ART

Llewellyn E. Foll

Gift books, or literary annuals as they were more often called, were one of the primary outlets for popular literature and popular art in nineteenth-century America. As such they provide one of the best records of the taste and ideas of the rapidly maturing new nation in the thirty-five years preceding the Civil War. At the same time, this popular art form also served as an essential medium for the promotion and development of elite American literature and art. Nineteenth-century American gift books are thus a curious combination of popular and elite art.

I

Definition and Description.
The definitional boundaries are vague, but lines must be drawn somewhere for the sake of bibliographic classification. The following six characteristics are typical of all gift books and by using these one can recognize a gift book at a glance. (1) Miscellaneous literary content: The letterpress of gift books is made up of a collection of poems, short stories, and essays, heavily sentimental and moral in nature, by a variety of authors. The key idea here is the miscellaneous nature. (2) Engravings: There are usually between five and twenty-four steel engravings scattered throughout the gift book, again by a variety of artists and engravers. (3) Titlepage and presentation plate: Most annuals contain an engraved or illuminated (colored) presentation plate with suitable places in the design for the giver's and the receiver's name and/or a titlepage with the title

16

of the book worked into an engraved or illuminated design. (4) Elaborate bindings: Gift books are usually fully bound in morocco, embossed with an elaborate, eccentric design, and stamped with gilt. (5) Sentimental titles: Titles generally contain the names of flowers and plants, for example, *The Violet, The Lily of the Valley, The Rose of Sharon, The Magnolia,* and *The Laurel Wreath*; or gems, for example, *The Pearl, The Talisman,* and *The Opal.* The subtitle usually explains the function of the book: "A Gift of Friendship for All Seasons" or "A Token of Affection for the Holidays." But somewhere the title invariably uses the word *gift* or one of its synonyms: souvenir, offering, memorial, keepsake, token, or present. A date is also a conspicuous part of the title: *The Magnolia for 1837* or more impressively *The Talisman for MDCCCXXVIII.* (6) Gilt-edged pages: This is a minor characteristic, but typical of nearly every gift book.

The terms "gift book" and "literary annual" are synonymous, the former being more popular now and the latter being the usual nineteenth-century expression. The two terms taken together pretty well sum up the phenomenon they describe: a book designed to be given as a gift which is primarily a collection of literature issued annually.

The above definition excludes three types of books that are often confused with gift books. The first is the glorified, finely decorated edition of a particular author's works, suitable for giving as gifts; however, these cannot be classified as gift books, as we are using the term, but simply another edition of an author's work. A second is magazines bound as gift books. Since some magazines imitated the gift book style and format, the publisher at the end of the year collected extra issues and issued them as gift books, often under a new title. But since these were originally issued as something else, we do not classify them as gift books. A third type of book often confused with literary annuals is the collection of engravings and prints, often accompanied with suitable letterpress, which were essentially art books rather than literary annuals.

II

Publishing History.
American gift books are only part of a world-wide phenomenon. During the nineteenth century literary annuals were published in England, France, Germany, India, Australia, Canada, and even Latin America.

However, the American type is distinctly different in its conception and development.

Gift books were the offspring of almanacs, which were issued annually and contained information such as weather forecasts and calendars. The basic almanac was altered in Europe in the eighteenth century when it was used to bring together each year the best prose and verse available. The first of these European literary almanacs was the *Almanach des muses*, begun in Paris in 1765. Five years later the Germans adopted the idea and improved on it with their *Musenalmanach*.

Meanwhile in England, and consequently in imitative America, the almanac was undergoing a somewhat different type of change which resulted in "pocket books" for ladies and gentlemen. These small books, which could literally fit into pocket or purse, contained the usual almanac information, "enlivened with riddles, small verses, etc."[1] The literary content increased every year, until they came to resemble the European literary almanacs. Then in 1822 the publishing house of Rudolph Ackerman, a producer of fine, illustrated books, issued an elegant, nicely bound pocket book called *Forget Me Not*, designed to be given as a gift. Thus two essential elements—engravings and impressive packaging—were added to the annual literary almanac to create that distinctive specie of literature, the gift book.

The change was sudden, but the idea soon caught on. A critic for the *North American Review* described the transition this way:

But suddenly by a change . . . indicative of the progress of society . . . the simple sententious, and prophetic almanack became metamorphosed into the ornamental, narrative and reminiscent *Forget Me Not, Memorial, Souvernir, Amulet, Token,* and *Talisman.*[2]

This "change . . . indicative of the progress of society" refers to the increasing role of women in the production and purchase of popular books. From the time of its conception, this unique type of literature was devoted almost entirely to the newly emerging woman, the Genteel Female.[3] Ralph Thompson, the first and foremost authority on gift books, says: "The evolution of the almanac into a decorative literary periodical was the result of an increasing regard for feminine taste."[4]

The enterprising Philadelphia publishing house of Carey & Lea soon made arrangements to become the American agents for the

English *Forget Me Not* of 1824. Henry Carey was impressed by the large American demand for the English gift books and quickly saw the opportunity for an American annual. As the publishers' historian, David Kaser, says, Carey "was convinced that an American annual, comprised entirely of new works written by Americans, illustrated by Americans, and published by Americans, would find an even greater public in this country than the *Forget Me Not* had found."[5]

Carey & Lea immediately requested leading authors to submit material, placing advertisements in newspapers to attract new talent. From a trip to England, Henry Carey brought back paintings by his brother-in-law, Charles Robert Leslie, suitable for engraving. Then he hired a young University of Pennsylvania graduate, Henry Gilpin, to edit the material and oversee the preparation of a gift book resembling the popular English annuals. The result was America's first literary annual, *The Atlantic Souvenir*, which appeared on 6 December 1825, just in time for the holiday season. The 2000 copies of this edition were sold almost immediately and the publishers, collecting nearly twenty-two per cent profit over costs, immediately began planning another volume for the coming year.

Carey and Lea's success showed that conditions for gift books were perfect in America. First of all, recent technical innovations in the printing industry meant that better looking books could be produced at lower costs, with steam-powered presses, stereotyping, and the new composing or type setting machine. In 1810 the process of steel engraving was introduced for the purpose of making bank notes. About 1822, with the arrival of a softer steel, publishers started using engravings for book illustration because it was easier to work on steel and because many more impressions could be taken from a steel plate than from copper plates.[6]

Coinciding with these publishing improvements were cultural conditions which all but demanded the type of aesthetic satisfaction yielded by gift books. More people than ever before were able to read and were reading—newspaper circulation nearly doubled in the fifteen years before the gift books appeared. But people wanted more than newspapers to read; therefore, they were turning to novels and poetry. Gift books with their miscellaneous literary content found a ready audience. In addition, the increasing affluence of the middle classes meant that there was more time and money to be spent on the pursuit of literature. Interest in art and letters had traditionally been associated with wealth and high social position; therefore, the newly rich middle classes were highly interested in literary and artistic productions which they hoped would bring them the culture they thought necessary for higher status. One authority of the period describes it as a "new spirit" at work in middle-class America: "A new prosperity was feeding aspirations for what was popularly called culture, a notion vaguely associated with the printed page. Books accordingly acquired a new importance in the life of the average American."[6] Gift books, with their low level of aesthetic sophistication, "were books ideally suited to an aspiring middle class. They appealed to the eye and the heart rather than to the mind; they were handsome and costly; they were 'artistic' and 'refined.' "[7] In short, they met the demand for culture in the young country.

With favorable cultural and technological conditions, the American version of the gift book was immediately and immensely popular. Within three years as many as thirteen literary annuals were being published. The phenomenon reached its peak between 1846 and 1852, when over thirty annuals a year were being published, then declined sharply thereafter. Gift books have a clearly defined time span: they lasted from 1825 when the first one was published to 1861 when they had all but vanished. This thirty-six year period can be roughly divided into two different phases: the first from 1825 to 1845 when the literary annual was taken seriously as a literary and artistic product; and the second, from 1846 until the Civil War, when gift book became fads and objects for display.

That a decline took place can easily be seen in the reviews of the gift books. Until the mid-1840's they were reviewed regularly, and seriously, in the important American periodicals. The *North American Review*, for example, contained over a dozen notices of annuals between 1826 and 1841, while *The Knickerbocker* regularly gave space to the annuals until 1846. From the first the critics were fair in their judgments, admitting that the literary content was barely respectable, regretting that American authors had to rely on "the magic of a beautiful edition" in order to be read. On the other hand, they respected the annuals as an attempt to establish a truly American literarure, and expressed high hopes that they would improve the cultural condition of the country.[8] As one critic said, "It is chiefly on account of our desire to see the improvement of art and taste among us, that we hope the publishers of the Souvenir, and of all

similar works, may always receive ample remuneration from the
public. . . ."[9] When the early reviews are compared to those found
in the magazines after 1845, it is apparent that deterioration has set
in. John Sartain, the most popular gift book engraver and also an
editor of an annual himself summed it up in 1849:[10]

The popularity of the first annuals brought into the market such a host of competi-
tors that the business was soon overdone. The number of annuals increased almost
ad infinitum on both sides of the Atlantic, and their quality deteriorated in the
same ratio, until at length they became a mere laughing stock.

By 1852, most critics would have agreed with the reviewer for the
Southern Quarterly Review who, after commenting on their gaudy
appearance, wrote:[11]

These books of beauty are not properly subjects *for* justice. Offenders they may
be, as a butterfly is a trespasser sometimes, and swims in the parlour, when he should
be sipping in the fields, But who breaks the butterflies over the wheel? Critics though
we claim to be, far be all such cruelty from us.

What had originally been a serious attempt to satisfy the popular appetite
for culture had degenerated into a more status symbol, which ladies displayed on their centre-tables as a sign of their taste for literature.
    All the gift books of any literary importance were published during
the early years of their popularity. Carey & Lea's *Atlantic Souvenir* was
published until 1832, when it was bought out by Samuel Goodrich of
Boston. *The Souvenir* established the pattern among the early gift books
of seeking out the very best the country had to offer in literature and
art. In 1828, two years after the first *Souvenir*, S. G. Goodrich of Boston
started *The Token*, which added the name *Atlantic Souvenir* to its title
in 1833, running until 1842. Its literary content is generally more respectable than the average annual because of the twenty-seven short stories by
Hawthorne which Goodrich published, and because of poetry by such
popular poets as Hannah F. Gould, Grenville Mellen, Lydia Sigourney,
and editor Samuel Goodrich, as well as poets of established reputation,
such as Holmes, Longfellow and Lowell.
    Probably the best of the gift books was *The Talisman*, published
in New York City from 1828 to 1830, largely the work of three talented
men: William Cullen Bryant, Robert C. Sands, a popular New York wit,
and Gulian C. Verplanck, the literate Congressman from New York City.
The letterpress of the three volumes has a unity unique among gift books

because all the work is supposedly by "Francis Herbert" who is personally involved, along with his friend De Viellecour, in almost every story. Furthermore, since each story or sketch usually leads into another, the volumes resembled a loosely constructed novel. Bryant, Sands, and Verplanck belonged to an artistic coterie, The Sketch Club, which included some of the country's best artists and engravers. Many of these gladly contributed to *The Talisman*, among them painters like John Inman, Robert Weir, Thomas Cole, and S.F.B. Morse, and engravers like A. B. Durand, G. W. Hatch, and Peter Maverick. The intellectual flavor of *The Talisman* was unique; sentimentality was kept to a minimum and good humor and wit, rare things in gift books, pervaded the entire production. A gentle but obvious masculinity, which often satirized women and things sacred to them, made *The Talisman* atypical among gift books.

The last annual to have any real literary importance was *The Gift*, published in Philadelphia from 1836 to 1845. It was here that Edgar Allan Poe published five tales, including "The Pit and the Pendulum" and "The Purloined Letter." *The Gift* also contained some of the finest work by William Gilmore Simms and the popular local color stories of life in Michigan by Caroline Kirkland. Other well-known contributors included Harriet Beecher Stowe, C. P. Cranch, William E. Channing, Jr., Longfellow, Lowell, and Emerson.

The end of *The Gift* in 1845 seemed to mark the end of the period in which gift books were taken seriously; later gift books seemed obviously meant more to be seen than read. Many were spurious—that is, an original literary annual reissued as a new book under a different title. This practice picked up in the 1840's until in 1845 more than half of the annuals published were such spurious reissues. The *Magnolia* for 1836, for example, appeared later under more than half a dozen different titles. Some publishers openly pirated material from other books or magazines while others bought old type and engraving plates, shuffled the contents, and issued the result as a "new" book. Carelessness in reorganizing the contents or in "borrowings" resulted in some ludicrous mistakes. W. S. Hunt tells how in one annual:[12]

devoted to a fraternal organization, a man leaning on another is the subject of a picture entitled "A Brother!" In the same year the editor of a temperance annual apparently was unaware that this engraving already had been spoken for and, with an eye to his cause, used it with the title, "The Inebriate!"

A second characteristic of the later gift books is specialization. The primarily belletristic interest of the earlier annuals was displaced by the desire to use them as a tool to promote a specific cause or memoralize a particular event. The anti-slavery movement, for example, published at least seven different gift books, the most important being *The Liberty Bell*, published from 1840 to 1858 by the Boston Anti-slavery Fair to raise money and spread the message of abolitionism. The temperance movement had at least three different annuals, while political parties issued gift books like *The Wide-Awake Gift and Know-Nothing Token* (1855) edited by "One of 'em." Lodges published annuals, such as the *Odd Fellow's Offering*, while *The Judson Offering* celebrated the return of a famous missionary to America in 1846, and there were books for specific domestic occasions, such as mourning or marriage. A host of religious annuals were issued in the forties, and there were also gift books for children which occasionally contained some respectable children's literature but were more often didactic Sunday school lessons.

The decline of the gift book began in 1852, when the number of titles dropped from the previous year's thirty to nineteen. By 1855 there were only nine titles being published and by 1861 the phenomenon had died out. The fad had worn itself out, but it had lasted for over thirty years. There are three basic reasons for the decline of the gift books.[13] First, and probably foremost, was the competition from the lady's magazines, which offered all the literary matter of gift books plus fashions and gossip, and which appeared monthly rather than annually. It is ironic that the gift book, which had prepared the way for the lady's magazines by educating women's tastes, was eventually to be overcome by them. Secondly, since people seldom bought gift books to read, when they did want to read they turned to cheaper publications, such as the literary weeklies which published whole novels in serial-newspaper form, the cheap, 50¢ books published in cloth, or dime novels. Thirdly, the tastes of the people were changing; readers were satiated with the fantasy world of gift book fiction, with the sentimentality of its verse; the urgent, bitter questions of the day—slavery, labor, violently partisan politics—demanded some other vehicle.

During the thirty-six years that gift books were in vogue, between 850 and 1000 annuals were published. Of these, only about 465 were original; in other words, nearly half of the total number were spurious reissues.[14] Most of the series lasted one or two years; only thirty-six titles published three or more issues. The average edition was probably about 5000 copies and the largest editions about 10,000; at the height of the fad there were at most only 150,000 issued in a year. Prices ranged anywhere from 37¢ for a cheap production to over $20 for the most magnificent folios; however, prices generally stayed between $2.50 and $4.50, which explains why great quantities were not sold—the lower class simply could not afford them. Geographically, gift books were chiefly confined to New England and the mid-Atlantic states; the West was too busy settling the frontier to be interested in something as impractical as gift books, although a fine annual was produced in Cincinnati in 1829, *The Western Souvenir.*

III

Literary Content.

Gift book literature defies description and analysis because of its great variety, the wide range of authors, and the variety of forms and subjects. The literary content was overwhelmingly moral and polite. The following excerpts from the prefatory poem to *The Rose of Sharon* for 1851 are not only typical of the poor quality of gift book poetry but are also characteristic of the moral claims made for the literary content of most annuals:

> Fear not to place it on your guileless bosoms
> And call't your own! . . .
>
> Each modest petal will some lesson teach you,
> If rightly read,
> And balmy odors, that will softly reach you,
> Be from them shed.
>
> Take then the Rose by gentle hearts and lowly
> Long years caressed,
> And may it wake but visions bright and holy
> Within your breast.

In the stories, the author commonly intrudes to point out the intended lesson to be learned, and poems usually end by explicitly stating the moral. Virtue is always rewarded and religion brings peace of mind; hard work, honesty, humility, and good manners are the keys to success.

In other words, the puritan-flavored Protestant ethic is constantly reaffirmed in gift book literature.

The somber tone which pervades much of the writing corresponds to this moral emphasis. Humor and comedy are rare in gift books, the notable exceptions being the *American Comic Annual* (1831). Sentimentality was another obvious feature of the gift book, whose writers seemed to believe that Truth is best perceived through tears. One gift book editor put it this way:[15]

That literature is most prized and longest remembered which appeals to the heart—which touches the feelings. No skill of art, no polish of expression, no rhetorical ornament, or sweetness of numbers, can make that lasting impression on us which is made by a single touch of genuine feeling.

The gift book reader wanted emotion that he could easily grasp and understand, rather than ideas or intellectual complexity. An anonymous writer for the *Athenaeum* magazine (1844) explained:

Reading with us is our pleasure, our relief, and we must have such literature as will afford us this relief with a pleasurable excitement, without any great expense of thought. We prefer, indeed, to cry rather than to think, and fancy it does us more good after our hard day's work. We are not ashamed of doing so.

An emotional experience "without any great expense of thought" is exactly the literary fare offered by the gift books. Gift book poetry, for the most part, was turned out by amateurs who emphasized conventionality rather than originality, for the nature of their audience made experimentation risky—as Robert Sands said of their similes, "None of them are new, or strage, or rare,"[16] terms that applied equally well to subject matter and prosody. This conformity was characteristic for gift books were meant to reassure, to conventionalize emotion and reinforce it. Writing poetry to match the book's illustrations, too, generally resulted in nothing more than mechanical, uninspired riming.

The most popular themes of gift book poetry were naturally those with the most emotional appeal: love and death, Nature and Country (nationalism). Since gift books were intended mainly as "tokens of affection" it is not surprising that many of the poems deal with love—the lover wasting away because his love ignores him; the lover inspired by love to solve any problem and overcome every obstacle; the importance of marriage and love to true happiness.

Death poems were popular not only because of the emotion-laden subject matter, but also because death was an ever-present fact of life in the early nineteenth century, when only about six percent of the country's population could expect to reach the age of sixty. The purpose of the majority of poems is consolation, and acceptance of fate, reassurance of the immortality of the soul, often accompanied by the reminder that the lost loved one is probably happier and better off out of this world. The mutability theme, or the grave as equalizer, is common element in these death poems.

Nature, as scenery and as a moral lesson, was another popular subject for gift book poetry. Many poems were built around the seasons of the year symbolizing periods of life: spring representing innocent childhood; summer, maturity; autumn, old age; and winter, death. The favorite season for poems, autumn, represented an opportunity to look backward to past happiness compared with the unhappy present, with the chance to look forward to death. Nationalism was a strong element in gift book poetry, with much emphasis on American history. The idea of America as the new Eden was popular:[17]

> Thanks be to God that our fair forest Land
> Was kept as in the hollow of His hand,
> Till, in the fulness of his gracious plan,
> The Pilgrim came—best type of Christian man!

The Romantic debate between city and country life, and the theme of happiness depending not on wealth but the simpler pleasures of life were common themes. As the poet of "Stanzas" in *The Talisman* for 1828 said: "Riches we ask not, nor on fortune call,/Save for our wealth of flowers, and chaplets gay" (p. 27).

The themes popular in the poetry were also popular in gift book fiction, which was generally much better than the poetry. One favorite subject was settlers versus Indians; the revolutions in Greece and Poland were also popular; so were tales of knights and their ladies, or of noble heroes in some exotic foreign country or incognito in our own.

Gift book fiction was made up not so much of short stories as it was of condensed novels and romantic tales. The short story as a separate distinct genre of literature had not yet fully developed; however, the requirements of brevity laid down by gift book editors helped to evolve the form. The language of the stories is ornate and flamboyant; for example, a girl running is described as "bounding over the frosty field with the fleetness of a frightened fawn." Dialogue is often ridiculously wooden, characterization generally weak, stock figures and stereotypes predominate, most of the stories are full of accident and chance. Gift book authors consistently tried to use American incidents, American locale, and American characters. Thompson has calculated that seventy percent of the stories have an American setting; however, the action in many instances, could have happened anywhere.

There was virtually no drama in the gift books, the only exceptions being a few translated excerpts of foreign plays. Besides the drama, a good deal of non-English poetry and even some prose were translated and printed in gift books. Translations from German, French, Spanish, Latin, and even Russian and Scandinavian authors are often good and raise the level of the poetry appreciably. Non-fiction was scattered throughout the gift books. Biographical sketches were popular; moral essays and exotic descriptions of faraway places (in America and abroad) were common fare. There were a few literary essays like those by John S. Hart who tried to popularize some of the English classics: in *The Opal* for 1849 he described Chaucer's Prioress as portrayed in the "General Prologue" and then gave her tale in Middle English. Later gift books contained some essays on social reform, but these were contrary to the original purpose of the genre and thus contained the seeds of its demise.

IV

Embellishments.

The engravings were responsible for much of the popularity of the gift books, for this was the first time pictures had been reproduced for wide distribution among the middle classes. People had been collecting prints for a long time, but the use of copper and wood for engraving material had allowed only a few reproductions, whereas the new steel engravings could be reproduced indefinitely. The gift books provided the first opportunity for many people to see good art paintings. Very few art galleries existed in early nineteenth-century America and most of these were in a few large cities; therefore the gift book engravings were popular because they were something new and smacked of culture. Some of the paintings that were engraved for gift books were obviously inferior, but there were also many of the best from Britain and America. The engravings themselves were usually good. David Stauffer, one of the foremost authorities on engravings, says:

It is among these small Annual plates, engraved by such men as A. B. Durand, John Cheney, Danforth, Prud'homme, and others that we find some of the most pleasing and best examples of pure line work executed in the United States.

The most popular of the engravers was John Sartain, though not necessarily the best. He used the mezzotint process and all his pictures have a unique quality, a soft, ethereal effect, that is unmistakably his. Landscape, genre paintings, and portraits of ladies predominated in gift book illustrations of Indian girls, or of European scenes, provided a flavor of the exotic and the faraway; "story" pictures added to the narrative flow of the fiction. Medieval subjects, the war for Greek independence, the lost grandeur of the American Indian—these and other topics reflected the interests of the era, as did formal painting itself.

V

Gift Books' Contribution to Elite Art.

In conclusion, it is evident that nineteenth-century American gift books are important cultural records. For one thing, they show the unsophisticated cultural tastes of the popular audience—the comfortable reaffirmation of conventional ideas, the emphasis on sentimentality, the liking for pictures rather than words. The annuals also help to show what the major ideas and attitudes of the era were—reverence for the genteel Female, fervent nationalism, love of nature, and an obvious concern with death.

But gift books are also important because they contributed a great deal to the development of American literature. Fred L. Pattee perhaps overestimates their importance when he says, "their coming more than any other single influence determined the direction American literature was to go"; nevertheless, they were a vital factor in promoting that national literature which the young country demanded. Frank L. Mott describes the situation eloquently:[19]

The patriotic desire to achieve a national literature, to throw off the shackles of literary dependence as those of political subservience had been thrown off, is a paramount motive in much that was written for a hundred years after the close of the Revolution.

This "patriotic desire" certainly in large part helped to motivate the writing of the gift books and their publication.

At their first appearance, in 1826, a critic for the *North American Review* wrote: "Their aim should be, as far as possible, to enlist the best writers in different parts of the country, to procure articles on American topics, and designs of American scenery. It will thus have a character and a value peculiar to itself. . . ."[20] Editors and publishers worked hard to make their annuals a means of developing an American literature by encouraging authors to use American subjects, and by printing mostly American authors; few English authors appeared in the gift books, with the exception of Felicia Hemans and Mary Russell Mitford.

One of the most important things gift books did was to offer struggling American writers an outlet for publication. After the failure of Hawthorne's first novel, *Fanshawe*, he was fortunate to have the gift books to rescue him. As Pattee has pointed out, "It was the one market that could be depended upon, and without it many who later achieved success might have surrendered in their discouragement and ceased to write."

Gift books also served as a training ground for young authors, as the *North American Review* realized as early as 1829: "Here seems to be fair and pleasant field for them to exercise together, to prove their powers and prepare them for future and nobler exertions."[21]

In addition, gift books trained the public taste for art and broadened the artist's audience; more important, they provided a rather lucrative market for both artists and engravers. In this it represents what may well be the first public support of the fine arts in America.

Thus, gift books are unusual, paradoxical creatures, for while they represent the exploitation of the fine arts and literature for financial profit (like other forms of popular art) they also provided one of the means of assisting the advancement of the elite arts and letters in America.

NOTES

[1] Andrew Boyle, *An Index to the Annuals* (Worcester, Eng., 1967); see the whole preface for a good discussion of the gift book predecessors.

[2] [H. Payne], "The Talisman for MDCCCVIII," *North American Review*, XXVI (Jan., 1828), 259.

[3] Clifton Furness, *The Genteel Female: An Anthology* (New York, 1931), has, in his preface, a definition and evaluation of the position of the newly emerging woman in nineteenth-century America.

[4]Ralph Thompson, *American Literary Annuals and Gift Books, 1825-1865* (New York, 1936), 3. The only thorough study of the gift book phenomenon.

[5]David Kaser, *Messrs. Carey & Lea of Philadelphia* (Philadelphia, 1957), 139.

[6]Ola E. Winslow, "Books for the Lady Reader, 1820-60," *Romanticism in America*, ed. George Boas (Baltimore, 1940), 90.

[7]Thompson, 4.

[8]*North American Review*, XXXVI (Jan., 1833), 276.

[9]*Ibid.*, XXIV (January, 1827), 230.

[10]*Sartain's Magazine*, I (Feb., 1849), 154.

[11]"Gift Book and Annuals," *Southern Quarterly Review*, XXI (Jan., 1852), 182.

[12]W. S. Hunt, "Gift Books and Annuals," *Proceedings of the New Jersey Historical Society*, LII (Jan., 1934), 102.

[13]Earl Hutchinson, "Gift Book and Literary Annuals," *Journalism Quarterly*, XLIV (Autumn, 1967), 470-74, on the gift book decline.

[14]Thompson, 102.

[15]"Preface," *The Evergreen* (Philadelphia, 1847), iv.

[16]*The Talisman for 1828* (New York, 1927), 5.

[17]Mrs. [Sarah J.] Hale, "The Pioneers, or The Mission of America," *The Opal* (New York, 1848), 145.

[18]*American Engravers Upon Copper and Steel* (New York, 1907), xxix.

[19]F. L. Pattee, "The Arrival of the Annuals," *Development of the American Short Story* (New York, 1923), 31; Frank Luther Mott, *History of American Magazines 1741-1850* (New York, 1930), I:183.

[20]John Everett, "Critical Notices," *North American Review*, XXII (April, 1826), 444-6.

[21]*Ibid.*, "American Annuals," XXVII (April, 1829), 483.

THE LITTLE BLUE BOOKS AS POPULAR CULTURE:
E. HALDEMAN-JULIUS' METHODOLOGY

Dale M. Herder

In a discussion of the Little Blue Books elsewhere I focused my attention on Haldeman-Julius' unique and sophisticated theory of popular culture.[1] That study concluded that he, as popular paperbook publisher, was motivated by the highest sort of idealism in his efforts to educate the masses.

Building on the two premises that (1) happiness is the highest good of mankind and (2) that knowledge is the key to happiness, Haldeman-Julius set out to ameliorate the popular ignorance by sending his "University in Print" to the doorsteps of American society. Each Little Blue Book that rolled off his presses was sent through the mail as a soldier in a war against ignorance; individually and in phalanxes the crisp blue-uniformed nickel booklets were to carry knowledge and culture to the masses. Haldeman-Julius theorized that the average man was a potential buyer of good books, who could and probably would read good literature if it came to him in a size small enough to be carried in his work-trouser pocket and at a cost he could afford.

The validity of Haldeman-Julius' hypothesis about "Mr. Average American" was substantiated by the phenomenal success of his thirty-two year publishing career (1919-1951). By the end of his first nine years as a publisher he had sold a hundred million Little Blue Books and established his Girard, Kansas, printing plant as the largest mail-order book publishing house in the world. Before his death in 1951 this second Gutenberg had almost unbelievably *quintupled* his 100,000,000 sales figure and published over 2000 different titles in the Little Blue Book

31

series.

It is the purpose of this paper to consider briefly the methods utilized by E. Haldeman-Julius in researching the American reading market and providing it with what it wanted during the nineteen-twenties. Before a discussion of Haldeman-Julius' methodology as a publisher of popular culture, however, it is important to comment on his business interest in the Little Blue Books. For despite his Socialist Party background and his many altruistic pronouncements about popular culture and the good it might accomplish for the common man, Haldeman-Julius was no stranger to capitalism and the profit motive. This statement might at first seem to compromise the idealism of his experiment in mass enlightenment, but clearly there would have been no Little Blue Books without such a motive. When asked whether he considered himself to be a philanthropist or a businessman, Haldeman-Julius answered without hesitation that he was in business: "I invested my capital in the Little Blue Book idea because I thought it was a sound business venture. . . . I was as interested in making a profit as Henry Ford."[2]

The Little Blue Books were indeed profitable. As Haldeman-Julius indicated in his autobiography, he was able to pay off completely, within the first year of operation, the $75,000 obligation he had incurred in purchasing his Girard, Kansas, publishing plant. During the 'twenties the plant produced annually between 13 million and 25 million books, and the business grossed approximately a half-million dollars per year.[3] Ultimately, then, it appears that Haldeman-Julius' Little Blue Books derived from a synthesis of his pragmatic business sense and his altruistic theory of popular culture. In 1928 he expressed pleasure in the fact that he "had been able to use good business toward the improvement instead of the exploitation of the masses."[4]

At the outset of his publishing venture Haldeman-Julius had only his intuition to guide him in determining popular reading tastes. He considered himself to be "Mr. Public—E.H.-J. multiplied hundreds of thousands of times," and judges his first manuscripts by one standard—"do I like them?" His intuition was seldom wrong. Public response to the publication of his first two books in the pocket series, Oscar Wilde's *The Ballad of Reading Jail* and Omar Khayyam's *Rubaiyat*, make it clear that his own literary taste differed little from that of the average Americ: Over the years, however, Haldeman-Julius supplemented his intuition wi a combination of more scientific market analysis techniques. He eventua relied heavily on sales data, advertising feedback, response to questionna and responses to published appeals for information about readers' likes and dislikes.

Since sales volume is such an important criterion for measuring the success of a popular culture medium, it came to be Haldeman-Julius' most valuable tool in determining what the public wanted. By offering something for nearly everyone in a standardized format at a standardized low price, Haldeman-Julius had only to advertise his product widely and then carefully study Little Blue Book sales in order to feel the popular pulse. Beginning with advertisements for his pocket books in his own paper, he rapidly expanded the exposure of his product in such nationally circulated newspapers as the *Kansas City Star,* the *New York Times,* the *New York Herald Tribune,* the *Chicgao Tribune,* the *Chicago Times,* the *Philadelphia Inquirer,* the *Detroit Free Press,* the *Los Angeles Times,* and the *Los Angeles Herald Examiner.* He also ran full-page advertisements in such popular magazines of his time as *Life, The Saturday Evening Post, Liberty, Nation, Popular Science, Popular Mechanics,* and the *Ladies Home Journal.* His advertising was successful largely due to its simplicity. By merely listing columns of book titles, arranged under such helpful subject headings as "Sexology," "Self-Education," "Evolution," "Health," "French Love Stories," "Religion," "Prostitution," and "Psycho-Analysis," he was usually able to bring a return of at least two to one, often as much as seven to one, and occasionally even ten to one, on the amount he had invested in advertising.[5]

It was important to the outcome of Haldeman-Julius' careful sales research that virtually all Little Blue Book advertising was "coupon advertising." Fully ninety-five per cent of the more than one hundred million Little Blue Books sold during the 'twenties were ordered on tear-out coupons which the customer sent directly to the factory in Girard. This enabled Haldeman-Julius, who was his own advertising manager, to test the "pulling power" of various kinds of advertising media and techniques, while at the same time discovering exactly what the public wanted. Relying primarily on the "key" advertising method, which required the customer to respond to a special "key" box number or "key" address, Emanuel could tell even before opening an incoming order which specific advertisement should receive credit for the business. The data he thus received was direct, controlled, immediately quantifiable, and valid.

Louis Adamic, in an article published in a 1930 issue of *Outlook and Independent* magazine, stated that Haldeman-Julius' sales were "a weathercock which shows which way the breezes of public taste [were] blowing."[6] A 1929 issue of the *New Republic* used another meteorological analogy in assessing the extent to which this medium of popular culture accurately reflected the attitudes and concerns of the society for which it was produced: "Mr. Haldemann-Julius' [sic] titles are so numerous and the volume of his sales so fantastic as to make his business almost a barometer of plebeian taste."[7] By the late nineteen-twenties Haldeman-Julius was sufficiently confident of the diagnostic validity of Little Blue Book sales figures that he could claim to have discovered even the comparative popularity of chess and checkers in the United States: checkers led by 20 per cent.[8]

An important corollary to an analysis of sales as a method of checking the popular pulse was Haldeman-Julius' basic premise that the Little Blue Books were *read* books. While other book publishers might *claim* to reflect public taste in their annual sales figures, Haldeman-Julius was convinced that his success reflected more accurately than that of other publishing houses the general psychology of American readers. Unlike many luxuriously bound "merchandise books," the Little Blue Books had no pictorial or luxury appeal. For this reason, and because the editorial policy in Girard was to select manuscripts for informative rather than prestige value, Haldeman-Julius could conceive of no reason for a customer buying a Little Blue Book other than to read it. In what was not wholly an overstatement, Haldeman-Julius asserted that "more than 99% of the Little Blue Books sold direct to the purchaser are sold to him because he wants to read them."[9] The Girard publisher frequently referred to his business as "the democracy of books"; the orders he received (sometimes 4000 in a single day) to him represented "votes" indicating the degrees of interest that people had in the great variety of reading matter represented in his series. His dual role of "campaign organizer" and "chief vote-counter" uniquely equipped him to keep his candidate in office.

Probably the second most valuable source of information about what the public wanted was direct feedback to Girard in the form of letters from readers of Little Blue Books. When in 1924 Haldeman-Julius published his five-hundredth Little Blue Book title, he used the occasion to publicize his "University in Print." He drew together and published in his monthly periodical, *Life and Letters*, several favorable letters received from prominent American Blue Book readers. An old

Milwaukee Socialist friend, Carl Sandburg, wrote the following:

The Haldeman-Julius hip-pocket library has a fine picked list of the best things men have thought and written. For a five-dollar bill it brings an amazing array of good things to read. It is the brick-layer's hope, the mucker's dream, the wop's wonder of an education.[10]

Upton Sinclair, whose muck-raking novel of the Chicago meat-packing industry, *The Jungle*, was published in a set of six Little Blue Books, saw the Picket Series as the solution to the problem of culture:

Haldeman-Julius has solved the problem of culture for the people. In a year or two he will be printing more books than all the rest of the publishers of the world. He is going to put all the comic strips, sports pages and Sunday supplements out of business. The most important invention since the art of printing is the art of printing five cent books![11]

Will Durant, author of *The Story of Philosophy*, was perhaps the most celebrated of Haldeman-Julius' "finds." After the editor had persuaded Durant to convert his lectures on various philosophers into manuscripts for publication in the Little Blue Book Series (Haldeman-Julius published these manuscripts in a dozen Little Blue Books selling for a total of 60 cents), the young scholar's work became famous, and his efforts were collected into a handsome edition that sold for $5.00 per copy. Eventually it became the best-selling non-fiction clothbound book in America. Durant wrote the following letter:

After wandering through all the radical and liberal political and economic movements of the 20th century I have been brought forcibly and inevitably to the conclusion that the only hope of political or economic redemption lies in the spread of knowledge and the enlightenment of understanding and judgment. We cannot change our institutions until we change ourselves; and we can change ourselves not by sermons but by knowledge and wisdom. If there is a utopia, Mr. Haldeman-Julius has found the road to it.[12]

Eugene V. Debs, another old Socialist friend, hailed the publication of the 500th Little Blue Book title with the following letter:

You have certainly built up a wonderful and unique publishing enterprise, and the millions of copies of books of all descriptions, containing literature in all languages, you have put into circulation, not only in this country but beyond the seas, must have a great cultural and educational influence upon the masses of the common people who have thus been reached and hitherto have been unable on account of the expensive cost to provide themselves with such literature. I hope you will succeed . . . , and that you will be encouraged to develop indefinitely your great educational and cultural enterprise.[13]

Letters from the common man were probably better indicators of what the average American reader wanted. The following letters, published in 1928, substantiate what the famous men above had said four years earlier about the Little Blue Books, and give an indication of what subjects were most wanted:

Letter Carrier—Boulder, Colorado
I am a regular reader and booster of the Little Blue Books. They have opened up new subjects for me, which I might not otherwise have become familiar with. They have contributed to a much broader culture than I ever might have achieved without them.

Starr G. Bennett—Student, Kalamazoo, Michigan
The Little Blue Books on marriage and its problems, health and hygiene, for example, are books everyone should possess. They contain practically all I have ever learned about sex and I consider them invaluable in this line of education.

Louis B. Greenberg—Lawyer, Kansas City, Missouri
Looking back on my five years in the University and considering the various educational forces with which I thus came into contact, I find that I cannot attribute to any single factor a greater portion of credit for the little learning I now possess than to the Little Blue Books.

W. L. Nelles—Telegrapher, Rawlins, Wyoming
The Little Blue Books, being pocket-size, furnish me with a means to employ my spare moments to advantage. They enable me to continue in isolation my studies in subjects that interest me. Large, cumbersome books are difficult to transport and cannot be kept constantly at hand to catch these exclusive, idle moments.[14]

Unfavorable responses were not infrequent. It is not surprising that most of Haldeman-Julius' "hate mail" was directed against him personally (he was an avowed atheist, and thought the Bible to be a dull book), rather than against the philosophy or even the content of his Little Blue Books. Bishop George A. Beacher, in the Ames, Iowa, *Tribune*, said, "Down with H.-J! Would you have a snake come into your parlor?" The Augusta, Kansas, *Journal* stated that "H.-J. is not a good citizen," and the Macon, Georgia, *Telegraph* castigated him for being "not conventional." In Greenwood, South Carolina, the *Index Journal* called Haldeman-Julius a "densely ignorant man," while the Holland, Michigan, *Sentinel* nominated him "for the position of president of the publicity grabbers for these United States." But perhaps the Perry, Iowa, *Chief* summed up best the position of all those who were unwilling to spend $2.98 for a college education in Little Blue Books; it stated quite simply that "H.-J. is a bad influence."[15]

More specific research is necessary before valid conclusions can be drawn about the effectiveness of other methods employed by Haldeman-Julius in determining what Americans wanted to read. Accomplishing one of his many firsts in the history of publishing, he at one point sent out 15,000 questionnaires to his readers asking for their preferences in books and inviting comments and suggestions. He received approximately 9000 replies, almost without exception selecting "good" books.[16] Haldeman-Julius also made direct appeals in his own publications for readers' responses. Responses to the following request, printed in the *Haldeman-Julius Weekly* of January 28, 1928, served as a partial basis for his conclusions in *The First Hundred Million* (Simon and Schuster, New York, 1928), the story of how he sold that number of books during his first nine years as a publisher:

What Have the Little Blue Books Meant to You?

You know the Little Blue Books—you have bought them—you have read them. I am asking you to tell me, in a brief letter, just what those books have meant to you. . . . Be explicit. Be candid. Tell me exactly what these books have done for you. Have you been educated—has your attitude changed since you have been a reader of this pocket series? Have you been debunked? Is your outlook wider and freer than it was before you bought some of these books? Perhaps you never were much of a reader before; perhaps you now make use of your spare moments in a delightful or helpful way with these handy books. Tell me about it. Write me a personal letter—200 words or so—and tell me what the Little Blue Books mean to you. Give me your age, your occupation, and tell me something about yourself. Your name will not be used if you so request; what I am after is the general opinion among Little Blue Book readers as to the educational and cultural value of the series.[17]

It is evident that Haldeman-Julius had at his disposal and utilized a variety of market research techniques during the decade of the 'twenties. The success of the Little Blue Books as a vehicle of popular culture was dependent to a great extent upon his willingness to experiment with these largely intuitive but nonetheless effective techniques.

Having briefly examined Haldeman-Julius' market research formula during the 'twenties, let us now look briefly at his methods for giving the public what it wanted. His original printing equipment consisted of the 12 x 18-inch job press he purchased with the *Appeal to Reason* plant. With this primitive device the printing of a single 64 page booklet—minus its cover—took three eight-hour working days.[18] As his pocket books gained in popularity, Haldeman-Julius judiciously introduced technological innovations into his system of production. Under his guidance what had originally been a relatively expensive manual operation became within a decade a totally electric system of mass production capable of printing 240,000 books per day.[19] The two most significant consequences of this change were that, first, the cost of a Little Blue Book could be cut to a fifth of its original price, and, second, the Little Blue Books became capable of virtually unlimited duplication and distribution. Had it not been for these two factors, the series could not have become such a powerful agency of printed popular culture.

Two of Haldeman-Julius' editorial innovations, the "Hospital" and the "Morgue," helped to insure that Mr. Average American got the kind of reading material he wanted. As indicated earlier, he made frequent and careful studies of sales, advertising, and inventory figures. Whenever he discovered a book that was not selling its quota of 10,000 volumes per year he sent it to the "Hospital," his "editorial sanctum sanctorum," where he attempted to diagnose the reason for its reduced sales. In most cases a change in title was sufficient to "cure" the ailing Blue Book. Once sent back to the advertising manager under its new name it was usually able to survive in the marketplace. Books with a sales figure that fell below 5000 and showed no signs of increase were condemned to the "Morgue" —or scrap-heap. On a few sad occasions Haldeman-Julius baled for scrap as many as 30,000 copies of a deceased Little Blue Book. When he discovered at one point that some of his Little Blue Books were not factual—that they were actually bunk books—he respected his pledge to his public and sent them to the Morgue.[20]

Perhaps the best example of a Little Blue Book that recovered after hospitalization was Guy de Maupassant's "Boule de Suif." This famous story was first made available in the Little Blue Book series under the accurately translated title *The Tallow Ball*. When in 1925 the sales record for this book was checked, it was discovered that it was selling only half as well as two other Maupassant Blue Books (*Love and Other Stories* and *Mademoiselle Fifi*). The title of the lagging book was changed shortly thereafter to *A French Prostitute's Sacrifice*, which, of course, is what the story is about. Within a year the book had increased its sales by more than three times—from 15,000 to 54,700 copies.

In some cases an ailing book needed only a "change of scenery" to restore its sales health. Such a change involved moving the book from one advertising classification to another. Experience indicated, for example, that some poetry, such as Longfellow's *Courtship of Miles Standish* and Elizabeth Barrett Browning's *Sonnets From the Portuguese*, sold much better under the classification of "Love" than under "Poetry." On more rare occasions a book that was selling poorly needed both a title change and a change of scenery—involving two or more return trips to the Hospital.

Haldeman-Julius refuted criticism directed against this rather free-wheeling editorial policy by stating repeatedly that his title and scenery changes were motivated by his concern for the welfare of the reader, maintaining that changes in title served not to deceive the reader but to enlighten him. One of his basic rules in altering a title was that the change "must advance some particular information as to exactly the book's contents."[21] As an enlightened pragmatist, however, Haldeman-Julius had no qualms about using a clever title in order to trick a buyer into reading—and actually becoming "hooked" on—good literature.[22]

Besides his actual printing equipment and his editorial techniques, Haldeman-Julius utilized a third important means to provide the public with the kind of culture that it wanted—advertising. Earlier in this paper it was pointed out that to him advertising served as an important diagnostic tool, telling the editor what the public wanted. In its more traditional role the printed advertisement—with its handy "keyed" order coupon—served to bring the Blue Books to the reader. Because the high cost of national advertising was almost more than his low profit margin could tolerate, it was impossible for Haldeman-Julius to print a "blurb" about each individual volume in the series. Consequently, he merely listed all of his books by name and number in a standard full-page advertisement, and left it to his carefully selected titles and categories to do the actual selling. In 1928, with 1260 different titles in print, Haldeman-Julius was buying more agate lines (in which advertising is measured) of nationally circulated newspaper and periodical space than any other book publisher in the world.[23]

Other advertising mediums used by Haldeman-Julius were less effective than newspapers and magazines as diagnostic devices, but they undoubtedly had a considerable influence on the number of orders he received. Inside the back cover of many of his early Little Blue Books the publisher printed lists of book titles and numbers currently available from the plant in Girard. Also, circulars and small 3½ by 5-inch "Little Blue Book Catalogues" were regularly stuffed into outgoing packages of books in the mailing room. On one occasion in January of 1924 Haldeman-Julius even took to the newly invented radio to advertise his ideas and product, reportedly reaching a million radio listeners. Speaking on the subject "Do the Masses Want Culture?" he closed his broadcast by offering a free Little Blue Book to any hearer who wrote in and mentioned the speech. Nearly 10,000 people responded.[24] This experiment with a non-linear means of advertising during the nineteen-twenties is particularly significant because it was conducted by a man whose entire life was devoted to the medium of typography. And to a certain extent this experiment in radio advertising foretold the impact that the revolution in electronic circuitry would eventually have on other agencies of American popular culture.

Since there is no reliable information at present regarding the effectiveness of Haldeman-Julius' final two devices for getting culture to the masses, it will have to suffice merely to mention them. In 1924 he opened in Cincinnati and New York City the first two of a projected series of "Little Blue Book Shops." The extent to which such shops were established in other cities across the country is still in need of further research. Several years later, in 1939, Haldeman-Julius contracted with a Chicago vending machine company to sell Little Blue Books in the same manner as five-cent packs of gum. An initial order of half a million books (including such titles as Kipling's *Gunga Din and Other Poems*) were sold in strategically-placed coin-operated machines under the following imprint: "Published for Automatic Libraries, A Division of O. D. Jennings & Company A National Institution."[25] In spite of the dearth of information about these two marketing devices it is safe to say that they probably did not contribute substantially to Haldeman-Julius' phenomenal total sales figures. The Little Blue Book business was (and still is) transacted almost exclusively by mail-order.

We might conclude, as Victor Willard did in an article published in 1926, that the success of Haldeman-Julius' unique publishing venture lay ultimately in his genius for understanding the American public.[26] "Haldeman-Julius," Willard said, "knew that a large part of our population was intellectually undernourished, that its diet consisted almost exclusively of winter bread and the jam of light fiction. He set out to supply the mental vitamines [sic] that make growth of the mind possible. He won because his diagnosis was correct."

NOTES

1"Haldeman-Julius, The Little Blue Books, and the Theory of Popular Culture," *Journal of Popular Culture* IV (Spring, 1971), pp. 881-93. The article also briefly outlines the background and training of Emanuel Haldeman-Julius (1889-1951), and describes the nature of the Little Blue Books.

2E. Haldeman-Julius, *The First Hundred Million* (New York: Simon and Schuster, 1928), pp. 39, 255, 256 (hereafter *FHM*).

3*Ibid.*, p. 237; *Nation* (May 10, 1952), p. 453; *Time* (August 8, 1949), p. 47.

4*FHM*, p. 256.

5*Ibid.*, chs. XV and XVI, p. 273.

6Louis Adamic, "Voltaire From Kansas," *Outlook and Independent: An Illustrated Weekly of Inquiry* (June 25, 1930), p. 285;

7*New Republic* (January 9, 1929), p. 206.

8*FHM*, p. 76.

9Quoted in Adamic, p. 285.

10*Life and Letters* (January, 1924), p. 3.

11*Ibid.*, p. 8.

12*Ibid.*

13*Ibid.*, p. 40.

14*Haldeman-Julius Weekly*, no. 1684 (March 10, 1928), p. 2.

15*Ibid.*; *Time* (August 8, 1949), p. 47; *Saturday Review* (April 12, 1969), p. 23.

16"Porter Library Bulletin," Vol. 3, no. 18 (May 15, 1969), pp. 3-4 (Haldeman-Julius Collection, Porter Library, Kansas State College of Pittsburg).

17*Haldeman-Julius Weekly*, no. 1678 (January 28, 1928), p. 1.

18*FHM*, p. 224.

19*Ibid.*, pp. 223-237, for a detailed description of how Haldeman-Julius mechanized his system of production.

20For a detailed discussion of the "Hospital" and "Morgue" see chs, VIII and X, *First Hundred Million*.

21*Ibid.*, p. 137.

22*Ibid.*, pp. 123, 132; William McCann, "Sex-mad Socialism," *The Progressive* (September, 1967), p. 45; *New Republic* (Sugust 15, 1960), p. 20; *New Republic* (January 9, 1929), p. 207.

23*FHM*, p. 339.

24Unidentified newspaper clipping dated January 14, 1924, probably from the Girard or Pittsburg (Kansas) newspaper. Gives an account of Haldeman-Julius' broadcast from the Crosley Radio Station in Cincinnati (Haldeman-Julius Collection document).

[25]Series of letters between Haldeman-Julius and the O. D. Jennings Company, dated March, 1939 (Haldeman-Julius Collection documents).

[26]Victor Willard, "Bringing the Light to Main Street," *Sunset Magazine* (January, 1926), p. 62.

THE PEDESTAL MYTH REINFORCED: WOMEN'S MAGAZINE FICTION, 1900-1920

Ellen Hoekstra

Women of the Middle Ages had little to compensate for their lowly social and economic position. What compensation they had was given to them by a combination of custom and a tradition of courtly love which placed them on a pedestal above men, their abject worshippers. Both women and the Church were able to grant or withhold grace through love to an unworthy man. It is difficult to ascertain the degree to which this tradition represented reality, or to which it was merely literary tradition. Assuming it was partially representative of reality, it must have been used by women as a means of obtaining power; presumably if they had possessed real power, they could have dropped the pedestal tradition. Yet, centuries later, twentieth century American women, who had considerably more socio-economic power than medieval women, seem unwilling to give up this tradition. Perhaps this conservatism shows a preference for power without responsibility. Possibly it reflects the fact that women in 1900 through 1920 did not have (and still do not have) equal socioeconomic power. Certainly it illustrated the reluctance with which society changes its attitudes.

The desire of women to remain on their historic pedestal is clearly illustrated in the fiction published in four of the leading women's magazines of the period 1900-1920: *Ladies' Home Journal, Good Housekeeping, Woman's Home Companion* and the *Delineator.* Presumably the fiction in these magazines reflected attitudes which their readers could accept. Although the individual reader need not necessarily agree with any one attitude, the popularity of these periodicals rested partially in their ability to reinforce what their readers already believed. All of these magazines illustrate the pedestal myth in two major ways. First, their plots consistently cast women in "spiritual" roles, roles considered inherently "feminine." Secondly, they reinforced several common taboos; a woman who steps off her pedestal to violate one of these taboos is certain to receive her "just deserts" before the end of the story.

In addition to their reinforcement of the pedestal tradition, these four magazines have other factors in common. All were started in the late nineteenth century as general magazines, containing fiction, poetry, recipes, fashions, and articles on child care, interior decorating, etiquette, beauty, and occasionally public affairs. The *Ladies' Home Journal* (under Edward Bok) was the most frequent advocate of causes among the four. The *Delineator* emphasized fashions and *Good Housekeeping*, appropriately, housekeeping and food. By the end of the nineteenth century, many other women's specialty magazines existed, including magazines which dealt exclusively with food, childcare, or fashions. Few such specialty magazines ever approached best seller status. The leading general magazines had the highest circulations. All four of these magazines achieved the then rare million mark in circulation within a twenty-year span. The *Ladies' Home Journal* was first, in 1904, followed by *Woman's Home Companion* in 1916, the *Delineator* in 1920, and *Good Housekeeping* in 1924. Along with two other magazines, the *Pictorial Review* and *McCall's*, which also reached the million mark during this period, these magazines were known as the "Big Six" because they led the field of women's magazines.

Ladies' Home Journal, Good Housekeeping, Woman's Home Companion, and *The Delineator,* from 1900 to 1920, published fiction which seemed to have two functions: to provide the female reader with escape and to reinforce her generally-accepted values. In other words, the fabulously wealthy and beautiful heiress always acted with virtue and decorum.

While a staff member on the *Delineator* under Dreiser's editorship, Charles Hanson Towne discovered how conventionally exacting the magazine's subscribers were:[1]

I soon saw that the fiction which was to go into a magazine like ours—we had not only the *Delineator,* but the *Designer* and the *Woman's Magazine*—must be selected with great care. There were certain inevitable restrictions. We must be highly moral, first of all; for our subscribers depended upon us to uphold the traditions of high and sound ethics. "Sister Carrie" could not have been one of our serials; and no one knew that better than Theodore Dreiser.

Eighty-five percent of the fiction published in these four magazines, over the first twenty years of the twentieth century, provided escape, or reinforcement of social and moral values, or both, through the use of six basic plots. These plots all place women characters in traditionally "feminine" roles, and nearly all end happily.

The largest group of stories belong in the boy-meets-girl category, rung through a variety of changes. Running a close second are stories in which someone learns a lesson through suffering, punished for wrongdoing. The "lesson" stories, while literally as old as Eve in basic plot, are particularly revelatory of the moral and social boundaries of the era. The third group unites a child and a parent, usually a mother, through reunion after separation, adoption, or after misunderstanding. Fourth are mother-centered stories, dealing with idealized children and centering on a mother's relationship to them. These stories are usually constructed about two major character types of children—the Pollyanna girl or the Tom Sawyer boy, that is, the ideally happy and sweet girl, and the lovable but mischievous boy. Fifth are problem-solving stories (predecessors of the Mary Worth comic strips) in which a wise older woman, by her valuable advice, saves marriages, restores domestic harmony, chastises the wicked and rewards the virtuous. Last is the "working-girl" story, in which a woman achieves success and personal fulfillment through employment—a type of story which increased in frequency after 1915. Not all stories published in these four magazines over this twenty year span fit into one of these classifications, of course, and some combine elements from more than one; but the use of one or more of these six basic plots characterizes by far the majority of the stories published.

Each plot has its own recurrent characteristics. The boy-meets-girl story, for example, except for a few humorous ones, always ends in marriage; there is no hint of premarital sex, and the final marriage ceremony chastely suggests the physical consummation of love. The girl is American, beautiful, young, and both naive and innocent. (Heroines defy the laws of genetic possibility in their tendency to be always blond and tiny.) With the rare exception of stories concerning widows who meet the right man (never divorcees) the heroine's love affair is her first emotional attachment to a man. In the stories that appeared early in the century, heroines were consistently reluctant to reveal their feelings, which tended to delay and complicate the plot. In "The Voice in the Choir" for example (*LHJ*, July, 1900), the young man's pride (he is poor, she is rich) and the girl's hesitancy delay their marriage for some years. Furthermore, the heroine is often quick to take offense; if the young man fails to write frequently, the affair may be delayed for months. It is important in these stories that the heroine be an absolute model of virtue, and an inspiration to her lover who sees the goodness shining through her beauty. Smitten men in these stories think things like (*GH*, Feb., 1920):

It was his dream of her, somewhere on the Big River, that had given him his great courage to believe in the ultimate of things.

Frequently it is inferred that men are spiritually weak creatures who stand in need of such inspiration, but even wicked men can be temporarily "lifted above themselves" by a good woman's example. Louis Aker, a self-interested revolutionist labor leader in a Mary Roberts Rinehart serial (*LHJ*, Aug., 1920) is the perfect example:

His insistent body was always greater than his soul, but now and then, when he was physically weary, he had a spiritual moment.

This type, who remains unredeemed despite the pure love of a beautiful woman, is responsible for the unwed mother in a hundred and twenty-five stories, and thus unredeemable even by love.

Heroes in the boy-meets-girl stories tend to be young, American, and endowed with all the Christian virtues. They don't drink and rarely smoke cigarettes; as Charles Hanson Towne pointed out, *The Delineator* never even ran drawings of characters holding cigarettes or of table settings with wine glasses. Heroes are, like heroines, in love for the first time and, it almost goes without saying, have only marriage in mind. It isn't necessary for them to be rich, but they must be able to support wives and they are generally upwardly mobile. A frequent plot variation portrays a young man who is looking for a way of earning enough money to be worthy of "her," since a man who would live on his wife's earning, or accept a position arranged by her family, is considered beneath contempt. In I.A.R. Wylie's

"Children of Storm," (*WHC*, Jan., 1910) a mother talks to her son who may, she thinks, allow "her" to support him:

We've got a son who's too fine just to earn an honest living. He knows how to get on better than that. . . . Your fine lady'll have money enough to keep you both, or her people'll give you a job, the sort of soft job they give to hangers-on. You're all right. You've feathered a pretty nest for yourself.

The young man must also adore his beloved consistently and absolutely; but although his love has to be absolute, it does not have to be articulate, for the smooth-tongued young man is viewed with suspicion. However, it does help if he is "manly," preferably tall, square-shouldered, firm of jaw, and ruddy-hued, with hair dark and slightly curling. In 1919 and 1920, he is frequently a returned soldier bearing battle decorations and lacking a hand, arm, foot, or leg. In general, he is the American Boy as much as his beloved is the American Girl.

Aside from the concluding matrimony and the standard characteristics expected of these fictional lovers, other conditions in these stories are variable, within limits. Many stories endorse love at first sight; in others love is discovered after a long acquaintance; but in both cases, "love" is as sudden and as definite as the measles. Its realization frequently occurs in a romantic setting—in China or aboard a ship—but it may also happen "next door." In this latter variation, it is customary for the boy or girl to choose a childhood friend over a more sophisticated competitor, often a visitor from a nearby big city. There are a few stories of love between the previously married "grandma" and "grandpa" of the community, but such stories are usually meant to be humorous.

The prevalence of boy-meets-girl stories reveals the fact that women of the period felt that they received their power vicariously through union with a man and the institution of marriage. For the vast majority of American women, this was probably an accurate perception. Also, the position of women characters as the "beloved" before marriage even more directly indicates the extent to which they were willing to remain on the pedestal.

There are two main patterns which recur in the stories in which someone learns a lesson. The less common rewards a character for doing something good; the more usual plot punishes a character for being foolish, irresponsible, or bad. Both are clear, straightforward expositions of prevailing social values and moral codes. Transgressions fall into two general categories. In the first, the character either faces up to, or does not, a responsibility to someone to whom he is emotionally committed. The second emphasizes the character's responsibility to society.

In the first group, many of the stories deal with a woman's responsibility to her husband. In Mark Lee Luther's story "Presenting Jane McRae," (*Del.*, 1906) a woman marries a man to spite the man she really loves because he has sown some wild oats. She comes to despise her husband, who subsequently kills himself stunting an airplane in order to prove his love for her—thus she learns her lesson, and lives to treasure his memory. In Margaret Widdemer's "Margery Marries" (*GH*, 1922) a woman learns to overcome her revulsion for a soldier-husband she feels she does not really know. Women also learn not to expect perfection from men, either before or after marriage. For example, in Edith Barnard Delano's "Face to Face," a woman who has turned down her fiance spends a night with her old seamstress whose son is saved at the last minute from a false accusation of murder (*LHJ*, June, 1900). From her the young girl learns the sweet joy of emotional commitment to another human being. In several lighter stories, girls who hesitate to announce engagements because they don't want their social life disrupted, set the date immediately when they learn that rivals are ready to snap up their swains.

Fiction which stresses the individual's responsibilities to society insists that the character show respect for socially-accepted values by preserving even the appearance of them. There is sympathy for the girl who gains a bad reputation for something she hasn't done, but she is also held partially responsible for her carelessness in allowing her acts to be misinterpreted. This is especially evident in the stories about "flirts" which begin to appear in profusion after the War.

In "Betty Bell and the Leading Man," (*Del.*, Jan., 1920) a young girl keeps her flirtation secret from her mother. After a while, guilt overwhelms her:

She had never dreamed that wickedness could be so exciting. . . . She kept thinking of her mother—There was no reason for this, yet her mother's plain, kindly face framed in with its grayish hair kept coming before her eyes . . . the thrill of adventure slipped farther and farther away. . . . The old standards, the old days had been too strong. She had lost her nerve.

The worst villain is the man who comes to town, wins the girls' hearts and turns out to be married, like the "no-good masher" who wins the hearts of two sisters in Mary Brecht Pulver's "The Wings of Love." (*GH*, Feb., 1920) Women who are flirts are punished more severely than men. In "Amy Up a Tree" by Eden Phillpotts, a girl is punished for having two suitors meet each other, instead of her, in a planned elopement; she is tied into a boat and left moored in the river all night. "Man-eaters" tend to be older than "good girls" and usually use more cosmetics. In Fanny Heaslip'Lea's "A Story Not Without Words," a villainess is compared to a virtuous girl:

Sara was twenty-five to Nelly-Lou's twenty-three—and as much like a somewhat overpowering but lovely gardenia as Nelly-Lou was like a wild rose.

Those who defy the rules of conventional courtship usually receive their punishment before the conclusion of the story. These straight-forward parables confirm in no uncertain terms the prevailing emphasis on sincerity, constancy, and virtue.

Motherhood in the magazine fiction is considered a sacred office, for which a woman's superior intuitions particularly fit her. To a woman, motherhood is the ultimate fulfillment; therefore a reunion with a lost child, or the gaining of a child, represents a deep desire for children. Stories which show women who are not completely fulfilled by having children are rare.

There are many reasons for the original separations in these "reunion" stories. A child may be separated from the mother by occupation or schooling, as in Ina Breroort Roberts' "From a Far Country," in which a daughter, studying voice in Paris, sends her parents a recording of herself singing "Home Sweet Home" on her birthday. Sometimes the mother isolates herself from her child by quarreling with her in-laws as in L. M. Montgomery's "The Knuckling Down of Mrs. Gamble." In this story, a mother unbends her pride concerning a daughter-in-law of whom she disapproves, to visit her children just in time to save their lives. Occasionally, the mother dies and the reunion takes place in heaven. A father's quarrel with a child may also cause the initial separation, as in Mary Heaton Vorse's "The Hidden World," in which the reunion with her alienated son brings a mother from her deathbed. Poor widows sometimes leave their children on the doorsteps of the wealthy, to be reunited when they learn their real parentage.

There are a number of "adoption" stories, especially around 1900, involving unhappy spinsters or lonely widows. In these stories the theme of the superiority of maternal love to sexual love recurs again and again. In "The Hidden World" it is suggested that a woman's child takes the place in her affections originally held by her husband:

Indeed, most women, as soon as they have a few little clothes to put away in the hidden treasure place, and a broken toy or two, incontinently throw out the dried flowers, the love letters, and all the other foolish and dear trivial things their hearts have bid them cherish. Most men who looked for the first gifts they made their wives would find in its place the tiny shoe of a little man.

Love for a man is considered suitable for the young, but the mature and experienced find more fulfillment in love for children. In Kathleen Norris's "The Heart of a Mouse" a widow with children of her own decides not to remarry because, she concludes,

To become a good man's wife might indeed be a promotion for some lonely girl, but she, Mollie, was a woman.

Similarly, in Octave Thanet's "In Place of Their Own," a spinster whose husband-to-be was killed while rescuing a child from an oncoming train considers her loneliness:

. . . it was not a husband who tempted her; it was a child . . . it was a wise woman who said to her, "We women may cease to regret the husband we might have had, but never the children who might have been ours."

One reason for the glorification of the maternal role is the attitude of the period toward children. This is, no doubt, a carry-over from the nineteenth-century Romantic view which saw children transcending ordinary human corruption by their still-intact innocence. The mother was very important, then, because she was the guardian of this inherent virtue. Stories which express this idea were frequently written for children, but from the adult point of view.

This view of children results in two general attitudes toward children in the women's magazine stories: condescension and awe. A kindly condescension seems to be the customary adult reaction to the Tom Sawyers who constitute about a half of the juvenile characters. These Tom Sawyer figures are continually getting into harmless mischief because of their naïveté. The other major juvenile character, Pollyanna, draws tears from strong men by her instinctive good deeds.

In the Tom Sawyer stories, adults, because of their awareness of good and evil, are depicted as kindly mentors, capable of unraveling the results of childish misdeeds. For example, in a selection from the Henry A. Shute series, "Brite and Fair"—subtitled "the story of a real boy"—a mother has to clean the dye off her son after he takes a job as "The Wild Man of Borneo" at a fair. The Pollyanna girl, too good to be true, is often endowed with special qualities denied to adults. In the James Hopper Story, "What Happened in the Night," a mother tells her husband that their two little daughters who dream the same dreams, may share other forms of extra-sensory perception. In Mabel Gifford's "Trot's Easter Offering," a tiny child, to whom the meaning of the special Easter offering has not been explained, instinctively comprehends its meaning by shyly putting a wilted pussywillow in the minister's hand.

The prevalence of these attitudes toward children seems extremely relevant to women's conception of their role, as it is viewed in these stories. By endowing children with innocence and special powers, the role of the mother as protector of their innocence and guardian of their virtues becomes very important. Motherhood is considered a mystery over which only a woman, because of her special spiritual powers, could ever be high priestess.

The "Mary Worth" stories similarly imply special powers to the good wife, mother, or sweetheart. In these plots an older woman dispenses earthly wisdom through advice or example; her judgment is considered surest on such matters as marriage, child-rearing, love, and charity. It is also made clear in these stories that "plain folks" are generally more good-hearted and more perceptive of the "real" values of life than the rich and sophisticated. The wise female counsellor, therefore, may derive from the lower social stratum and speak ungrammatically or in dialect. This kind of reverse snobbism is present in many of Zona Gale's stories, such as "The Charity Ball," in which a group of small-town, uneducated women goes as special guests to a charity ball. When a small ragged boy walks in and appeals for help for his sick mother, the wealthy board of directors shows no real compassion for the child, but the small-town women (and two of the "good" rich people) go straight to the child's home and apply chicken-soup-style aid. The most extreme use of dialect in this type of story is found in Dorothy Dix's "Mirandy" stories, as can be seen by this excerpt from

"Mirandy on the Truth":

> . . . de onliest thing dat keeps us from scratchin' out each odder's eyes is de way we wuks de circumlocution of de veracity.

Many of these "Mary Worth" stories are written in dialect, in an attempt at folk humor.

Women's magazine fiction of the period also assumes that women are wiser than men about social and ethical problems. Mirandy is continually straightening out a too-textual male preacher; when, in "Mirandy on Vanity," the preacher warns her against vanity, she points out the necessity of pride to human achievement. And in the anonymous "Josiah and I Go A-Visiting" series in the *Ladies' Home Journal*, it is Josiah's wife, never Josiah, who solves the problems they encounter in the course of their visits. Just as the men in the boy-meets-girl stories learn goodness and virtue from the girls they love, so in the "Mary Worth" tales do they find moral inspiration in the advice of older and wiser women. In Wanda Petrunkevitch's "Madame Joy in Life," an older woman joins a class of art students, inspiring and improving them all by her wisdom and her earthy cheerfulness. In all of the stories in this group, a woman's spiritual superiority makes her an authority on ethical and social matters.

The last major plot pattern concerns women who achieve success through employment that carries some responsibility. There were few such stories in the women's magazines at the turn of the century, in all of which the heroine goes to work only through absolute necessity. The stories in the magazines throughout the period warned women of the dangers of ignoring their natural and noble calling of homemaker. Josephine Stricker in "It Won't Do! A Warning for Business Women" unequivocally stated,

> The young, ignorant and inexperienced girl goes into business with an outlook on life that is mentally and morally feminine and in almost every particular different from her brother's . . . She is pretty and lovable and by all the laws of nature she should be nest-building and not pounding a typewriter.

Edward Bok, in an untitled editorial in the *Ladies' Home Journal*, stated a common theme of the day: women were neither physically nor temperamentally suited to stand the strain of employment. Few but Bok would claim divine support, however, for his view:

The fact is that not one woman in a hundred can stand the physical strain of the keen pace which competition has forced upon every line of business today. . . . God made her a woman and never intended her for the rougher life planned out for man and each step she took proved this uncontrovertible fact to her. It was not man that stood in the way; it was herself. . . . Commercial atmosphere . . . is distasteful to the sensitive feminine mind and fine womanly temperament.

This attitude toward working women is borne out by the magazine fiction. Generally, "business" is considered an interlude before marriage, and not a life work. Stories in which women continue to work once they are married are rare. In one exception to this, "A Letter to Miss Douglas" by Ellis Parker Butler, a woman who marries her co-partner in an antique store does continue to work. But instead of retaining the majority vote in the antique store, she opens a little wicker shop upstairs and sells novelties. Fictional characters who work without economic necessity tend to enter fantasy occupations. For example, in Kate Corbal's "A Pair of Blue Rompers," a mother of grown children stumbles into a career as a motion-picture actress playing dowager empresses. And in Ruth Sawyer's "The Glorious Comedy," an ex-dramatics student, currently a tired housewife, sells a play that is immediately a smash hit on Broadway.

Again and again, especially after World War I, the stories explain that a woman should not take a job that a man needs; many magazine heroines give up their jobs to returning soldiers. The heroine of Mary Stewart Cutting's "Perfectly Safe" needs the job to support herself, but she cannot bear to see a handicapped veteran vainly search for work. She quits the job on the pretext that she is getting married, and the story ends with her engagement to the soldier. Many stories which deal with a working girl end with her happy marriage, frequently to the boss, which ends her career in the office.

The general attitude in these stories, concerning women who work, is clear—the world of business is neither suitable nor satisfying to them, for her real fulfillment lies in her home, her husband, and her children. The anonymous voice of "An American Mother" in the *Ladies' Home Journal* (June, 1920) speaks for many when she says:

But to claim that these (careers) are nobler occupations than her own craft—the high calling of wifehood and motherhood—is the most shallow and dangerous of cant.

The six plot patterns, whatever their differences, all place women on a pedestal; the female is seen as desirable love object, guardian of innocent children, spiritual and moral guide, mistress of the home. Bearing these responsibilities, she need seek fulfillment nowhere else.

A minority of the stories—about fifteen percent—published in these four women's magazines over the twenty-year span after 1900 do not fit into these six categories. Some are simply stories for children and young people, such as Kipling's juvenile stories, adaptations of classics like *Little Men*, or "Nature" stories about animals. There is a small group of adventure stories, apparently aimed at the male reader, such as a series of hunting stories about the "Blue River Bear" that appeared in *Ladies' Home Journal* in 1900. There are also a number of comic sketches, built about domestic stiuations such as the servant problem, the difficulties of renting a house, or the problems of remodeling, in which a harried husband and resourceful wife battle against a world of comic maids, inept contractors, and hostile landlords. Some sketches deal with the "battle of the sexes," in which the wife or sweetheart usually wins; the sketch titled "Remodeling a House" in *Woman's Home Companion* is subtitled, "Proving that if you give a wife an inch she will build on a couple of ells." There are also mystery stories, some fictionalized history—such as the history of a New England Thanksgiving—and a few additional types. Such miscellaneous stories derive from the attempt of these magazines to interest other members of the family, a trend which more recently culminated in *McCall's* "togetherness" campaign of the nineteen-fifties.

Whatever the category of plot pattern, however, the stories aimed at the woman reader contain very clear rules of behavior; violation of these taboos places the character in great danger of losing her spirituality, wisdom, and womanliness. Interest in sexuality is forbidden; physical attraction can be expressed only in etherealized romantic love; the only other allowable love is maternal.

The ban against physical sexuality expresses itself in a number of ways. Masculine sexuality is pictured as coarse and brutish, something which no decent woman could anticipate with pleasure. Male villains are frequently described by reference to their obvious sensuality like Louis Akers of Mary Roberts Rinehart's "A Poor Wise Man." The office anarchist of Mary Stewart Cutting's "Perfectly Safe" (*WHC*, June 1920) is:

Mr. Pulver, a pale, thin lissome young man with a lisp, anarchistic sentiments and an uncomfortable habit of affectionately touching one's hand, or arm or shoulder. . . .

Women characters are repelled by physical affection, with the exception of the engagement kiss. For example, the young war bride in "Margery Marries" reacts to her husband's return with revulsion:

He stood with his arm still around her—would he never stop touching her? . . . Then, as he caught her hand in his, quite undisguisedly this time, and held it under his arm, the repulsion came back.

Women control sexuality in a double-standard society. Josephine Stricker's article "It Won't Do! A Warning for Business Women" (*Del.*, Jan., 1920) stresses this:

With rare exceptions, the morality of a situation is always ultimately in a woman's hands. She can always say "NO."

Yet the initial responsibility is generally credited to the man. In "A Poor Wise Man," a woman who has an affair is quick to name her lover as the tempter. She also suggests a kind of numerical sexual morality:

I was a good girl until I knew him. I'm not saying that to let myself out. It's the truth.

Strong women not only avoid sexuality but serve as example and inspiration to the sensual males, as in the "Mary Worth" stories, since the moral superiority of women is an uplifting influence. For example, in Frederick Orin Bartlett's "They Who Walk in Darkness" (*LHJ*, June, 1920) an errant husband compares himself to his faithful wife, saying "I'm a cad and you're a pure white angel . . ." while love for a pure woman changes masculine sensuality to adoration in James Oliver Curwood's "The Valley of Silent Men," (*GH*, Feb., 1920) in which the hero then sees his beloved ". . . not as a creature to win, but a priceless possession. . . ." In some stories, women display a rather macabre preference for a dead man's memory over a live husband. For example, in Kathleen Norris's "The Heart of a Mouse," a widowed woman who considers remarriage to a decent and sincere man is reprimanded by her mother, who tells her, "There ain't a woman breathin' any luckier than you—be who she may. You got Anthony's memory—."

The daughter agrees quickly and somewhat guiltily. In "In Place of Their Own" an aging spinster ponders on her loneliness:

She was not tempted to take a husband as cure; on the contrary, less than ever she thought of such a course. Her dead lover, whose memory the years had dimmed even while they consecrated it was become in some subtle and incommunicable way more vividly dear. . . .

A dead man, apparently, is somehow safer and much less physical than a live one.

The taboo against sexuality in these stories suggests that physical love is an unsatisfactory substitute for the "higher" joys of life. Mature women find their affection for men supplanted by love for their children; maternal love is deeper and more lasting than sexual love, the child being a "blessed innocent" rather than an undeniably physical grown man.

It is also made clear in the stories that women should never act in a masculine way, that the sexes are different, and follow different life styles. Smoking is masculine, a de-feminizing habit, which well-bred women do not even approve in the male. Only "vamps," like Sara, "an overpowering but lovely gardenia" of a woman, smoke. Women must be relentlessly domestic, constantly tidying things up, as opposed to male indifference to household confusion; a woman of careless habits loses some of her appeal. Men too are tougher and stronger than women; when a meek younger sister happens to beat her brother in a footrace—in Myra Kelly's "Spirit of Cecilia Anne"— she gives him the prize, a bundle of firecrackers, because she is afraid of noise. Nor should women ever assume responsibilities which rightfully belong to the male. In Basil King's "The Thread of Flame" a man refuses to take money from a woman, since it is not her role to help him do what he should do himself. Frederick Orin Bartlett's serial, "They Who Walk in Darkness" is the story of a woman whose erring husband returns to the path of virtue under her influence. Later, after he is crippled while dashing in front of a train to save a child, she works to support the family, much to the pity of her friends and her husband's shame. If a woman is placed in a position of responsibility above a man, both are unhappy. Miss Douglas, of "A Letter to Miss Douglas," finds it embarrassing to have the deciding vote in an antique store owned with a male partner. When he marries her, and she hands him the store, both are content.

Competitiveness is a male characteristic, dangerous for a woman to imitate. In an article appearing in *Ladies' Home Journal* in June, 1900, a doctor states:

You are here (in the marketplace) in competition with men . . . I do not like that . . . The exceptional successes and vigor of the rare few serve but to lure the mass of women into the belief that the continuity of work of the man can be imitated with no more risks than are his.

According to Edward Bok, the competitiveness of the marketplace means, for a woman, increased illness, a higher divorce rate, and a childless home. In Ida M. Evans's "The Eternal Triangle" (*GH*, Feb., 1920) a woman warns her prospective daughter-in-law:

"I don't know," said Reeve Hycomb's mother defiantly, "that a knack at fast promotion in a modern young woman shows that she'll do the wife act to a husband's best happiness . . . if he should happen not to set his two hands chockful of success, God pity him! His wife won't."

Women have a higher calling, the stories suggest, and if they want success, it is enough that they attain vicarious status through their husbands. This attitude results in a third taboo, strongly under-lined in women's magazine fiction—a woman should not marry beneath herself, which can be defined in various ways. In Katherine Holland Brown's serial, "White Roses," the heroine cannot marry the charming Count Morgan because his antecedents are unknown, and his standing as mysterious as his origins. The girl in James Oppenheim's "Lovers" will have nothing to do with her sweetheart when she overhears him tell a lie; he is unworthy of her, and though he repents, he convinces her only with difficulty that he belongs at her moral level. The girl who marries into a lower class, as the heroine of "Children of the Storm," faces the pity and contempt of her parents and sister—"The same thought flashed through all three of them—after all, a common young man." The girl in Zona Gale's "The Lovingest Lady" who falls in love with a young clerk is saved when it is revealed he is really a law student, working his way through school. Numerous stories emphasize the point that the man a girl marries must be at an economic level sufficient to guarantee a life of security; the girl who marries below that level is in real danger. Before he can win her he must win the promotion or find the better job.

Whatever the claims for female "emancipation" in the opening decades of the twentieth century, and whatever the impact of the First World War on the position of women in society, the patterns and taboos of the fiction published in the women's magazines, of which these four may be taken as representative examples, reflected less change than one might suppose. In the stories, women tended to take traditionally feminine roles and traditionally conservative positions in the depiction of relations between the sexes, affairs of the home, and responsibilities of parenthood. In the overwhelming majority of these stories, women remained on the pedestal where the nineteenth century had placed them. So long as the majority of readers were content to accept this as their biological destiny, no legislation and no demonstrations were likely to affect the feminine status quo.

BIBLIOGRAPHICAL NOTE

Thirty-one issues drawn from four magazines were used in this study. These were: *Good Housekeeping* 30 (January to December, 1900) and 70 (February and June); *Ladies' Home Journal* 17 (July to December, omitting September, 1900) and 37 (January and June, 1920); *Delineator* 76 (July to December, 1910); and *Woman's Home Companion* 37 (January and June, 1910) and 47 (January and June, 1920).

The major source for circulation figures was N. W. Ayer & Son's *American Newspaper Annual & Directory*, Philadelphia: N. W. Ayer & Son, Newspaper Advertising Agents, for 1901, 1911, 1921, and 1924 (The phrase "& Directory" is absent from the 1901 title).

Other works, secondary sources and biography, were useful in providing the history of these magazines:

Bok, Edward. *The Americanization of Edward Bok*. New York: Charles Scribner's Sons, 1920.

Mott, Frank Luther. *A History of American Magazines*, Vols. 3-5. Cambridge, Mass.: Harvard University Press, 1938-1968.

Peterson, Theodore. *Magazines in the Twentieth Century*. Urbana: The University of Illinois Press, 1956.

Thayer, James Adams. *Astir, a Publisher's Life Story*. Boston: Small, Maynard & Company, 1910.

Towne, Charles Hanson. *Adventures in Editing*. New York: D. Appleton & Company, 1926.

Wood, James Playsted. *Magazines in the United States*. New York: The Ronald Press Company, 1949.

NOTES

[1]Charles Hanson Towne, *Adventures in Editing* (New York, 1926), 125-6. In subsequent reference to the magazines, titles are abbreviated and placed in parentheses.

THE "CELEBRITY" MAGAZINES

Maureen Honey

Assuming that "popular culture" can be defined as "a set of art forms characterized by wide popularity and an emphasis on recreational or entertainment values"[1] and assuming that high sales are a positive index of "wide popularity," celebrity magazines are obviously to be classified as a form of popular culture.

A brief history of the celebrity magazine reveals an immense popularity. From 1911 to 1937, for instance, at least 12 celebrity magazines came into existence, and during the 1920's and 1930's reached an audience of about 3,000,000 adults. By the early 1960's, two dozen had a total circulation of 8,000,000 copies per month, and by 1968, 10 movie-radio-TV magazines were among the 120 most widely sold publications of the year. In 1968, *Photoplay* alone had a total circulation of 1,106,047 copies per month while *Modern Screen* followed close behind with 830,726. If the monthly sales of *Motion Picture* and *Movie Mirror* are added to these figures, one discovers that a staggering total of 3,596,773 top celebrity magazines were sold each month, not including the large number of less successful publications. Again in 1969, *Photoplay*'s monthly counter sales (566,697) added to its subscription sales (595,993) yield a grand total of 1,162,690 copies sold per month. For the same year, *Modern Screen*'s monthly counter sales (396,156) added to its subscription sales (406,369) came to a total of 802,525 copies sold each month.

Because the celebrity magazines have such a wide circulation, they may have a significant impact on American attitudes and beliefs. It is important to study them in order to determine just what attitudes and beliefs are being reinforced, and to determine what functions such magazines may serve for the reader. If high popularity indicates successful fulfillment of audience needs, then to study how these needs are met is to gain some insight into the surrounding culture. Therefore, this study aims at defining the attitudes and perspectives conveyed by the celebrity magazines in order to better understand the American culture.

In establishing the bases for this study, it was first necessary to formulate a composite picture of the reading audience. Data for this was obtained by writing to the publishers of those magazines studied and by analyzing the appeal of their advertisements.[2]

All letters received from the publishers indicated that their readers were almost exclusively female, a conclusion borne out by the large number of ads directed specifically toward women, e.g., those dealing with female fashions, sanitary napkins, vaginal deodorants, and bust developers. Second, Bartell-Macfadden's *Photoplay* is read primarily by women 25-40 years in age. Dell's *Modern Screen* readers range in age from mid-teens through their 50's and 60's. Sterling Publishers' *Movie Mirror* fans are either pre-adolescents (11-14) or older women (40-65+). Although adolescents do make up a portion of the celebrity magazine market, the advertisements indicate that most readers are considerably past puberty. For example, ads dealing with the relief of acne are vastly outnumbered by ads dealing with the relief of hemorrhoids, varicose veins, sagging muscles, and age spots. Also, assuming that "The Lawrence Welk Show" appeals primarily to the older person, the high proportion of celebrity magazine articles dealing with Welk and his performers indicate a mature reading audience.

Third, all indications are that the reader is white. Advertisements use only white models, while articles concerning people of color are directed toward the prejudices and concerns of whites: "The Touch of a Black Man!" (*PNov69*), "John Lennon's Interracial Love Affair—The Shocking Inside Story!" (*MSOct68*), "Peyton Place: The Problems Began When the Negroes Moved In!" (*SLJan69*).

Fourth, the typical reader has a low income and little education. Out of approximately 300 randomly selected ads,[3] 95 had to do with earning, winning, or borrowing money. Most products advertised are low-cost items, such as synthetic wigs for $4.95 or second-hand dresses for $3.98. In addition, the reader is encouraged to get a high school diploma by enrolling in Correspondence Schools or to improve her job opportunities by learning to "speak and write like a college graduate." Fifth, both Bartell-Macfadden and Sterling Group Inc. claim their best-selling geographical location to be the Midwest. (Dell Publishing did not have available an area breakdown of sales.)

Thus, the composite of the typical celebrity magazine reader emerges as that of a white, middle-aged or older Midwestern female of a low socio-economic class (low socio-economic class being here defined as little education coupled with low income). To find out what attitudes were being reinforced for this reader, the most popular subjects and most oft-repeated themes were examined. Topics of interest that frequently recur are as follows:[4] Love (Romantic and Marital), Sex, Marriage, Adultery, Divorce, Birth, Parent-Child Relations, Every-Day Life of the Stars, Unhappiness of the Stars, Death or Illness, Religion, Drugs or the "New Morality," and Race Relations.

The most popular personalities are TV performers, movie stars, and political figures. Assuming that there is a correlation between popularity and cover story, Jackie Kennedy/Onassis was the most popular celebrity of these years. Out of a total of 65 magazines studied, Jackie Kennedy appeared on 18 covers, Elizabeth Taylor on 14, the Lennon Sisters on 12, Mia Farrow on 11, Connie Stevens on 8, and other members of the Kennedy family on 8. (For an explanation of the popularity of Jackie Kennedy, Liz Taylor, and the Lennon Sisters, see Appendix B.)

There were a number of major themes culled from the articles, which appeared with amazing frequency.

First, there is the theme that the stars may *seem* to want for nothing but that they are in fact unhappy, bored, and dissatisfied. "For [Gregory Peck] being a movie star has been one physical ordeal after another, not hardly as glamourous . . . as the general public may believe movie-making to be." (MovMJe68) "Ava [Gardner] sounds like she leads a romantic life in Spain but those who know Ava say she is a lonely, moody woman driven by deep passions and a restlessness that can never be satisfied." (MSJan68) Story titles also reflect this theme: "Hidden Heartaches behind the Academy Awards" (MSMay68), "Liz and Burton's Desperate Search to Find a World without Pain" (PJy69), "Mia Farrow Haunted by Family Tragedies." (MPA,p69)

Predictably enough, the second most popular theme contrasts the happy life of the ordinary woman with the unhappiness of the stars, since the celebrity must face public scrutiny and is denied the simple, homely rewards of the commoner. "The girls I grew up with have mostly married the boys they dated then or in college. They've settled in the same environment. When I go back to Dallas, their happiness seems fabulous to me." (Dorothy Malone in *P*Ap68) In an issue of *Modern Screen*, Connie Stevens is quoted as saying: "It would be difficult enough for two people to work out the kind of problems we've had if they were just ordinary citizens who could live their lives in privacy." (*MS* Je68)

Related with these two themes is a third, that wealth and power don't bring happiness. Only love, which is accessible to all people, can guarantee harmony and well-being. Without "the basic standards of love, helpfulness, and kindness," (*MS*Dec69) one can have all the money and fame in the world and still not be happy. "Money and power are fine, but tenderness and love are what make two people happy." (*P*Jy69) "The most important gift of all is the gift beyond price—love . . . and whether that love takes the form of a million-dollar plane or a dime-store ring really doesn't matter at all." (*MS*Jan68)

Next to love, the main ingredients for a happy life are family and religion. "Sophia has tried to keep her ambitions simple. . . . Her basic values have been stated by her clearly and simply: 'A husband to love, a baby to hold, and a meal to cook—no woman should ever ask for more.'" (*MS*Feb68) Home and family, in fact, are considered to be the very foundations of civilization. "We have to save our homes if we are going to save our nation. The ladies who put a home first—well, I admire them very much." (Lawrence Welk in *P*Jan68) "The very foundation of society [is] a happy home for children." (*MM*Dec69) "Family. A marvelous word. . . . We are to be grouped together, and brooded by love, and reared day-by-day in that first of church [sic] the family." (*MS*Oct69)

Several themes concern the nature of the star's relationship to the public. First of all, it is constantly emphasized that stars are very much like the average person. "[Doris Day] has hopes and fears like any other woman—she's no different from the woman next door, widowed and working." (*P*Nov69) "By this time, you have gathered that being around Eddie and Connie is really no different than being around any other young couple with a new baby. Sure, they're famous, and they have more money than most . . . but apart from that, they're just as proud and excited and happy, with the same joys and worries all parents share." (*MS* March68)

Secondly, stars are believed to have a duty to serve the public as moral guides. "The public needs images for its young people to imitate. Goodness and virtue must be shown to exist in this world." (in praise of the Lennon sisters, *MM* Dec69) "Sally [Field] has always been deeply concerned about her fans. She knows that they may be influenced by things she does and says, and she does not like to be presented by anyone as an impulsive, wild youngster." (*MS* Jan68) In fact, stars are often asked for advice. *Photoplay* has a regular feature, "All About Baby," in which various celebrities give their views on child raising, e.g., "Paul Burke discusses when and why to spank," (*P* Sept67), "Sandra Dee discusses a child's religious training." (*P* Je68)

Though stars must serve as moral examples, it is also assumed that some, at least, engage in immoral behavior. Indeed, Hollywood is often seen as a veritable den of iniquity. "Through the years, Hollywood has lived a dual life –a symbol of . . . success on the one hand, and a hotbed of sin, sex, and scandal on the other." (*MM* March70) References to homosexuality, promiscuity, and drugs abound.

Take, for example, the rugged star whose fans have only recently begun to guess his secret preference for boys . . . or the father, everyone in the business knows, who rarely goes home to his wife, and is frequently seen with young starlets. But his wife isn't worried—she knows that because of a necessary operation performed on the q.t., her husband is *unable* to cheat on her! (*MM* March70)

But whatever the star's set of values, or his or her conformity to conventional behavior, it is always assumed that the fan controls the star's life, and that the celebrity is ultimately responsible to, and must depend on, the reader's approval. "Just about every Hollywood star, like a fashion trend in women's wear, can become outdated, outmoded practically overnight. A sort of instant annihilation perpetrated by a fickle public. . . . It's absolutely true . . . that the fan magazines and fan clubs made [Rock Hudson] a star." (*MS* Jan68) The fan magazine reader is even encouraged to give advice for the stars. The June, 1969, issue of *Movie Life*, invited readers to write Nancy Sinatra about her second marriage. Similarly, the June, 1968, issue of *Photoplay* asked readers to vote on which of three bridal gowns Jackie

Kennedy should wear in her supposedly imminent marriage to Lord Harlech.

Several themes relate to the proper role of the American woman. First, the "good" woman gladly subordinates her own needs to those of her husband and serves him with obedient devotion. "It's Carol's year because she's smart enough to put Joe first. It's the life she must live to keep her husband happy. And this is truly how a real woman lives." (*P*Ap68) "Jeanne was there with her man, seeing that all of the problems with the children were solved before he came home; making sure that his dinner was ready when he wanted it; doing all the countless things that a truly devoted wife accepts as her role." (*MP*Je68)

A woman's role is also to provide emotional stability to her family. Woman is mistress of the heart and the great civilizer: "A husband's pride is his manhood; a wife's boundless love is her womanliness." (*P*Ap68) Audrey "will provide the womanly control that envelopes an impulsive man." (*MM*Ap68) "Building [a] harmonious family life is a womanly job." (*MP*Nov67) Thus, woman is the benevolent manipulator, building up her husband's ego and providing wise counsel to him and her children: "It was Jeannie who spurred Dean on to become the absolute giant of show business that he is." (*MS*Feb68)

To a woman, the magazines make clear, the ultimate happiness comes in being a housewife. In describing Kathy Lennon's reaction to her new home, *Photoplay* informed its readers that "she was absolutely beside herself. She was ecstatic. She ran from room to room, through arches, down hallways . . . a woman loose in a childhood dream." (*P*Je68) The Lennon Sisters' greatest ambition, the article continued, is "to stay home and tend their families," while they live "in anticipation of the beautiful day when they can quit being entertainers and just be happy housewives." But housewifery in itself is not enough—the woman's ultimate fulfillment and personal glory come only from motherhood. "[Patty Duke] talked about having babies—a woman's ultimate fulfillment." (*MS*Jan69) "[Liz] is not dominated by passion or ego. On the contrary, she is a real woman, for whom the birth of a child was to have been the supreme consecration of the love she bears for her husband." (*MS*Oct69) "With impending motherhood, Connie, once fiery and independent, suddenly changed. She became totally dependent on Eddie; she radiated happiness . . . like a bride!" (*MP*Je69) "[Lawrence Welk] has repeatedly said that the mother is the heart of the home, that she is the soul and center of it and that motherhood is the highest calling for any woman." (*MS* Dec69)

Women who do not devote themselves to home, husband, and children, and who violate the "good woman" norm are assumed to be miserable, guilt-ridden, and unhappy—or in Marya Mannes' words, "The apron is the mark of a good woman, the career the sign of a frustrated one, the single existence, the proof of a desperate one." "Only a woman understands how heart breaking it is to see her friends fall in love, get married, have children, make a home and simply foam with happiness. Those of us who are not that lucky sit by and wonder why *we* can't have that too. We ask ourselves what's wrong with us?" (Barbara Parkins in *MM* Je68) Commenting on the love failures of Mia Farrow and Barbara Parkins, *Modern Screen* revealed: "Both suddenly became terrified of the press, as if they feared that a word spoken in haste, a photograph taken unawares, would somehow reveal to the world what they were afraid to admit even to themselves—that for all their stardom, they felt they had somehow failed." (May68) Career women, however successful, are suspect as unfeminine, not quite womanly enough. "Success is lovely, but it can be lonely. Especially difficult for a woman as an actress, because in this business it is so easy to lose your femininity; you find yourself constantly battling for your rights—even against men." (Faye Dunaway in *P* Je68) Julie Andrews, *Photoplay* editorialized in January, 1968, would soon have "to choose whether to be an actress or a woman," a choice on which the magazine had definite ideas.

A recurrent theme in articles concerns the threat of the "other woman," based on the unspoken assumption that women are naturally competitive, and constant threats to each others' marital harmony. "It's not unheard of for a woman to dare another woman to steal her man . . . because it does her ego good to know that another woman finds him desirable and wants him, and can't have him. Most women are competitive creatures. They don't want a man no one else wants. If another woman tries to get him—and fails—doesn't it prove that the one who has him is the more desirable woman?" (*MS* Jy68) The more valuable the prize, the more threatening the other contestants: "[Mia's] presently the winner and new world's champ [because she caught Frank Sinatra] and she's relishing every moment of it. . . . Can she hang onto the crown, when there are contenders who are hungry?" (*MS* Jan67) Even daughters are seen as potential rivals for a man's affection: "Is

Joanne Jealous of Paul Newman's Daughter?" (*MS*Jy68) "Is Sybil's daughter coming between Liz and Richard?" (*MP*Je68) One of the reasons Liz Taylor has received such extensive coverage is that she has captured the hearts of two married men. As *Movie Mirror* points out: "Most women consider Liz a threat" (Dec69) because she has an uncanny ability to attract men.

The celebrity magazines unanimously agree that a man must dominate the relationship, and that women like to be dominated by a virile male. "He's my boss and I'm not being subservient or smug, but he's smarter than I and that's it. It's a very smart woman who knows this. It's an even smarter woman who says it." (*PA*p68) "[Janet Lennon's husband] is the boss and she adores it." (*P*Jan70) "[In an early picture] Clark Gable calmly trod on Barbara Stanwyck's hand, and during the preview of the picture, women screamed with delight. . . . [In another picture] there was a scene in which he had to hit Norma Shearer and push her around. That scene was the beginning of his huge success." (*MS*May68) It is not simply that men must dominate because women respect authority in the male, but because women need protection from a confusing and often hostile world. "A woman without a man is like the proverbial ship lost out at sea." (*ML*Je69) "[Doris Day] lost a man—a real man—who was her strength, her best friend, the center of her existence as only a real man can be. He shielded her from a confusing world. He solved all of the serious problems in her life." (*SS*March69) Commenting upon Patrick Nugent's being sent to Vietnam, *Photoplay* sympathized with Luci Johnson: "They had been a family in Austin—husband, wife and child, building a life together. Now that life lay in ruins at her feet. Without Pat to guide her, how could she manage?" (Je68) Though women have superior charm, men have superior skill in dealing with the outside world. "[Jackie Kennedy] went to Cambodia . . . at the behest of President Johnson. [Lord] Harlech's mission as a skilled diplomat . . . was to see that Jackie was not tricked in a diplomatic gambit by the shrewd Prince Sihanouk." (*P*Je68) If a husband is not available, a woman may even turn to her son for leadership: "[Doris Day] has turned for manly guidance to some extent to her only child—her son." (*P*Jan69) In addition to protecting the woman from worldly machinations, the good man provides for her financial security; in fact, his masculinity depends on it. "[Dora Malone's] dad was a full-time provider, a marvelous example of the secu

a girl needs if she's to believe in the nobility of men." (*P*Ap68) "A
man works to give his family security and educational advantages."
(Lawrence Welk in *ModM*Dec69) "[Mahlon's] pride would be rubbed
raw, as he watched brave Kathy helping to pay the bills." (*P*Ap68)

On the other hand, those men who fail to live up to their responsibilities are judged to be irresponsible, exploitative, unworthy of a
"good" woman's respect. Warren Beatty, the reader is told, "never
worries. . . . When he falls in love, he focusses in, and . . . marriages
crumble, homes break up." (*MS*Je68) When Eddie Fisher married
Connie Stevens three months before she gave birth, the fan magazines
were filled with articles such as: "Pregnant Connie forced to share
Eddie with Debbie Reynolds—Connie Stevens Fisher has suffered
just about every humiliation at Eddie Fisher's hands that is con-
ceivable." (*TV&MovP*Sep68) "[It is said that] the deejays are
giving a lot of airplay to Eddie's recording of 'Call Me Irresponsible.' "
(*MP*Je68)

The world of the celebrity, as the magazine writers see it, is a
world of dark and mysterious forces. Happiness arrives and departs,
fortunes accumulate and fail, reputations rise and fall, seemingly
without explanation. Life among the famous, the magazines imply,
is largely controlled by fate. Astrology plays a major role in determining the celebrity's future. *Motion Picture* has a regular feature
entitled "Hollywood Star-O-Scopes—See what you have in common
with the stars that share your sign." *Movie Life* has a similar column
called "Star Revelations" which gives astrological analyses of the
stars' personalities. *Photoplay* explains the surprise marriage of
Jackie and Onassis by referring to the zodiac: "According to their
horoscopes, it was all in the stars for them." (Jan69) If not the
planets, chance plays an important part. "How else," asked *Popular
Screen* in September, 1967, "can you explain what each of the Kennedy women went through for the men they loved?" Similarly,
Movie Mirror, September, 1969, choosing Elizabeth Taylor, Kim
Novak, and Marilyn Monroe as "Unlucky Ladies," believed that
"Fate has singled them out to pay a high price for fame and fortune.
. . . They are marked for success and unhappiness, wealth and poverty
of heart." "Faye Dunaway: Afraid She'll Give Her Lover the Kiss of
Death! . . . It was as if a perverse quirk of fate had control over her
life. . . . She searches for love and fulfillment, all the time aware of
the one thing she fears the most . . . the love jinx." (*MM*March70)

Since fate is uncontrollable, the most that can be done is to prepare oneself by consulting horoscopes and reading "seers" such as Jeane Dixon and Peter Hurkos. *Modern Screen*'s lead article in its January, 1970, issue was "Hollywood in the 70's" in which Peter Hurkos used his "psychic powers" to predict what would happen to favorite celebrities in the next decade. At the end of the article, it was proudly announced that "Hurkos will give a psychic reading, in *Modern Screen*, to five lucky readers each month."

Yet there is, the magazine's articles suggest, much to be said for the powers of love and faith and morality in solving life's problems, and in confronting fate. Love is considered as a secret, potent mechanism for securing harmony, success, and peace. "Something which has united Sophia and Carlo every day of their married lives [is] love, pure and unselfish." (*MS*Oct69) "Connie has determination and love so things will turn out fine." (*MS*Jan68) "Love is blind to all problems" (*ML*Je69) Faith in God is also believed to be a positive force sweeping away problems and causing things to "turn out right." "It was Susan who helped shape the boys—even hammer them—into men. What helped her was her faith and strength and an unfaltering belief in God." (*MP*Je68) "There was something within her that forced her onward—faith. Sophia has more than once credited her marriage, her success, her son to Almighty God. Without Him, she feels, she would still be wandering the streets of Puzzuoli or Naples, hunger tearing her apart." (*MS*Oct69)

Several conclusions can be drawn about the reader from an examination of these magazines' contents. For instance, the high value placed on self-sacrifice, piety, self-reliance, loyalty to the family, honesty, simplicity, and obedience to God indicates traditional, puritanical code of ethics—a code that promises rewards for hard work, clean living, and faith.

Several thematic elements reflect ambivalence and massive insecurity. "Wealth and power don't bring happiness," "The common girl is happier than the star," "The stars have problems too," "The housewife is happy," "The mother is fulfilled." All these themes continually reassure the reader that she is happy and that her values are correct. The stars themselves repeat these themes as do the psychiatrists. On the other hand, there is evidence that the reader secretly believes that wealth and fame do bring happiness. As was so perceptively observed by *Movie Mirror* in an interview with Michael

Caine: " 'People used to say 'Remember, money doesn't buy happiness.' It's not true—I am rich and I'm happy. I don't understand people who find success and money a problem. . . . When I travel, they pay my first class fares, I sleep at the best hotels, and eat in the best restaurants. Perhaps because it's fashionable nowadays to pretend that money isn't important and millionaires have to insist that they only want the simple things of life, everyone is amazed by Michael's frank admission that he loves money and what it can bring. But he has the courage to say straight out what most people secretly believe." (Je68)

Several themes reflect the reader's insecurity about the validity of her way of life. Perceiving other women as direct threats indicates status insecurity; because selfless devotion to one's mate is no guarantee against divorce or adultery, a woman may find herself single and lonely with little warning. The fact that the "good woman" is often scorned in favor of a more attractive one provides evidence that adhering to cultural norms doesn't necessarily bring happiness. The fear of growing old is directly related to the fear of the younger, sexier woman; thus the magazine advertisements indicate that the reader is preoccupied with making herself appear young and beautiful. Out of approximately 300 advertisements, 124 were directly concerned with improving one's physical appearance. There is a plethora of products which develop the bust, remove unwanted hair, reduce weight, put on weight, make the hair glisten, whiten teeth, improve the figure, and generally increase sexual allure. There is some reason to believe that the reader of these magazines senses certain dissatisfactions with her every-day life, and finds justification in the lives of the stars. The preoccupation with conspicuous consumption, sexual behavior, and glamorous romance can be seen as a measure of the extent to which these things are denied in real life. This dissatisfaction often results in the symbolic punishment of the celebrities. The articles concerning the misery of the stars function as modes of scapegoating for women who are denied access to the forbidden fruits of licentious behavior, emotional fulfillment, and luxurious wealth. Because the reader has limited economic and social freedom, she enjoys seeing the privileged elite suffer for its monetary and moral excesses.[21]

The readiness to believe that stars have feelings similar to those of the ordinary citizen can be seen as both an attempt to order reality according to the evidence of one's own experiences and as a manifestation of the desire for reassurance that even successful people have the same problems as the average girl. At the same time, the belief that the world is run by uncontrollable forces–the heavenly bodies, fate, chance, luck–reflects a feeling of powerlessness. As adherence to cultural norms may fail to bring success and happiness, so the reader turns to superstition and astrology for explanation of why things work the way they do. Even advertising reflects this "Now you can learn what life holds for you . . . Love, good fortune, a new job, travel. The answer is in the stars. Hollywood stars pay hundreds of dollars for readings and some owe their success to it . . . Could be the beginning of your fondest dreams." (*MovS*Ap68) A magic device advertised in *Movie Stars* (Ap68) is described as follows: "Make people do what you want! This is worth a million dollars in the success, love, admiration and riches it will bring to you."

There are six major reasons why the celebrity magazines appeal to a market of readers made up of educationally and economically deprived women. First, they are relatively inexpensive. *Photoplay* and *Modern Screen* sell for 50¢, most others for 35¢. Second, the cover pictures and headlines are eye-catchers; the magazine is filled with colorful, visually appealing pictures. Third, they are placed in stores which these women would be most likely to patronize, such as drugstores and supermarkets, and are easily accessible. Fourth, they are easy to read–the language is simple and the subject matter familiar. Fifth, there is much use of pictures to explicate theme. For example, a story may be entitled "The Games Liz and Richard Play to Tantalize Each Other," while superimposed over the title are pictures of Liz Taylor on the right and Richard Burton on the left, both staring at a disrobed sexy starlet in the middle. The combination of picture and title are clever enough to attract attention, yet clear enough to be readily understood. Sixth, celebrities make excellent material for escapist reading. They are intriguing to the general public because they represent the incarnation of the American Dream, which promises to all untold luxury and wealth. People read about them because they are extraordinary–talented, wealthy and, most important, famous. The reader can pretend for a while that she too is one of the beautiful people.

Not only are celebrities rewarded with wealth, power, and adoration, their success is incomprehensible "in a society whose ethos rests upon hard work and virtuous deportment." Hence, the insatiable curiosity to find out how these super-beings live, to discover their secret key to success. The reader believes that perhaps some of her idol's magic qualities will rub off on her: "Ah, she'll sigh, if only I could be like her—if only I could *be* her—then I would be completely happy!" (*MP*Ap69)

Celebrities also make good copy for escapist literature because the public will believe almost anything about them. The public's view of the celebrity is one-dimensional; that is, the movie, TV screen, or newspaper page reflects only one side of the individual on display. They are not, in a sense, "real" people, but pictures on a screen, faces in an illustration, names in a column. What they do and say has little relation to reality, and the public is prepared to accept the illusion as the fact. Celebrities make good copy, and because of their high visibility make good scapegoats. As not-quite-real people with beauty, wealth, and fame they attract the reader's secret envy, and one can readily understand why celebrities serve admirably as whipping-boys for those with little economic power or social mobility. The fan magazines successfully exploit these escapist potentials by providing reams of gossip and "inside information" to satisfy curiosity about the stars' daily lives, their sexual standards, and their presumed unhappiness. And in addition, the magazines actively promote what Frank Getlein has called the "personality cult,"[5] the creation of a person who does not exist except in the imagination of the reader. Thus *Motion Picture* for December, 1968, rhapsodized about the possibility of Warren Beatty co-starring with Mia Farrow, "Warren and Mia would be an irresistible combination. How ironic it will be if it turns out that Frank inadvertently handed his ex-wife to another man on a solid gold platter. How ironic! How delightful! What a fabulous story! And it's one we'll keep you posted on if it should come to pass." (*MP*Dec68)

Though the celebrity magazine reader may obtain vicarious satisfaction through reading about the privileged elite, she is likely to feel frustration at the contrast between her life and that of the stars. Thus the celebrity magazines continually editorialize and reassure the reader by using the stories of the stars as moral lessons, providing guidance as well as fantasy. The reader is told that there is no need to desire that which she cannot have, since "Wealth and power don't bring happiness," "The stars are unhappy," "Women are fulfilled through marriage and motherhood."

This study raises some interesting questions concerning the nature of popular culture. Does all such popular literature function dually as escapist diversion and value reinforcement? Are the themes which appear in a popular medium like the celebrity magazine reflected in "elite" art? If so, what implications does that have for the relationship between elite and popular culture? Perhaps it is not true that popular art is aesthetically inferior because it is directed to a mass audience. It may be that those needs which can be most profitably met by the mass media lend themselves to artistically inferior productions. For instance, the celebrity magazine reader's need for inexpensive, easily accessible diversion could perhaps be met in more creative ways than by the exploitation of her insecurities and fears. It may be that the mass media's desire for sure profits causes it to meet needs in artistically unsatisfying ways.

What do the themes in a popular art form like the celebrity magazine tell us about the workings of the culture from which it derives? And what is the impact of themes relating to proper role behavior such as are found in the celebrity magazine? For example, one reason women may be so reluctant to assume positions of authority and "wordly" power is perhaps due to the fact that they have internalized popular themes which preclude competition with men and self-assertive behavior. The mass media may be as significant a socializing force as the family and the school. If so, it is essential to study such examples of popular culture—its content, its ramifications—in order to be aware of how and in what direction it molds those it reaches.

APPENDIX A

Titles of articles dealing with these subjects of interest:

Love (Romantic and Marital)

"Eddie Fisher finds instant love" (*PN*ov69)
"David Janssen's love trap: The girl who fell in" (*PA*ug69)
"The shocking sacrifices Andre Previn makes for Mia's love" (*MS*May69)
"Why Welk and his wife are still married lovers" (*MP*March70)

Sex

"Jackie and the dirty movie scandal" (*MS*Jan70)
"Husband saves Julie Andrews as sex maniac comes at her" (*MP*March70)

"Jackie and Mia: The wild nights they try to hide" (*MovW*Feb70)

Marriage

"Natalie Wood weds with doctor's help" (*P*Oct69)
"Tom Jones: The truth about his marriage" (*MS*Dec69)

Adultery

"Glen Campbell: The day his wife found him in bed with another woman"
    (*ML*March70)
"David Janssen, you committed adultery with 31 women!" (*P*Oct69)

Divorce

"How a mere girl took Dean Martin from his wife's arms" (*MP*March70)
"Frank Sinatra: Is he really divorced from his first wife?" (*MS*Dec69)
"Ted Kennedy: The truth behind the divorce rumors" (*MS*Dec69)

Birth

"Sophia Loren: Is she hiding a new pregnancy?" (*ML*March70)
"Elvis and Andy: The heroes have babies" (*P*Nov69)
"Jackie to be a mother again" (*MM*Dec69)

Parent-Child Relations

"Connie, Mia, Jackie: How their new way of life can harm their babies"
    (*ML*March70)
"Paul Newman: His fight to win back his son's love" (*MP*March70)
"Dean Martin tells his daughters about love" (*P*Oct69)

Every-Day Life of the Stars

"George Hamilton at Home" (*ML*March70)
"Marlo Thomas: Special hometown report" (*MP*Ap69)
"Close-up with the stars" (*SS*Sept69)

Unhappiness of the Stars

"Lucille Ball recalls the mistakes in her life" (*ML*March70)
"Doris Day: Her midnight tears" (*P*Nov69)
"Famed astrologer predicts 3 Liz tragedies for 1969" (*MP*Ap69)

Death, Illness

"Steve McQueen: The physical handicap that threatens him" (*MS*Jan70)
"Doctors fight to save Liz Taylor from life of crippling pain" (*MP*March70)
"Jackie: Did Ari have a heart attack?" (*MS*Dec69)

Religion

"Leonard Nimoy: The religious ceremony that brought his family back together"
      (*MS*Jan70)
"Jackie Kennedy and Kathy Lennon: How each defied the Pope" (*MP*Ap69)

Drugs, the "New Morality"

"Sidney Poitier: My suitcase full of pills" (*P*Oct69)
"Tony Curtis: I made my father take dope!" (*P*Oct69)
"Bob Cummings' wife accuses him of being 59 year old speed freak" (*ModM*March70)
"Shocking new discoveries about the hippie life that led to the Tate massacre"
      (*Mp*March70)
"Martin kids go nude" (*ModM*Dec69)

APPENDIX B

There are at least three reasons why Jackie Kennedy, Elizabeth Taylor, and the Lennon Sisters are so popular in the period studied. First of all, they receive publicity in three major media—movies, television and newspapers—and they are all ideal models for the American woman. Liz Taylor has the image of a "vamp" who collects men's hearts the way other women collect store stamps, and she "has for years reflected the American woman's idea of beauty." (MSJan69) The Lennons are wholesomely attractive girls who insist on doing their own housework and who obey their husbands, their father, and God—the idealized girls-next-door. Jackie Kennedy was America's sweetheart. She represented the epitome of cultured refinement, aristocratic beauty, and feminine dignity. Liz Taylor, the Lennon Sisters, and Jackie Kennedy represent respectively the sexy bad girl, the virtuous Madonna, and the queenly aristocrat—all disparate but connected elements in the American woman's idealized image of herself.

These women provide the reader with vicarious experiences in romantic ecstasy, domestic bliss, and worldly power. Liz Taylor's marriages to five attractive men earned her the envy of thousands of American women, tied to unimaginative husbands and tedious household chores. However, not only do women perceive her as a threat, they simultaneously wish to identify with her: "She has . . . been the embodiment of the turbulent and sometimes tormented emotional heights millions of American women secretly wish they could attain themselves. She has known the inexpressible ecstasy of young love, wild love, mature love, even irresponsible love. She has been a wife, mother, divorcée, widow. She has been a rebel and a conformist; sweet, kind, hateful, sympathetic, obstinate, submissive, and indiscreet." (MSJan69) To identify with Liz Taylor is to identify with all that is romantic and glamorous in life.

The Lennon Sisters provide a different kind of idealized escape. They reassure the reader that she can have domestic bliss if she is submissive, sweet, and humble. " 'I just want to stay at home and scrub floors and take care of my husband,' Kathy insists, and Janet agrees: 'Lee and I just like to spend an evening watching television together. We hardly ever go out.' " (Look, Oct. 21, 1969) "Probably some people would say this kind of marriage is a big bore. If it is, we're certainly enjoying boredom." (Peggy Lennon in MMJe68) Women feel reassured by celebrities who affirm traditional morality in a confusing, often frightening world. "The girls are best known for slow, sweet songs done in close harmony . . . a kind of music that is out of style now, except with all the people who find folk-rock harsh and a little frightening. Many Americans don't want to hear songs about death and drugs and war. They demand music to think nice thoughts by—and the Lennons specialize in it." (Look, Oct. 21, 1969) The Lennon Sisters serve as nostalgic reminders to those who remember "the good old days" when life was clear-cut and simple.

Jackie Kennedy's popularity is a more complex phenomenon because her image underwent a drastic change after her marriage. At first, "Jackie Kennedy could do no wrong. She was . . . America's queen . . . the queenly symbol of courage and honor." (PAp68) She was the ideally compassionate, benevolently manipulative, womanly tower of strength, made the "living custodian of her husband's immortality." (MSJan67) The mechanisms involved in this kind of heroine worship are far too complicated to be dealt with here. It is enough to say that from 1963 to 1968, Jackie Kennedy served as celebrity magazines' aristocratic ideal. Her marriage at the close of 1968 came as a blow, or as *Photoplay* put it in January, 1969, "The man-in-the-street responded with almost unanimous displeasure." If she had married for money, or disregarded her children's welfare, or turned her back on her country, or disobeyed her family heritage, she had violated a number of cultural norms and betrayed her widow's trust to boot. "If JFK could look down and see his wife as she is today, he would undoubtedly find that she has become a complete stranger to him. What would he think of this stranger? What do you think?" (MPDec69) But this reversal of roles did not lessen curiosity about her. For now Jackie, as well as Liz, plays the seductive Eve to a Lennon sister's Virgin Mary and serves as an admirable scapegoat for envious readers. Thus, Liz, Jackie, and the Lennons represent three facets of the American woman's secret aspirations—beauty (wholesome or seductive), power (direct or indirect), and emotional contentment (through romantic ecstasy, domestic bliss, or great wealth).

NOTES

[1]John Cawelti, "Popular Culture Programs," pamphlet publication of the Popular Culture Association, 1970, 8. In this study the term "celebrity magazine" refers to what is commonly called the "movie magazine." This term is preferred because "movie magazines" are actually concerned with TV stars and political figures as well as movie stars. With the advent of television in 1950 and the appearance of the Kennedys in 1960, fan magazines have devoted less and less space to personalities who are strictly stars of the Hollywood screen. Magazines used in this study for the period 1966-1970 were *Photoplay* (*P*), *Modern Screen* (*MS*), *Motion Picture* (*MP*), *Movie Mirror* (*MM*), *Modern Movies* (*ModM*), *Movie Life* (*ML*), *Movie Stars* (*MovS*), *Photo Screen* (*PS*), *Screenland* (*S*), *Screen Life* (*SL*), *Silver Screen* (*SS*), *Movie World* (*MovW*), *TV & Picture Life* (*TV&PL*), *TV & Movie Play* (*TV&MP*). Footnotes following quotes from the magazines will be in parentheses with the magazine title italicized and the date represented by the month and year. For example, a quotation from the June issue of *Photoplay* in 1969 would be immediately followed by this notation: (PJe69)

[2]Letters were written to the following publishers: Magazine Management Co. Inc. (*Screen Stars*), Actual Publishing Co. Inc. (*Screen Life*), Sterling Group Inc. (*Movie Mirror*), Dell Publishing Co. (*Modern Screen*), Ideal Publishing Corp. (*Silver Screen, Movie Stars*), Stanley Publishing Inc. (*TV & Movie Play, Photo Screen*), Macfadden-Bartell Corp. (*Photoplay, Motion Picture, Silver Screen, Screenland*).

[3]Ads were selected from the following magazines: *Photoplay* (Nov., 69), *Motion Picture* (Nov., 69), *Modern Movies* (Dec., 69), *Movie Stars* (Ap., 68), *Modern Screen* (Jan., 67), *Motion Picture* (Nov., 66).

[4]For examples of titles relating to these subjects, see Appendix A.

[5]Frank Getlein, "Movies and the Modern Mind," *Dramatic Arts and the Modern Mind,* Edward Cardinal Mooney Lecture Series, Sacred Heart Seminary, Detroit, Mich., 1963-64, p. 11.

THE DEATH OF THE SATURDAY EVENING POST, 1960-1969: A POPULAR CULTURE PHENOMENON

Stephen Holder

The death of *The Saturday Evening Post* did not come as a major surprise for most of its fans. For years we had watched the gradual decline of our magazine; many of us continued our subscriptions long after the *Post* had any but nostalgic use for us. The shocking thing about *Post*'s death in February of 1969 was the realization it brought for many Americans: the realization that a whole chapter of American Popular History had ended.

While the life of the *Post* is a fascinating story, it is similar to many American success stories and is relatively simple. *Post*'s death, on the other hand, provides a number of speculations about changing trends in American Popular Culture and is extremely complex. A study of *Post*'s death is more than a simple consideration of the failure of a magazine; it is a study of the role of the magazine in a society of increasingly complex media. And, during the *Post*'s seventy year life span, American thought, economics and values underwent tremendous change.

Marshall McLuhan has said that the "medium is the message," that is, that the means by which a message is transmitted is more important than the message itself. If this statement is true, it goes a long way in explaining the demise of *The Saturday Evening Post*. Certainly, television had a number of specific advantages over linear media at the outset. The first of these, and one of the most important, is simple novelty. New experiences, regardless of category, have traditionally attracted the American people. Novelty does not, of course, account for the continuing popularity of television as a communicative channel. But it does offer one explanation for the initial impetus for television; the makers of television sets were on firm ground with their first efforts. Americans had long expressed a need for visual experiences. Witness the phenomenal growth and development of the movie industry . . . as well as the rapid growth of related visual forms: the home movie and the slide projector.

A second big push for television came from the traditional American fascination with possessions. As soon as television became at all dependable, it was a "must" for every middle-class household. And, once the set arrived (for whatever reason), a definite obligation to use it accrued. Definite family behavior patterns are a result of this obligation; television has so firmly established itself over the past decade that it can now be viewed as ritual experience.

A most important characteristic of any ritual is that it be performed always in exactly the same way: variation is contrary to the whole idea of controlling processes or participating in rites by observing systematic regularities.[1]

And so television became firmly entrenched in the average, middle-class, American home. That *The Saturday Evening Post* had filled at least a part of this ritual need formerly is fairly obvious. All the signs point to it: the continuing reader participation, the virtually static layout, the regular features (such as "The Perfect Squelch," "You Be the Judge" or "What's Happening Here"), etc. The implications of television as a new ritual experience are almost as obvious: assuming a fairly fixed number of hours of leisure time for the average American family, *the intrusion of a new ritual must result in the exclusion of a former ritual.*

Why, one might ask, didn't the same thing happen to radio? That answer is a fairly easy one. First, radio is an audial medium, not a visual one. One can listen to radio and read magazines simultaneously. Moreover, radio is a portable medium; we can listen as we drive our cars, sun ourselves at the beach, etc. Secondly, the producers of radio shows were quick to perceive that the market for programs which demanded close attention was ended. They saw radio's new function as a kind of "filler" for the times between regularly planned activities. Note that even the afternoon "soaps," the last close-attention programs to die, have been replaced by rock music, capsulated news, and other brief communications. Magazines, as linear media with relatively fixed readership groups, simply are not in the position to make such a shift.

It is likely that *Post* did, however, retain some of its value as ritual experience. We see that subscription figures during the 1960's remained practically static. Had nothing changed, those six and a half million people might still be reading *The Saturday Evening Post*.

But many things about *Post* did change, perhaps in an attempt to compete more effectively with the visual media. A comparison of any *Post* issue from 1960 with any issue from 1969, for example, reveals a number of obvious visual changes. Covers depicting traditional American experiences were replaced by covers screaming sensationalism. The issue of January 25, 1969, the next-to-the-last issue, boasted on its cover that it would tell us "How Barney Rosset Publishes 'Dirty Books' for Fun and Profit." Inside we note that the traditional "The Cover," a paragraph explaining the nuances of the cover experience, is gone. The editorial occupies its place. The quality of paper, too, changed in favor of glossier stock; photographs became larger and brighter, illustrations smaller and fewer. Type styles changed in favor of darker, bolder characters. Eye appeal was the keystone of the 1969 edition; mind appeal marks the earlier ones, and content of articles and fiction changed to correspond with the new image.

What was the net result of all these changes in favor of high visibility? For those six and a half million readers, scattered across America, those "silent majority" types, *The Saturday Evening Post* had lost whatever they subscribed for. The habitual reading experience that *Post* provided for them was gone. *By changing image and format, Post lost its value as ritual experience.* Its competitor in the family-readership market, *The Reader's Digest*, changed format little if any, in recent history; its relative position in the market improved while *Post*'s dwindled. In 1960 there was one *Reader's Digest* for every 14.9 Americans; in 1968 there was one for every 11.5 Americans. In 1960 there was one *Post* for every 28.2 Americans; in 1968 there was one for every 29.5 Americans. If (and it seems a reasonable hypothesis) *Post*'s value as ritual was a mainstay in supporting it during its declining years, the changes wrought by the new editorial regime effectively knocked the support out from under an already heavily leaning magazine.

The "message" part of McLuhan's statement deserves attention too. TV took several pages from *Post*'s book in this area, for many of the traditional *Post* favorites appeared in one form or another on the TV screen. Situation comedies, travelogues, family dramas, all in their stock form, still fill most of the "prime time" hours.

Just as the mass magazines had supplanted the Novel of Manners as escapist fare, television began to supply an endless stream of situation comedies, horse operas, and detective stories to entertain the audience the Post claimed as its own. Indeed, even "Hazel" became a TV show.[2]

Even the most superficial examination of such TV shows as "Mayberry, R.F.D.," "Green Acres" or "Gunsmoke" demonstrates their sameness in content, from week to week. This repetition of basic format is essentially the same formula that worked so well for *Post* with continuing stories such as William Hazlitt Upson's "Alexander Botts" series or Norman Reilly Raine's "Tugboat Annie."

While all this was taking place in TV's "message," *Post* cast about for new content, new ways to titillate the public. If TV's success was indicative of the "message" the public wanted, *Post* would have been better advised to turn out more of the old things that it was so good at. (It seems ironic that one of Curtis's last presidents was a former television executive.) The changes in content (discussed later in this study) upset readers. One reader wrote the following letter, published in the issue of January 25, 1969:

Where are the stories that give man good thoughts, that leave man with a pleasant inner glow and relieve him for a moment of the worldly tensions? To help people emulate the good, instead of the permissive bad, is a goal that is worth more than a man's life. This I believe. This I would write, to help my fellow man, I hope.[3]

This was a definite plea for the *Post* to align itself with the generally acceptable, conforming ideas that were indigenous to the media of popular culture in which the magazine moved.

Another important consideration in the relationship of the *Post* to television was the cost factor.

. . . TV licenses were granted as federal monopolies in every city and region, in what advertisers called "markets." These were not national markets in the old sense, but something new: conglomerations of special markets offered to advertisers at rates magazines could never meet. To get its stories into a home, a magazine has to bear the cost of buying paper treating it with ink and words at a printing plant, and then shipping it. Television sends its stories over airwaves provided "free" by the FCC.[4]

As the number of television sets in American households skyrocketed, more and more advertisers shifted from magazines to the new medium, believing their advertising dollars would allow them to reach more people than they did with magazines—and a family that owned a television set was a family with purchasing power. *Post* and the other big magazines attempted to fight back, but to no avail.

The answer of the big magazines to the threat of TV was to get as many readers as TV could show in its Nielsen ratings: to fight numbers with numbers. As the numbers went up, so did the cost of paper and printing. Only very rich advertisers could afford to buy a page at $40,000. Smaller advertisers were closed out. The effects of the "numbers game" were synergistic and final.[5]

The small, one or two inch advertisements that formerly dotted the pages throughout every issue of *Post* disappeared. At the same time, bigger advertisers, the producers of durable goods, life insurance companies, etc., began to question the value of *Post*, too. Editor William Emerson's answer relied heavily on the value of *Post* as ritual experience. When asked by the advertisers, "Why should there be a *Post*?" Emerson said:

Because it is unique. Because it will, in time of turmoil and anxiety, be an expression of common sense, of belief in America and its traditional political and economic systems, of belief in both civil rights and law and order, of belief in the American people and their basic decency and wisdom. If this sounds conventional or platitudinous, we would do well to remember George Orwell's dictum, in *1984*, that truisms are true, and that the basic right is the right to know that two and two make four.[6]

The effect, then, of television on *The Saturday Evening Post*, and on magazines in general, was tremendous. Many of the visual changes in *Post* during its declining years can be attributed directly to the competition of television and the demand for visual presentation, a definite trend away from linear communication and a move toward spatial stimuli. The result of this move was probably an alienation of many readers. Compare, for example, the visual reinforcement of values offered by the typical *Post* format . . . that is, in issues up to about 1965 . . . with the "jazzy" layout and sensational photography of the last issues. If there is a lesson to be learned here, it is probably this: *spatial communication is the proper province of the spatial media*; linear media cannot compete well in a spatial arena. For the *Post* to compete with television at its own game was almost as absurd as a six foot man attempting to swim competitively against a six foot shark.

During the years that George Horace Lorimer reigned in the offices of Curtis Publishing Company, *Post* had a definite policy toward its readers. That policy was a very simple one: *readers are important.* And the readers knew that they were important. Thousands of letters from concerned people all across the country arrived at the *Post* offices yearly. People responded to *Post* because they felt that they had personal stakes in it; they were quick to praise or condemn features which they felt added to or detracted from "their" magazine. Their letters were invariably answered, many by Lorimer himself. Lorimer's morning routines were rigid. After looking at some manuscripts,

. . . he attacked the mail. There were three formidable piles of it. The right-hand file was personal mail, the usual potpourri of requests for everything from speeches to articles to money, and a batch of fan letters. These he read first and set aside to dictate the answers after lunch. The middle pile was addressed to the *Post* and he read those with care, because they helped him to keep his finger on the public pulse.[7]

The mail enabled Lorimer to make intelligent decisions about what to include in *Post* and what to leave out. His criterion for accepting or rejecting any article was simple: "Will the *Post* audience like it?"

Just how great the readers' sense of participation was, and the importance of that participation, were not recognized by the regime that made the decision to cut subscriber lists in the last year of *Post*'s life. Many readers, not only those on the unwanted list, felt that their relationship with *Post* had changed:

It was not just that the subscribers had a legal and moral right to their magazines but that they seemed to believe they had a personal relationship with the *Post*. They thought that when they subscribed, the editor rejoiced, and when they canceled, he grieved. Now they were learning that they were nothing but names on a computer tape.[8]

One fact seems to stand out about many forms of popular culture: *constituent loyalty is a prerequisite to success.* This phenomenon seems very similar to the situation in the auto industry. A man who has owned one make of car for years may tolerate one, even two "lemons" before opting for another. This was indeed the case with *Post*; long after the magazine stopped meeting their needs, many subscribers hung on tenaciously, remaining faithful until *Post* literally kicked them out of the ranks by removing their names from subscriber lists. Reader reaction to the cancellations was astounding. *Post* offices were swamped with letters. The office staff designated for correspondence was unable to handle the added volume of mail; many letters received absolutely no attention.

In retrospect, we can see that *Post* was less an institution than a commodity like other commodities—in fact, a remarkably successful one during most of its life. But, as is the case with any commodity in an open market, *Post* had to live with certain economic facts of life, and its failure to do so contributed considerably to its decline and ultimate death.

Perhaps the most obvious problem was *Post*'s failure to maintain its position relative to the increased population. In the years 1960-1968 *Post* not only failed to increase its subscription lists substantially, but its per capita advantage declined. This would seem a typical symptom of any dying publication, not a cause of death, but the symptoms themselves became causes for further symptoms. Between 1960-1968 *Post* increased only .027 as much as U. S. population (584,343: :21,080,000); the number of potential readers for each issue moved from 1:28.2 to 1:29.5. The *Post*, therefore, was increasingly less attractive to advertisers. With fewer advertisers, *Post* had less advertising revenue; less advertising revenue meant less operating capital, which pointed to smaller production. Smaller production meant, ultimately, a smaller readership, and smaller readership made the magazine even less attractive to advertisers. At the same time the *Post* was plunging into its downward spiral, operating costs soared. Not every magazine was adversely affected by the trends of the 60's, however. Note that *Newsweek* almost doubled in circulation, improving its ratio from 1:138.1 to 1:94.5. The odds seemed to be stacked against the loser, and advertisers, naturally, were more interested in the lower cost-per-page rates of a growing concern. Moreover, since it was a family magazine, *Post* advertising came from concerns selling products that appealed to families. But as shown elsewhere, the small advertisers were beginning to be drummed out; this left only the bigger companies. Meanwhile as leisure-time activities became increasingly centered outside the home, family-style advertisements proved less appealing than those featuring beautiful girls in bathing suits or exotically dressed swingers.

Business trends also hampered *Post*'s efforts to stay alive. Big business in America moved increasingly toward conglomerate structures, a tendency which cut down the number of potential advertisers without diminishing greatly the number of products to be advertised:

As a matter of fact, what was good for General Motors would soon leave the *Post* on the beach. Many of those forty advertisers that had backed Lorimer in 1914 were now divisions of General Motors. By the fifties, competition by producers in the mass market had noticeably ebbed, and as the tide of the distributive society went out, so did potential advertisers.[9]

The *Post* then issued "A" copies of the *Post* in an attempt to attract more big advertisers, notably auto makers. Issue number 12A, for example, carried 36 full page ads as compared to 25 in regular number 12. But even these "A" issues failed to achieve the desired effect on advertisers, and *Post*'s courtship of the auto makers did not meet with consistent response.

The laws of price, supply and demand were also operative. The size and quality of *Post* diminished greatly, while the price per issue climbed rapidly. In November, 1960, the *Post* was a weekly magazine selling for 15¢ an issue, or $6 for a year's subscription. In January, 1969, the *Post* was a bi-weekly magazine selling for 50¢ an issue, or $8 for a year's subscription. The November '60 issue carried 124 pages; in January, 1969, *Post* had only 84 pages. Content diminished at the same time. The November, 1960, issue contained 4 stories, 8 articles and 2 serials; the January, 1969, issue carried 1 story, 8 articles and no serials. Thus the price of *Post* more than tripled while content was cut to about a third, within the space of eight years. Readers responded to this change in much the same way that they would respond to any increase in price and decrease in quantity; they simply stopped buying it. In its last years *Post* was, frankly, not a very good buy, either for advertisers or for consumers.

As with most popular culture media, *Post*'s fiction was essentially a reinforcement of traditional American values; all of the things held dear for generations appeared on *Post*'s pages, from Apple Pie to the Girl Next Door, until it ran into trouble in the sixties. It is important to note that the quality and quantity of *Post* fiction did change, drastically, in its declining years.

For many years, *Post*'s fiction remained much the same. Although the kinds of fiction being written changed rapidly during the first sixty years of the twentieth century, the new trends did not often find their way into the pages of *Post* until their popularity was thoroughly tested. As editor until 1935, Lorimer was shrewd enough to understand the reasons for not following literary trends.

The *Post*'s moral standards were about the same in 1935 as they had been in 1900. If they had been any different, there is little doubt that the *Post* would have ceased to exist. The application of the American novel's standards to a mass-circulation magazine would have been fatal, and Lorimer knew it.[10]

It is also true that during most of this period, *Post* did not have great competition; many subscribers bought the magazine for its fiction. That *Post* fiction *was* read is evident in the tremendous volume of letters expressing satisfaction or disapproval with each issue. Many readers, in fact, wrote directly to the authors themselves by way of the *Post* editorial offices. Readers never forgot the boundless optimism and good cheer of William Hazlett Upson's "I'm a Natural Born Salesman," the first of the Alexander Botts stories:

The Farmers' Friend Tractor Company
Earthword City, Ill.

Gentlemen: I have decided you are the best tractor company in the country, and consequently I am giving you first chance to hire me as your salesman to sell tractors in this region. I'm a natural born salesman, have a very quick mind. . . . When do I start work?

Believing that the *Post* needed a change of fiction formula which would place its stories more in the mainstream of the literary fashions of the sixties, the editors shifted quickly into a quite different vein. The distance between the world of Botts, the most likeable salesman who ever trimmed a satisfied customer, and the world the *Post* editors created in their later issues can be best measured by comparing the closing paragraphs of the single piece of fiction which appeared in January, 1969:

"Ah," Perkins said, "Did you have a roll in the hay miss?"
David did not want to witness this.
Myrna said, with astounding vindictiveness, "Did you give it away?" Her smile seemed at one moment to express pleasure and good will, at the next the

most vicious hatred.

"Give what away?" Tucker said.

"Why, your little maidenhead, dear," Myrna said. "Don't you even know the name of the merchandise?"

"We didn't go all the way, if that's what you mean," Tucker said. Her father took one step and slapped her so hard she fell down. Hoarse bleats came from her mouth.

Readers who wanted Botts did not welcome the change; those who liked sex and violence found it done better on television and in the paperbacks.

Lorimer, during his years as editor, knew how to balance old and new. He did, after all, publish Willa Cather, Joseph Hergesheimer, F. Scott Fitzgerald, Theodore Dreiser, Ring Lardner, Sinclair Lewis, William Faulkner, and many more; he knew also that his readers wanted entertainment too.

He understood that the magazine had to be edited for a broad middle class of readership, but he wanted to reach the upper level, too, and consequently he deliberately published stories he knew would appeal only to about 10% of the audience. They had to be stories, however; he was scornful of intellectuality for its own sake. The formless products of the little magazines were not for him.[11]

On the other hand, Lorimer did not avoid the controversial, nor did he shun the edges of the taboo; he simply knew how to do it and still retain his readers' trust. Writes John Tebbel,

Time and again he was right and the experts were wrong. It was said that no popular magazine could print a story about miscegenation, least of all the *Post*. Lorimer printed one by Charles Brackett . . . a story carefully hedged in several ways, it is true, but nonetheless unmistakably concerned with a subject tabooed.[12]

These matters of controversy became moot points, however, as the *Post* grew farther and farther from active concern for readers' wishes and as interest in *Post* fiction declined. A cursory examination of the appendices to this study will show how great was the change in the relative percentage of fiction in *Post* in the years 1929-1969. While we cannot say that the decline in fictive content was a major cause of *Post*'s death, we can note that fiction was one of the magazine's original selling points and that fiction seemed to have very little to do with promoting *Post* at the end of its life.

It does seem, however, that the editors' perception of changing American morality was incorrect. If *Post*'s concern for traditional morality may have waned over the years, the American public's—as represented by the *Post* clientele—apparently did not. An examination of the kind of story published by the *Post* between the years 1967 and 1969 reveals a sharp change in the subject matter and tone of its fiction, as well as a decline in quantity from eight stories per issue to as few as one. Whether this drove the final nail in the magazine's coffin cannot be determined, but since the *Post*'s main selling point over the years was the consistency and predictability of its own brand of fiction, it seems likely that the change contributed.

There is more, much more, of course, to the *Post* story. Erratic editorial policy, massive internal disorganization, palace feuds—all these factors played their parts. But the decline and fall of the *Post*, one of the most popular magazines ever to exist on the American scene, may reveal something of the nature and parameters of popular culture. Drawing on the *Post*, it would seem that success in the mass market derives from providing a conforming rather than a transforming experience. The medium that most closely follows the concerns and desires of the majority of people, which relies on their approbation, finds most success. When a separation between the public and the cultural media occurs, the media is invariably the loser. And the *Post* lost.

This separation can occur in a variety of ways. The public can, as with television, move its allegiances to a new idiom, leaving the old one with a diminished audience or none. Sometimes, as did radio, the old idiom can effect a successful change, finding for itself a new role. But failure to change, and obviously too much change, is certain death. The *Post* changed, but its role did not; it remained a family magazine when family magazines were in decline, when television and radio had captured the family market (as *Collier's* also found). Meanwhile the changes that the *Post* made—more articles, jazzier articles, "advanced" fiction, toying with the "new morality"—did not fit the family market nor open up another kind. A medium of popular culture must supply what the public wants. As any economist knows, demand must be met with a supply of goods as near as possible in both quantity and quality to what the public wants, else a new competitor will win the field. That *Post* failed to satisfy its constituency is obvious.

Still another obligation of a popular medium is that it recognize and accept its role. Trouble comes when the idiom's real self and ideal self are separated by too wide a gulf. *Post* saw itself as "America's interpreter"; in fact, it felt it was the essence of America itself, an ambitious stance for a relatively unsophisticated, family magazine. Perhaps because *Post*'s aspirations were out of line with its achievements, because it could not accept the fact that America had a new interpreter in TV, it failed to readjust its operations to the proportions of its continuing role. Letting go of the bird in the hand, *Post* failed to capture the two in the bush.

By the time *The Saturday Evening Post* was officially absent from the news stands, it was long dead in the eyes of those who had loved it for years. *Post* died, it seems to me, for each of its readers at the point when it ceased to be something to believe in. When George Horace Lorimer took over the *Post*, writes John Tebbel,

the hit song was "School Days, School Days." On the day Martin S. Ackerman became president of Curtis, "Mrs. Robinson" was on the top of the charts. Sensible men will notice the difference. On the day King Post finally died, there in New York after "the press" had finally gone, the editors gathered in what was now a ghostly layout room to watch themselves and their parting words on the evening news. Yes, sir, just as the TV crew chief had said, it was worth about a minute.

NOTES

[1] Richard Carpenter, "Ritual, Aesthetics, and TV," *Journal of Popular Culture*, Fall, 1969, 253.

[2] Michael Mooney, "The Death of the *Saturday Evening Post*," *Atlantic*, November, 1969, 73.

[3] Guy W. Korman, Jr., *The Saturday Evening Post*, January 25, 1969, 10.

[4] Mooney, 73.

[5] August 20, 1960.

[6] Mooney, 75.

[7] John Tebbel, *George Horace Lorimer and the Saturday Evening Post* (Garden City, 1948), 207.

[8] Otto Friedrich, "I am Marty Ackerman," *Harper's*, December, 1969, 112.

[9] Mooney, 73.

[10] Tebbel, 49.

[11] *Ibid.*, 42.

[12] *Ibid.*, 43.

THROUGH ROSE-COLORED GLASSES: SOME AMERICAN VICTORIAN SENTIMENTAL NOVELS

Leslie Smith

It was a beautiful, orderly world, that world of the sentimental novel. Everything was black or white, or it soon became so if it were rash enough to be gray. Good people were always rewarded, usually with a devoted spouse and an immense fortune, or—if translated to the hereafter—with a place among the angels in heaven. Bad people inevitably reaped the whirlwind in the here-and-now with the promise of worse things to come when they passed in the vale beyond. Or they might repent and join the ranks of the saved—after suffering sufficiently, of course. Either way, everyone received his just deserts.

There was no question about what was true, or just, or right. Values in the novels were clear-cut, based securely on home, mother-hood, the Protestant church, and decorum. And, perhaps most appealing of all, terribly significant things were constantly happening to people they were always falling in love, having babies, going to parties, or dying It is no wonder that American ladies bought these novels by the thousan for they admitted them for a brief time to this fascinating, supremely secure world. Each novel, like the drug addict's "trip," must have made the dull, real world the reader lived in seem even duller by contrast. An the less exciting the real world, the more need to escape once again to a better one. In *The Sentimental Novel*, Herbert Ross Brown suggests briefly the nature of the escapism the novels offered their readers:[1]

Here are to be found the compensations in fiction for the coveted values life had failed to give them. Nowhere outside their books could these women have encountered a delicacy so fastidious and a poetic justice so immutable. Nowhere beyond their pages could womanhood have survived with such glory the fiery ordeals of hot pursuit, hairbreadth escape, and uncomplaining endurance.

That thousands of people found a respite from their own demanding and unsettling society in the pages of sentimental novels is testified to by the millions of copies they bought.

It would be a mistake to assume that, because the novels were certainly escapist and unrealistic, they were therefore completely disconnected from the real lives of their readers. Rather, it was their similarity to real life that made them so immensely popular. The novels' heroines were like the lady readers, only a little more beautiful and good; they experienced all the joys and trials the readers had, only theirs were more extreme, more dramatic, or heart-rending, or happy. If children were always cherubic and charming in the novels, weren't they sometimes like that in real life? And if home and hearth were heaven, and fashion merely folly, what could be more natural and true than to read it in the pages of a book? The exaggerations in the sentimental novels, after all, derived from the era's popular myths and ideals. Escapism? Yes, but escapism into a sentimental utopia, bearing enough resemblance to reality so that one wonders if the readers fully realized that they had stepped through the looking glass.

Of all the novelists, three of the most popular were Mrs. E.D.E.N. Southworth, Mrs. Mary Jane Holmes, and Sylvanus Cobb, Jr. Mrs. Southworth published sixty novels in fifty years, many of them originally as serials in the *New York Ledger*. Nearly all of her books sold in six figures, and two of them, *Ishmael* and its sequel *Self-Raised,* sold over two million copies apiece, placing them among the top ten best sellers of the nineteenth century, while *The Hidden Hand* came close to the two million mark. Frank Luther Mott relates that when Mrs. Southworth visited England in 1859, ". . . she found London shops featuring Capitola hats and Capitola suits for girls [named after the heroine of the Hidden Hand] and three of the city's theatres producing dramatic versions of her story at once."[2]

Another immensely popular author was Mary Jane Holmes. After a slow start, her first book, *Tempest and Sunshine,* eventually caught the public's fancy. Republished in paperback, *Tempest* and *'Lena Rivers* both sold over one million copies. Beginning in 1854, she wrote thirty-nine novels over a fifty year span, selling novels year in and year out. Although most of the popular sentimental fiction of the fifties, sixties and seventies was written by women, a few men were also successful. Among the half-forgotten authors who most certainly should qualify as popular in the sentimental-female market was Sylvanus Cobb, Junior, whose output verged on the incredible. Most of his work was done for the *New York Ledger*, for which, in thirty-one years, he wrote one hundred and thirty novels and novelettes, eight hundred and thirty-four short stories, and two thousand thirty-five sketches, according to his own compilations. Before joining the *Ledger* he had already published thirty-six novelettes and two hundred short stories, as well as numerous articles for several magazines. That it is impossible to find only a very few of them outside the Library of Congress today is a silent commentary on the ephemeral value of such mass-produced literature.

Mrs. Holmes, Mrs. Southworth and Sylvanus Cobb were all, in varying degrees, formula writers. They were all writing for a living (or a substantial secondary income, in Mrs. Holmes's case), and had neither the time, and quite possibly not the talent, to write masterpieces. Certain elements appear and reappear, interminably throughout their novels. Some of these are common to all three, and to the sentimental novel tradition; others are their own distinguishing trademarks. Each of the three had his own personal formula, quite aside from the sentimental formula.

Mrs. Holmes's books were what are commonly called "domestic." Many critics and literary historians have used the terms "domestic" and "sentimental" interchangeably when dealing with the novels of the period. Domestic novels are simply one type of sentimental novels, distinguished by a glorification of the home and family and frequently by detailed descriptions of humble people and places. As a result, the confusion that has resulted is no doubt the reason why Mrs. Southworth is often called a "domestic" novelist, which she certainly is not, while Mr. Cobb is rarely classed as a "sentimental" novelist, which he certainly is. Mrs. Holmes' work, however, belongs in both categories.

The basic plot that Mrs. Holmes used in nearly all her books is typical of the domestic novel. She begins with a young heroine, usually seven to twelve years old, almost always a desperately poor but cheerful orphan. She is forced to live with an aunt who is jealous of the child's superiority to her own daughters. (As a variation, the girl's widowed father may remarry a clever, domineering woman who is ambitious for her *own* daughter.) The heroine is not as beautiful as her cousins, since she is undernourished, uncultured and poorly dressed—but she has an inner beauty that shines with innocence and goodness. For years the cousins, as well as the aunt, treat her cruelly, taking advantage of her in numerous ways. (For example, in *Dora Deane*, cousin Eugenia cuts off Dora's long black hair to sell in order to buy herself a new dress for a party.)

However, there is always hope that Cinderella will be rescued, more often than not by an unexpected benefactor. A rich old man who was once in love with the heroine's mother learns where the girl is living and sends her money from India. The cousin unscrupulously opens the heroine's mail and, of course, takes the money. About this time, a handsome and rich young man falls in love with the heroine, who by now has become a beautiful, cultured young lady. By various tricks, her wicked cousin who wants to marry the young man herself, manages to separate the lovers. Heartbroken, the heroine turns to religion and becomes a devout Christian. At last, "purified by suffering," she has proved herself worthy of the happy ending. Her fairy godmother arrives in the form of the rich old man from India. The cousin's theft is discovered; she confesses and either goes insane, dies, repents, or lives to be a miserable old maid—all terrifying fates. The heroine finds a husband, a huge fortune, and Christian salvation. And, of course, she lives happily ever after.

This basic Cinderella, rags-to-riches story is common to all sentimental novels after the mid-1850s, but many of the elements in Mrs. Holmes's formula are peculiarly part of the domestic type, a sub-genre of the mainstream of earlier sentimental fiction. During the first half of the century, novelists eulogized the patient Griselda—the pure, long-suffering wife whose mission was to teach moral wisdom to her children and to suffer all the injustices her husband heaped upon her, while quietly trying to save his soul. Sometimes she succeeded and was rewarded with a charming domestic life with angelic children and a permanently repentant husband. At other times her efforts won her an early flight to heaven, after converting her husband and other sinners during a long deathbed scene, winning her victory anyway.

These same basic values and the same emphasis on pathos mark later domestic fiction of the sixties and after, but with an interesting shift of plot. Having the heroine die was no longer considered a sufficiently happy ending, so such inspirational deaths were shifted to other good women who were less important to the plot than the heroine, who is now no longer a wife but an adolescent. It is her trials which engage the sympathies of the reader, and her marriage, or at least engagement, which provides the triumphant ending. Proving her worth through suffering brings her not to death, or the peace of a happy family and reformed husband, but to the threshold of a happy future marriage. This is the basic plot of most of Mrs. Holmes's books. Dora Deane works in the kitchen, scrubs floors, and is put to numerous trials before she wins Howard Hastings. 'Lena Rivers is scorned, poorly clothed, and generally mistreated before she is worthy to be Durward's wife. Fanny Middleton suffers near-total collapse and skirts death before she triumphs at last. The path of true love is invariably strewn with thorns, boulders, and many puddles of tears.

Mrs. Holmes's *Family Pride, or Purified by Suffering* (also published as *The Cameron Pride*) furnishes an excellent example of her fusion of the two plot formulae, the suffering wife and the mistreated girl. At the beginning of the book little Katy tells her uncle that she is planning to have an easy path through life.

> "Can't tell what path you'll take," the deacon answered. "God knows whether you'll go easy through the world, or whether He'll send you suffering to purify and make you better."
> "Purified by suffering," Kate said aloud, while a shadow crept for an instant over her gay spirits.

This is, of course, exactly what Katy's fate turns out to be. She falls in love with a handsome, wealthy young man who is also egotistical, jealous, and totally selfish. Consumed with pride, determined to make his wife be the belle of New York society, he plans to mold her to the Cameron family ways. He refuses to let her visit her family or home; he gives their baby to a nurse in the country so Katy will be free for the giddy social life he prefers to fatherhood. All this is heartbreaking to Katy, but valuable to her moral growth. "Katy was very white next morning, and to Helen she seemed to be expanding into something more womanly, more mature, as she disciplined herself to bear the pain welling up so constantly from her heart. . . ."

But Katy's trials have only begun. She loses her health in the gay, dissipating life of the city, her baby dies of cholera, and her husband accuses her of unfaithfulness and deserts her. But throughout it all she remains the perfectly faithful, devoted, loving wife, her love for the errant Wilford still unfaltering. When she returns to her old home, her uncle says to her,

> "That chap has misused you the wust way. You need not deny it, for it's writ all over your face," he continued as Katy tried to stop him, for sore as was her heart with the great injustice done her, she would not have Wilford blamed.
>
> He was her husband still, and she had loved him so fondly that, whether worthy or not of her love, she could not turn from his so soon.

Eventually, to everyone's relief but Katy's, Wilford dies repentant, leaving her free to marry a far worthier man who has loved her all along. Now Katy is better able to appreciate her second love, for "Truly she had been purified by suffering; the dross had been burned out, and only the gold remained, shedding its brightness on all with which it came in contact."

Family Pride is an interesting combination of the long-suffering wife formula and the oppressed young girl story. Katy's trials come mainly from her husband, although her mother-in-law is anything but kind to her. Yet in the end her reward is another husband, a good man who has had his own share of suffering and is thus the ideal reward for our heroine. The subplot of *Family Pride* features Katy's sister Helen's victory over a clever and unscrupulous rival by the power of her goodness and virtue. She too must suffer, but in her case it is from female competition and the Civil War rather than male pride. Helen, too, gets her man in the end, and is a more noble woman because of the misery she has borne.

The domestic novel is, of course, thoroughly and pervasively sentimental. Providing the reader with "a good cry" seems at times to be the writer's chief goal. The first paragraph of Mrs. Holmes's *Dora Deane* strikes the proper note:

> Poor little Dora Deane! How utterly wretched and desolate she was, as she crouched before the scanty fire, and tried to warm the little bit of worn-out flannel, with which to wrap her mother's feet; and how hard she tried to force back the tears which would burst forth afresh whenever she looked upon that pale, sick mother, and thought how soon she would be gone.

Following this, the entire chapter is given over to a detailed description of the death of Dora's mother, closing with an exhausted Dora falling to sleep against her mother's body:

> At last, as her arms grew purple with cold, she moved nearer to the bedside, and winding them around her mother's neck, laid her head upon the pillow and fell asleep. And to the angels, who were hovering near, waiting to bear their sister spirit home, there was given a charge concerning the little girl, so that she did not freeze, though she sat there the live-long night, calmly sleeping the sweet sleep of childhood, while the mother at her side slept the long, eternal sleep of death.

By the end of that first chapter, any Victorian lady (or gentleman for that matter) who had not yet wet the page with tears must have been hard-hearted indeed.

The emotionalism that manifested itself as maudlin sentimentality in the domestic novels appeared as melodrama in Mrs. Southworth's stories, who specialized more in suspense and excitement than in tears. Mrs. Southworth provided these in abundance, sometimes adding the tears for good measure. Frank Luther Mott finds in her novels "an indefatigable story-telling talent, a strong feeling for blatant and primitive melodrama, a love for sensational effects in both incidents and characterization, and a faculty for passionate declamation." Alexander Cowie speaks of her "tawdry world of glitter and glamor" where she is so much at home[3] with millions of readers equally enamored of that same world. Her stories were exciting, and the mere fact that they were also often outrageously unlikely and maudlin did not detract from their appeal.

Most of Mrs. Southworth's novels had all the sensational elements of stage melodrama. Her stories are often set in a dark, dingy castle or old family mansion; her characters tend to be either blond and good or brunette and evil, with names that reveal their personalities with unmistakable clarity. The action involves diabolical plots, terrifying murders and near-murders, kidnappings, disappearances, thefts, baby switches, and various forms of fiendish cruelty. Consider, for an example of her tempo and tone, the opening of *Skeleton in the Closet:*

> "Brandon Coyle! Are you mad?"
> She had stolen up behind him noiselessly. She had snatched the loaded pistol from his desperate hand and hurled it through the open window into the bay below. And not one instant too soon to save him from the crime of self-destruction.

He whirled round upon her, and they stood facing each other with eyes flaming defiance.

How like, yet unlike, were those fierce, beautiful creatures—twin sister and brother!

She with her slender, well-rounded, lissom form, supple as a serpent's; with her small, fine features and clear, deadly-pale yellow face, darkened by great, deep hollow black eyes; the whole over-shadowed by heavy, clustering auburn curls—a subtle, wistful, most seductive face.

He, somewhat taller, fuller and more supple, like another human snake, of a little larger growth, with a paler complexion, darker eyes and darker hair.

They were the orphan niece and nephew of Christopher Coyle, Esquire, an old bachelor, living on his ancient patrimonial estate of Caveland in the North of England.

Now they stood glaring at each other a full minute in silent menace. Then both spoke at once.

"Aspirita!"

"Brandon!"

Obviously, Mrs. Southworth wastes no time getting started, while the reader has already a fairly accurate idea what the rest of the volume and its sequel, *Brandon Coyle's Wife*, must be like. Brandon has just been foiled at suicide, and the reader soon finds that the girl he loves plans to marry his best friend. No nineteenth century reader would miss the significance of his attempted suicide, a crime against God. Clearly, then, he is the villain, and since the serpent metaphor is applied to both twins, his sister is a villainess. To underscore the point, there are the names, Brandon Coyle (Coil), Aspirita (Asp), living at Caveland. Especially fond of titles, peerages and ancestral estates, Mrs. Southworth used them whenever there was the remotest possibility that a character might have one or more. Perhaps in her own way she had something of Hawthorne's idea that "Romance and poetry, ivy, lichens, and wall-flowers, need ruin to make them grow." Though the atmosphere of her tale is considerably more Poe's than Hawthorne's, she recognizes the effectiveness of placing her tale in a locale far removed from the reader's everyday life.

Skeleton in the Closet must rank among the most sensational of Mrs. Southworth's books, but none of them can be considered dull. For example, in *The Missing Bride, or Marian the Avenger,* the heroine, Marian, waits alone on a beach at night, in the midst of a terrible storm, for her lover Thurston who is planning to carry her away to England. Instead, her friend Jacquelina's madly jealous husband, Grimshaw, has found the note arranging the meeting and believes that it was meant for his wife. While Marian is waiting for Thurston, Grimshaw arrives and thinking her to be his wife, stabs her as she turns and looks into his face. He sees his terrible mistake too late. Horrified at what he has done, he staggers home to the evil Jacquelina who planted the note in order to make him jealous. She has succeeded all too well.

> Yes! her frolic was brought to an eternal end. She saw at a glance that something fatal, irreparable, had happened. There was blood upon his hands and wristbands. . . . His fingers, talon-like in their horny paleness and rigidity, clutched his breast, as if to tear some unutterable reproach upon her face! Thrice he essayed to speak, but a gurgling noise in his throat was the only result. With a last great effort to articulate, the blood suddenly filled his throat and gushed from his mouth.

Grimshaw falls on the floor and dies in front of his horror-stricken wife. Meanwhile, Thurston has been detained and doesn't appear; by morning, Marian's body has disappeared. While everyone assumes that she has been murdered and her body washed away, Jacquelina keeps quiet and retreats to a convent. Many deaths, near-deaths, and chapters later, the innocent Thurston is on trial for Marian's murder. A veiled, mysterious woman sits in court listening to his testimony, visibly agitated. Suddenly Jacquelina appears, forced by her conscience to tell the truth before she takes her final vows as a nun. When she has told all, the veiled lady suddenly rushes forward and reveals herself as Marian. It appears that she had been picked up by a boat as she lay unconscious on the beach and had been taken to England, where she stayed because, due to a trick of light in the storm, she believed that Thurston had attempted to murder her. They are, of course, happily reunited. Such melodramatics are peculiarly Mrs. Southworth's own, her interpretation of the sentimental-domestic formula; no one else of the same school wrote novels in quite the same way or with Mrs. Southworth's wildly imaginative dash.

Far different from the gentle sob-stories of Mrs. Holmes and the sensational melodramatics of Mrs. Southworth were the adventure tales of Sylvanus T. Cobb. He has more in common with Mrs. Southworth, sharing her taste for melodrama, although she outdid him. In exotic settings, however, he is far ahead, for her dark, Gothic ancestral mansions pale before his fantastic cities of the Middle East. Cobb's plots are considerably shorter and less complex than either Mrs. Holmes or Mrs. Southworth's, but they are always sentimental, exciting and full of mystery and adventure. They are also always exactly the same.

The Cobb formula begins with a description of a setting placed in the far-away and often long-ago, perhaps a magnificent ancient city well equipped with palaces, dungeons and secret underground passages. "In a spacious marble building overlooking the grand piazza of Parma, its walls somewhat discolored by the touch of time" lives the *Painter of Parma*. *The King's Talisman* opens,

> In the midst of ancient Idumea, like a giant sentinel, pointing its granite finger heaven ward, towers aloft the barren, rugged peak of Mount Hor.
> The hot sun was pouring down its scorching rays upon the rocks and sands, and as the shadows of the craggy clifts fell upon the smoother surfaces, they told to the practiced eye that the day-king had reached the meridian of his noontide powers.

As soon as the locale is established, the hero is introduced, young, handsome, muscular, multi-talented. He is well-educated but poor, very brave, and an expert swordsman. Cobb writes of the hero of *The Caliph of Bagdad*,

> He was a young man, certainly not more than five-and-twenty, though much exposure to the changeful moods of the elements, and long-continued toiling and marching . . . had given his skin a depth of bronze, and imparted to his frame a massiveness of development, that might have betokened more mature age. Tall; stout; erect; of perfect proportions; and, despite the bronze upon his face and the dust upon his garb, as handsome as the handsomest.

Ruric Nevel, of *The Gunmaker of Moscow*, is a no less striking figure. He "possessed a frame of more than ordinary symmetry and muscular development. . . . His features were regular, yet strongly marked and eminently handsome . . . while his eyes . . . lent a cast of genius to the intellect of the brow." No matter how unlikely it is, given the time and country, the hero is always a Christian.

Setting and character taken care of, Cobb swiftly gets on with his story. The exotic city is ruled by a cruel, cowardly, heathen tyrant, perhaps the chief advisor to a just king who believes the villain to be an honest man. The tyrant hopes to marry—by force—the beautiful, virtuous, and always Christian, heroine, for her money, for political reasons, or simply for her beauty. However, just as she is being carried towards her fate, the hero arrives to rescue her. One look and they fall in love, politely, virtuously, and Christianly—a star-crossed love, it turns out, since he is far below her noble station.

The hero now returns the lovely girl to the protection of her guardian (or father) who is the leader of a secret political group plotting to overthrow the tyrant. (It may also be an organization of Christians hiding from persecution.) But now the hero himself is in danger from the enraged tyrant who has his men seize him. The secret organization has secret passages into the dungeons as well as numerous spies throughout the palace, so before long the hero is rescued.

Eventually, a wise old man who has been the hero's adviser manipulates events so that the tyrant is caught in his own political trap and revealed for what he really is. Various unpleasant fates await him, although he usually evades the worst by dying of shock, apoplexy or a broken heart. He never gets there, however, for "his proud heart broke on the road, and he died, unknown and uncared for, in a peasant's cot among the rugged mountains of Uralia." Meanwhile, the hero is restored to his true noble title and heritage of which the tyrant deprived him when he was an infant, so he can marry his aristocratic heroine. Once again, evil has been defeated and good has triumphed. And if the reader liked this story, *The Gunmaker of Moscow,* he could enjoy it over again in *The Painter of Parma,* or *The King's Talisman*, or many, many others.

Different as the Holmes, Southworth, and Cobb formulae are, there is one fundamental similarity among them. All three wrote success stories, and the rewards of success are always the same: love and marriage; fortune and social position; Christian salvation. Occasionally the protagonist is already wealthy, or already loved, or already saved, but by the end of the story he has gained whatever elements he lacked of the Victorian trinity. All three components are necessary for the ideal life, the novels say, and any ending to be happy must include them all. Furthermore, all three novelists wrote what were basically love stories, frequently more than one. Mrs. Holmes might have as many as four or five love plots in operation, besides the main one, being careful to resolve all of them by the end of the book. For both Mrs. Holmes and Mrs. Southworth, the complicated entanglements of love provide most of the plot's complexities. In Cobb's stories, the hero is always in love with a beautiful, high-born damsel, but since her character is rarely fully developed, she is merely another reward for him at the story's end. Because she is highborn and wealthy, and the victim of the villain's plot, the problem is solved simply when the tyrant is disposed of and the hero elevated in rank and fortune. Marriage to the woman he loves is his ultimate reward, since it is love, not wealth, that he has been seeking all along.

It is important to note that the difficulties Cobb's heroes encounter have nothing to do with love, misunderstood or unrequited. Between the hero and the girl there is perfect understanding, derived from love at first sight. There is none of the pain and suffering of love the reader finds in Mrs. Holmes, none of the Gothic evil and melodramatic emotionalism of Mrs. Southworth. But it is *true* love in all the books—the instant love of Cobb, the constancy of the victimized in Mrs. Southworth, the rewarding love of the mistreated and betrayed in Mrs. Holmes.

The sentimental vision of love that is basic to all the novels undoubtedly takes its origin from both the earlier nineteenth-century sentimental novels and the contemporary female ideal. In the "patient Griselda" books of the first half of the century, no amount of pain could dim the love of the good wife. Love was her life, and when she could do nothing else with her wayward man, she continued to love and pray for him. In the end, when he returned to the fireside, loving and appreciating his good wife, the idyllic picture was complete. In these novels the husband caused his troubles, and those of his patient, saintly wife.

The later novelists in the tradition, beginning at mid-century, shifted the formula. The happy ending became not a marriage repaired, but true love rewarded and a marriage made. The complications of the plot, and the obstacles overcome, were provided not by an errant husband but by another woman, a designing, malicious rival who either hoped to gain the hero for herself or at the least destroy the heroine's chances. The conclusion was thus shifted from the rewards of a marriage rescued to the future of married happiness. The plot becomes a struggle between the powers of good love and selfish love, or Eve versus the serpent. But true love wins and the picture of the couple, reunited and married, sitting at their fireside, provides the same happy ending as the earlier novels.

The change in formula, however, meant an additional character to dispose of—the other woman who caused all the heroine's problems. Her punishment was just, fitting, and in the context of the novel's values, terrifying—spinsterhood, or worse, a loveless, cruel marriage of her own. The lesson was clear, that good women get good husbands. In *Family*

Pride, for example, Mrs. Holmes sees that they do, except sister Juno, cold, proud, unscrupulous, who gets no man at all. As Mrs. Holmes has a happily-married character comment, "You ought to see Juno. I know she envies me, though she affects contempt for matrimony, and reminds me forcibly of the fox and the grapes . . . every year her chances lessen, and I have very little hope that father will ever call other than Bob his son. . . ."

But bad as spinsterhood was, marriage without love was worse. In *'Lena Rivers*, John tells his cousin,

". . . I have no particular love for Mabel, although I intend making her my wife, and heartily wish she was so now."

'Lena started and clasping John's arm, exclaimed, "Marry Mabel and not love her! You cannot be in earnest. You will not do her so great a wrong—you shall not."

Characters who marry for any reason but love are invariably miserable, as Mrs. Southworth makes clear in both *Retribution* and *Self-Raised*, sequel to *Ishmael*. The entire second half of *Retribution* concerns the results of a marriage based on selfish passion rather than unselfish love. In *Self-Raised*, Claudia must suffer the tragic consequences of having married for prestige rather than love. Her husband a suicide in prison, her name disgraced, Claudia lives in tragic loneliness. Meanwhile, Bee has married Ishmael, whom Claudia loved but rejected because he was poor. Claudia bitterly reviews her fate (and the book's moral):

This splendid career of Bee was the very thing to attain which she had sacrificed the struggling young lawyer, and taken the noble viscount. And now it was that very young lawyer who introduced his bride to all these triumphs; while that very viscount had left *her* to a widowhood of obscurity and reproach! In eagerly, reckless, sinfully snatching at these social honors she had lost them all! While Bee, without seeking or desiring them, by simply walking forward in her path of love, and duty, had found them in her way!

Obviously, the rewards of fame and fortune are inextricably bound up with the right kind of marriage, but they are never found when sought, and true love is its only basis.

The attitude of an era which glorified love, and the constant idealization of love in the sentimental novels must naturally have reinforced each other. In *The Victorian Frame of Mind*, Walter Houghton suggests that the great stress on love and the emotions was a protection from the rude realities of the industrial world. It was also a protest against the materialism of the era and the marriage of convenience. He writes,[4]

> Paradoxical as it may seem, the Victorian emphasis on romantic and wedded love was as much a protest against marriage as it was a means of protecting it from extramarital temptations. In this respect it was a revolt against a system which denied its impulses, and which, in the absence of love, was a source of personal distress and social evil. In 1854 G. R. Drysdale described the contemporary situation: "A great proportion of the marriages we see around us, did not take place from love at all, but from some interested motive, such as wealth, social position, or other advantages; and in fact it is *rare* to see a marriage in which true love has been the predominating feeling on both sides." It was therefore "chiefly in works of fiction" that "the romance and impetuosity of love" were to be met with; for there "people indulge in a day dream of what should be the feelings between the sexes."

When Dora Deane exclaims, "I would rather die than marry a man I did not love, because of his gold," she is voicing the inner protest of a whole generation of women who dreamed about love and married for security. But, after all, money was necessary, too—a fact the novelists never ignored.

In various ways, nearly all the domestic-sentimental novels are rags-to-riches, Cinderella stories. Depending on the personality and situation of the hero or hreoine, his or her rise is usually a result either of the character's own efforts, or virtues, or both. In a newly industrialized society where the survival of the fittest was fast becoming the code of many people even while love and gentility were idealized, the novelists ignored the contradiction and reinforced both ethics. Their heroines and heroes survived and triumphed because they were morally worthy of their successes, not because they sought them. They won their vast riches because of virtue, love, and gentility, and precisely because they did *not* seek the wealth they received as a reward. A heroine must be sweet and humble and never lift a delicate finger in her own behalf, but inevitably God and a rich uncle would see how deserving she was and would shower her with wealth. The men in the novels generally had to work harder for their success, but their substantial material rewards were unsought and came by way of helping others. Though Mrs. Southworth's Ishmael, for example, refused wealthy clients and devoted his law practice to winning cases for poor, oppressed widows, his charity eventually earned him a reputation which carried him on to vast fame and wealth.

Money is never an end in itself in these novels, but its possession is never belittled, either. Poverty builds character through suffering, but it has its limits and should never be permanent. No character ever rejects money; the novelists were certainly not about to strain their readers' credulity by condemning wealth. Herbert Ross Brown comments in *The Sentimental Novel* on the materialism found in the novels:[5]

> At a time when things were in the saddle, and America was in the midst of a boastful materialism, the sentimentalists felt a need of enveloping the new industrial order in an aura of approval. Accepting without critical scrutiny the sanctions of the philosophy of acquisition, they dangled the tempting bait of material prosperity before the eyes of every reader. . . . Drugged with the opiate of materialism, these writers succumbed without a struggle to the national acquisitiveness. Seldom have novelists been so thoroughly at the mercy of contemporaneity. "The public table laden with lavish gifts is barred only to the vicious," boasted Miss Leslie in *Althea Vernon*. . . .

The popular novelists simply reinforced the prevailing conservative ethic. Love and money went together as naturally as love and marriage; that the old virtues were enough, in the novels, to insure prosperity, was no doubt comforting to millions of readers. The novelists knew what they were about when they reinforced the happy myth of Cinderella in an era when the greedy stepsisters of industry were making their fortunes. Who could help wishing that it were true?

The third component of the protagonist's reward was Christian salvation. Whether he or she learned religion through his sufferings, or served as an example of Christianity throughout, the protagonist was always piously and outspokenly saved by the story's end. In the course of the plot there might be several conversions, one at least in a tearful deathbed scene, until most of the characters had joined the fold. In *Tempest and Sunshine*, Fanny sees the light after much mental suffering, and then converts her father and her husband. Her wicked sister Julia finds religion and repentance for her sins through the agency of a pious friend who died, leaving Julia her Bible. Thus, on the last page, all the major characters gather in the family parlor on their knees, to read the Bible and thank God for their blessing.

At a time when traditional Christianity was being shaken to its foundations, it is not surprising that many people hung more tightly than ever to its crumbling walls. The popular novelists did their best to reassure their readers that the Christian supports were as sturdy and trustworthy as ever. In *Retribution*, Colonel Dent tells Hester, "No, Hester; no human being need ever suffer loneliness. The most perfect communion of spirits that can be conceived, is the union of the human soul with the Divine Spirit of its Father and Creator." The code was basically simple: have perfect faith and do good works, and reap the blessings of this life and the hereafter. Anything less would bring misery. In *Family Pride*, Mrs. Holmes explains all the catastrophes that have befallen the Camerons:

> It had not been a house of prayer—no altar had been erected for the morning and evening sacrifice. God had almost been forgotten, and now He was pouring His wrath upon the handsome dwelling. . . .

Still, it is not too late for Katy and Wilford. Since Katy's redemption is paid for in suffering, and Wilford repents on his deathbed, both find God's mercy. Katy is blessed with a good second husband and Wilford, presumably, goes to heaven.

Deathbed scenes like Wilford's were popular since they assumed the double function of reinforcing religion and providing reassurance of a happy afterlife. Walter Houghton comments cogently on the purpose of these scenes.[6]

> The death scenes which fill the Victorian novel are clearly connected with the religious crisis. They are intended to help the reader sustain his faith by dissolving religious doubt in a solution of warm sentiment. When the heart is so strongly moved, the skeptical intellect is silenced; and when feelings of profound love and pity are centered on a beautiful soul who is gone forever, the least religious affirmation . . . was sufficient to invoke a powerful sense of reassurance.

The high mortality rate of nineteenth-century America made death a sober reality; few households were without a dying, aged parent or a sickly infant. Books that assured them that their loved ones were not really dead and that it was never too late to be forgiven for one's sins fulfilled a reassuring function. In *Dora Deane*, Ella Hastings led a gay, thoughtless life; the realization that she is dying terrifies her. A clergyman is sent for, and, in practically no time she is saved and safe.

> There was no more fear now—no more terror of the narrow tomb, for there was One to go with her—one whose arm was powerful to save and on him Ella learned to lean. . . .

In *'Lena Rivers*, Mabel is comforted when she is dying because she "trusted in One who she knew would go with her down into the lone valley—whose arm she felt would uphold her as she crossed the dark, rolling stream of death. . . ." The novels constantly emphasize the calm that faith brings those facing death. If it can give such security in the greatest of all crises, how powerful it must be in all other emergencies! This is the lesson taught by the novelists, learned by the various characters, and eagerly accepted by their readers.

Every hero and heroine created by Mrs. Holmes, Mrs. Southworth and Mr. Cobb was a true Christian, abounding in faith, hope and charity. They went through it all—suffering, excitement, self-sacrifice, poverty, chance, disappointment, happiness—to rewards as great as their trials and virtues. It was life viewed through the wrong end of a rose-tinted telescope, a world the reader loved because wouldn't it be nice if . . .

NOTES

[1] Herbert Ross Brown, *The Sentimental Novel in America 1789-1860* (Durham, North Carolina: Duke University Press, 1940), 322.

[2] Frank Luther Mott, *Golden Multitudes: The Story of Best Sellers in the United States* (New York: R. R. Bowker Co., 1947), 141.

[3] Mott, 142; Alexander Cowie, *The Rise of the American Novel* (New York: American Book Company, 1951), 419.

[4] Walter E. Houghton, *The Victorian Frame of Mind 1830-1870* (New Haven: Yale University Press, 1957), 381.

[5] Brown, 361.

[6] Houghton, 277.

OF FEW DAYS AND FULL OF TROUBLE:
THE EVOLUTION OF THE WESTERN HERO IN
THE DIME NOVEL

Daryl E. Jones

The dime novel western, and particularly the character of its
hero, was not innovative, but instead a continuation of the traditional Eastern response to the West. It has been shown by G. Edward
White that "the primary concern of Eastern chroniclers of the West
in the half century beginning with the 1830's was not the drama of
internal social relationships in that vast continent beyond the frontier
but rather the degree to which society (or lack of it) in the wilderness
represented an alternative to the social structure of the East."[1] The
dime novel, itself an Eastern literary expression, accordingly drew
upon this longstanding Eastern vision of the anarchic West.

The roots of the traditional Eastern response to the West are
to be found in Cooper's *Leatherstocking Tales*. The first of the
novels, *The Pioneers*, establishes the pattern of conflict which runs
throughout the remaining four; the anarchic world of the wilderness
personified by the old trapper Natty Bumppo comes in conflict with
the ordered, law governed society of civilization personified by Judge
Temple. The conflict between wilderness and civilization is irrecon-
cilable; Natty explains, ". . . our ways doesn't agree. I love the
woods, and ye relish the face of man; I eat when hungry, and drink
when a-dry; and ye keep stated hours and rules." Seeking escape
from civilization, Natty heads for "the setting sun." His flight,
however, is paradoxical, for his journey west is a harbinger of the
eventual downfall of the wilderness he loves so well. As Cooper's

107

final statement in the novel indicates, Natty is himself the vanguard of civilization, "the foremost in that band of pioneers who are opening the way for the march of the nation across the continent."[2]

Cooper's deification of Natty and the wilderness freedom which Natty represents sets the tone for the general nineteenth century response to the dichotomy between the Wilderness West and the Civilized East.[3] Although Cooper also dwelt upon the manner in which the unrestrained freedom of the West could be misused (Hurry Harry in *The Deerslayer*, Ishmael Bush in *The Prairie*), his ultimate contribution to the American experience lies in his portrayal of the West as a realm entirely divorced from the eastern social order, and his creation of a character representative of such a realm. The long range effect upon the popular imagination of Cooper's response to the West becomes clear in a study of the evolution of the hero of the dime novel western. By the publisher's own admission, the first popular western hero of the genre was patterned after Cooper's Leatherstocking.[4] The buckskin-swathed trapper was the first of a long line of pulp Western heroes, each of whom, like Leatherstocking, was distinctly characterized by his asocial, or even anti-social, status. An understanding of the importance of this status to the popularity of the western hero, and a recognition of the new dimension which this status assumed with the rampant industrialization of the last half of the nineteenth century, become crucial to an understanding of the dime novel's appeal to the American mind.

The most extensive treatment of the development of the hero in the dime novel Western is found in two chapters of Henry Nash Smith's *Virgin Land: The American West as Symbol and Myth.*[5] In his pioneer study, Smith examines various stereotypes of the Western hero that developed in the dime novel: the aged trapper proficient in wilderness skills (derived from Cooper's Leatherstocking); the young trapper possessed of innate nobility; the daredevil scout or plainsman of the Buffalo Bill variety; the cowboy as romantic cavalier, a virtual knight of the plains; and, the semi-bandit Deadwood Dick. In tracing the evolution of the hero stereotypes, Smith recognizes a progressive abandonment of traditional social and moral codes of behavior, complemented by a simultaneous increase of sensationalism, iron-willed self-reliance, and moral turpitude.[6] Suggesting that these "changes in the characters reveal a progressive deterioration in the Western story as a genre," Smith argues that the changing stereo-

type of the hero was a deterioration from a "saint of the forest" to
a rebellious outlaw; and, second, this deterioration was inevitable,
for the choice of an outcast as the representative hero of a growing,
civilizing, industrializing society doomed the dime novel western to
ethical and social irrelevance.[7]

Smith's argument, however, fails to account for the immense
popularity of the dime novel western. If the novels were actually
"devoid alike of ethical and social meaning," why did they sell in
such vast numbers? If the hero as self-reliant isolato was not relevant to an industrializing society, how does one account for the
way in which Buffalo Bill, Deadwood Dick, and Jesse James fired
the popular imagination for nearly forty years? Popularity alone,
then, strongly indicates the presence of social significance in the
dime novel western; it is probable that much of the significance can
be discovered by reexamining Smith's conclusions. What explanation lies behind the apparent paradox of a society which, while
seemingly "committed to the ideas of civilization and progress,
and to an industrial revolution," could venerate in fact only those
men who defied these ideas by their very life styles? And, what
accounts for the trend in the evolution of the hero-stereotypes
toward the progressive abandonment of traditional social and
moral codes in favor of sensationalism, self-reliance, and amorality?

To suggest that the dime novel western lacks social significance
because its characteristic hero lives apart from society is to disregard
powerful forces which worked beneath the surface of late nineteenth
century society—forces which initially motivated the mass veneration
of such a figure, and which ultimately found expression in popular
literature. Although Smith states that it "is the presumably close
fidelity of the Beadle stories to the dream life of a vast inarticulate
public that renders them valuable to the social historian and the
historian of ideas," he fails to examine the full proportion of this
fidelity, or to trace its meaning to an ultimate logical conclusion.[8]

The fact that a progressive, industrializing society chose a
Leatherstocking figure as its hero, "a child of the wilderness to
whom society and civilization meant only the dread sound of the
backwoodsman's axe laying waste the virgin forest," is a paradox
which closely resembles the paradoxical attitude of later nineteenth-
century society toward the machine. Simultaneously worshipping
and fearing the machine in 1840, society gradually entered a period

of psychological backlash against the effects of widespread industrialization on both the individual and the recently virgin American landscape—a backlash which has become a crisis in today's polluted environment.[9] It seems likely, then, that the popularity of the stereotype hero as a rebel, as fugitive from civilization, is related to the American mind's growing rejection of the values of a civilization dominated by industrialization, materialism, and suppression of the individual by a rigid socioeconomic structure.

In an age of increasing industrialization, labor strife, hazardous working conditions, the dehumanized factory system, and the control of society by big business and the international agricultural market, the public's need was not for a hero who would represent and promote such a way of life, but for one who would reject it. The self-reliant hero, fleeing the restraints of civilization, embodied the individual American's desire to flee these same restraints. The Western hero lived in an unfenced world, was solely responsible for his own fate, and provided a vicarious freedom for the fenced-in, powerless individual. Thus, the dime novel's social significance arises not from the fact that it mirrored the overt and often expressed ideals of a progress-hungry, materialistic society—because it did not—but rather because it revealed, and gave form to, the suppressed fears and desires of that society. The trend toward an increasingly rebellious hero in the dime novel western corresponds with society's growing psychological disaffection with its manner of existence and style of life.

During the span of more than sixty years in which the dime novel flourished, the evolving stereotype of the Western hero passed through four major phases: the trapper, the plainsman, the cowboy, and the outlaw. An examination of each of these hero types will serve to illustrate the degree to which the popularity of the western hero was dependent upon his asocial status and his inherent rejection of societal restraint.

II

"Buckskin Bravo: The Trapper"

The dime novel western was preceded by a large body of literature which concerned the real life exploits of the famed men of the West.[10]

Two basic types of protagonists emerged from this pre-dime novel western tradition: the "self-reliant, naturally civilized, independent forest or prairie scout in the tradition of Leatherstocking and Daniel Boone," and the "violent, rough, Indian killing adventurer" drawn from the "ugly white man tradition" of Crockett, Bird (Bloody Nathan), and Cooper (Hurry Harry March, Ishmael Bush, etc.).[11] The dime novel, drawing from this tradition, not surprisingly contains a preponderance of characters who fall into one or the other of these categories, but the protagonist of the early dime novel is usually a wilderness trapper modeled after Leatherstocking. Although he is sometimes young, he appears most often in the early dime novels as an aged, dialect speaking, innately virtuous hero possessed of a high degree of ability in all of the wilderness skills, as in Edward S. Ellis's *Kent, the Ranger; or, The Fugitives of the Border.*[12]

However, the trapper is not always the kindly hero derived from the Leatherstocking-Boone tradition. Sometimes he is the ugly white man drawn from the tradition of Crockett, Cooper's Harry March or Old Tom Hutter, and especially from Bird's *Nick of the Woods.* The stereotype of a villainous trapper whose character is the reverse of Cooper's virtuous Deerslayer appears most clearly in *Buffalo Bill's Leap for Life; or, The White Death of Beaver Wash* by the "author of 'Buffalo Bill.' "[13] Quite appropriately named Wolfslayer, this mysterious trapper hates both red and white men, and assumes the form of an avenging apparition known as the "White Death" in order to commit a series of blood-curdling murders. The similarities of his character to those of Bird's Bloody Nathan, the Jibbenainosay, are readily apparent.

However, the two traditions which gave rise to the trapper figure also endowed the trapper's image with a certain degree of ambiguity, which dime novel writers were quick to exploit. They played upon the reader's uncertainty as to whether the trapper introduced in the first few pages was a virtuous hero or a blood-thirsty villain. In J. Milton Hoffman's *Slashaway the Fearless,* Slashaway, a trapper, is characterized as a gruff and surly lunatic capable of murder. Edward Hale, the tenderfoot hero who plans to rescue the lovely heroine Margaret from the Indians, accordingly seeks the aid of a different trapper, the good-natured Onion Bob. But Hale and Onion Bob are also captured, and it is not until they are rescued by a sane and courageous Slashaway that they discover that Slashaway is actually Margaret's father, and that his temporary insanity was caused by grief resulting from the recent murder of his wife by her brother. At the novel's conclusion, Edward and Margaret marry, and Slashaway lives with them for a short while. But characteristically, "he soon tired of the restraints of civilization and went back to his traps and guns."[14] This involuted story suggests the manner in which dime novel writers employed the dual traditions of the trapper figure for the purpose of plot intricacies, heightened suspense, and surprise endings—items necessary to vary plots based essentially on flight and pursuit.

Dime novelists often took advantage of the trapper's traditional dialect as a means of exploring the character's comic possibilities. Once again, they drew upon traditions already in existence; the trapper shows signs of both the Southwestern and the Down East traditions of frontier humor.[15] In one of the earliest Davy Crockett novels, *Kill-bar, the Guide; or, The Long Trail*, the Southwestern backwoodsman, boiling over with braggadocio, uses the traditional longbow to recount his efforts to evade a lovestruck termagant: "I'm Killb'ar, slid from t'other side of the Rocky Mountains on a greased whirlwind, to get rid of Suke Spoon, who are arter me though she knows I are a married man."[16] In contrast to the swaggering self-assertion which marked Southwestern humor, the Down East tradition derived its humor from the presentation of a lowborn character whose pretensions to gentility were repeatedly undercut by his appearance and pattern of speech—a highly affected vocabulary marred by awkward pronunciation and senseless repetition. Edward Ellis's trapper in the famous Beadle western, *Seth Jones; or The Captives of the Frontier*, bears all of the character traits of the traditional Yankee peddler. Possessing "a long, thin Roman nose, a small, twinkling gray eye, with a lithe masculine frame, and long dangling limbs," he introduces himself to Alfred Haverland in a voice that is in a "peculiar, uncertain state," and which when excited makes "sounds singular and unimaginable": "How de do? How de do? Ain't frightened, I hope; it's nobody but me, Seth Jones, from New Hampshire." Warning Haverland of the proximity of Indians, he says, ". . . if you vally that 'ar wife of your bussum, and your little cherubims, (as I allow you've got,) you better be makin' tracks for safer quarters."[17]

As the dime novel progressed, the use of the trapper hero with a comic dialect waned. Throughout the late 1870's and early 1880's, the dialect peculiar to Southwestern humor was either assigned to ancillary, supposedly comic characters such as Old Avalanche of the Deadwood Dick series, or, as in the case of Edward L. Wheeler's Arkansas Alf Kennedy the Danite Ghoul, to ruffians in the ugly white man tradition.[18] Similarly, the burden of comedy was gradually shifted from the hero to minor characters whose bumbling actions are reminiscent of Cooper's David Gamut in *The Last of the Mohicans*. In the dime novel, however, this type of character—whether he be Josephus Doublebee, the Massachusetts green-horn gone west to "strike somethin' of a romantic nature," or Professor Reuben Springs selling exploding alarm clocks to the Indians—serves only as a means of introducing the comic element that was no longer associated with the hero.[19] This tendency to shift the burden of comedy away from the hero is important, for it was a change that was necessary in order to establish the trapper as a character more in accordance with the traditional image of the hero as a naturally noble and inherently superior figure with whom the reader could easily identify.

The concept of the hero as an elderly trapper had long posed major problems for the dime novelist. An intrinsic fictional problem arose from the fact that the aged trapper was, in the first place, simply too old to partake in the love interest which the audience demanded, and which, therefore, inspired most plots. Secondly, the trapper's dialect and ensuing comic role confined him to a lower class status, a position which doomed him to the bachelor life in an age of genteel sentimental heroines. Both the eastern dime novelist and the class conscious eastern audience for whom he wrote would consider it an indisputable social impropriety for the common and boastful—even if virtuous—trapper to marry even the silliest of the anemic upper class heroines. Like any other popular artist striving to sell books, the dime novelist tried to meet the public demand; if the reader wanted a hero who could participate in the novel's love interest, it would be necessary, the writer realized, either to reshape the elderly lower class hero the Cooper tradition had provided, or to find some way of avoiding the problem entirely.

Not surprisingly, dime novelists displayed amazing ingenuity in avoiding the problem. In *Seth Jones; or, the Captives of the Frontier*, Edward Ellis managed not only to evade it but to provide his tale with a surprise ending as well. Throughout the novel, the obvious hero is Seth Jones, the traditional older, comic, dialect-speaking hero the reader expected. But the plot twists, however, when, after rescuing the beautiful daughter of Alfred Haverland from the Indians, the old trapper reveals himself to be genteel, handsome Eugene Morton in disguise. After divesting himself of buckskin and casting off his Down East dialect in favor of romantic rhetoric, the caterpillar turned butterfly leads his sweetheart to the altar.[20] Perhaps suggested by the actions of young Oliver Effingham (alias Edward the trapper) in Cooper's *The Pioneers*, this device, although every bit as jarring as it was in Cooper, managed to become a major dime novel technique, repeatedly proving itself useful until the demise of the genre in the late 1920's.

Another common device for providing the dime novel with a love interest without reshaping the traditional Leatherstocking figure appears in *Gunpowder Jim; or, the Mystery of Demon Hollow*. Gunpowder Jim, forty-five years of age, dressed in buckskin, and accompanied by his dog, Misery, fills the role of the dialect-speaking trapper. The author, however, provides the story with a marriageable hero in the form of Edgar Allison, an Eastern gentleman traveling in the West. As usual, the heroine, Lotta Anderson, is captured—first by Indians, and later by an insane fiddle-playing hermit, musical Mike, and his hunchback assistant Venom. Gunpowder Jim and another elderly trapper by the name of Button Hole Jack aid Allison in his successful attempt to rescue Lotta from a "fate worse than death." Following their marriage, Allison and Lotta "often try to induce their trapper friends to change their mode of life, but all their efforts are in vain." After answering the lovers' plea with the reminder that "the leopard" cannot "change his skin," the stalwart woodsmen retire to the mountains.[21]

Although the tale could be inspired with a love interest by introducing a wellbred hero from the East, this device was infinitely inferior to the fusion within a single character of the best of both worlds: the wilderness skills and unlimited freedom of the traditional trapper, and the youth, gentility, and love interest common to the Eastern hero. The trend toward the development of such a hero, which of course demanded that traits long associated with the Western hero be dropped, was gradual, and it was not until the creation of Kit Carson and Buffalo Bill that a hero of this unique status consistently appeared. However, the beginning of the trend is clearly discernible.

As early as 1860, this hybrid hero appeared in Edward Ellis's *Nathan Todd; or, the Fate of the Sioux' Captive.* Not only is Nathan a Leatherstocking figure who speaks dialect and shows a strong element of Down East humor, but in addition, he displays many of the marks of the genteel Easterner; he is young, speaks an elevated rhetoric in the presence of ladies, discourses on religion, and eventually makes the heroine his bride.[22] But Nathan was a rare occurrence, for although young western heroes frequently dominated the action of the early dime novels, their dialect and the manner in which they were exploited for comic purposes usually kept them in the lower classes. For example, *Kill-bar, the Guide; or, the Long Trail*, published in 1869, portrays Davy Crockett as the typical barrel-chested frontier braggart. With the publication of *The Bear-Hunter; or, Davy Crockett as a Spy* in 1873, though, Davy has developed considerable polish, and by the time of his appearance in 1879 in *Daring Davy, the Young Bear Killer; or, the Trail of the Border Wolf*, he has evolved even further toward natural nobility.[23] However, he still would have little appeal for the sentimental heroine.

While Davy Crockett was slowly gaining nobility as late as 1879, other young trappers made much faster progress in novels written by Joseph E. Badger. In *The Forest Princess; or, the Kickapoo Captives. A Romance of the Illinois*, published in 1870, two Leatherstocking figures exist side by side. Pete Shafer, the elder trapper, speaks in dialect and provides comedy. Young Uriah Barham speaks without a dialect, and wins the hand of Myra Mordaunt.[24] Three trappers appear in *The Border Renegade; or, The Lily of the Silver Lake.* While two of them have thick dialects, the third uses the conventional rhetoric of the sentimental novel, and it is he who weds the heroine.[25]

Thus, it can be seen that the movement toward a young, naturally noble, inherently superior hero was not direct, but gradual; however, the importance of the general trend remains clear. The hero's abandonment of his dialect and his comic traits—traits which Eastern audiences considered inferior in the 1860's, and which branded the Westerner as a member of the lower class—corresponded with his accumulation of a natural nobility irrespective of social class. Although the Western hero was, in a sense, "being civilized" for the Eastern audience, it was a manner of "civilizing" which implicitly denied the rigid social structure of the East. The assumption by the Western hero, a man of lower class origin, of a natural nobility long considered to be the sole possession of the upper class, served only to prove to the reader the artificiality of the social code dominant in the East. The movement of the Western hero away from the restraints of an artifical social order based upon birth and wealth, toward the unrestrained freedom of a more open order based upon the individual's innate worth as a person, reflects the trends of social change during the latter half of the nineteenth century. The West, then, as it was presented in the dime novel, offered the common man a fantasy realm where the rigid socio-economic restrictions of Eastern reality did not apply, a realm which posed an alternative to the status quo.

III

"Hero on Horseback: The Plainsman"

As the American frontier moved westward, the hardy woodsman forsook dark forest paths for the open plains. It was in this sunlit, grassy country that the dime novel's trend toward the establishment of a young, naturally noble western hero reached its climax. The dime novelist needed only to seat his handsome trapper on a horse, and to replace his trusty flintlock with a percussion cap Winchester and a Colt handgun, in order to update a hero who had already a wide and devoted audience. The transition was made largely through the use of an historical personage, Kit Carson, who was already famous when dime novels began. As early as 1862, Edward S. Ellis seized upon Carson as the protagonist for a story later entitled *The Fighting Trapper; or, Kit Carson to the Rescue.* Kit arrives just in time to rescue a party besieged by Indians in the Black Hills.[26] As the title indicates, his appearance marks the first fusion of plainsman and trapper. Although Carson appears as an aged, dialect-speaking trapper of the Leatherstocking variety as late as 1879 in the hard-cover edition of Thomas Harbaugh *Kiowa Charley, the White Mustanger; or Rocky Mountain Kit's Last Scalp Hunt* (New York, Beadle and Adams), he is more commonly portrayed as a young bravo—handsome, athletic, and minus a dialect. Eventually, the growing popularity of young heroes led to Major Sam Hall's creation of Kit Carson, Jr. in *Kit Carson, Jr., the Crack Shot of the West.*[27]

In choosing Carson as his hero, Ellis initiated the transition of the

Western dime-novel hero from trapper to plainsman, but the movement came to full flower seven years later in the work of another
novelist who often worked for the Beadle firm—Edward Zane Carroll
Judson, better known as "Ned Buntline," who introduced Buffalo
Bill to the world. Small in stature but large in confidence, Buntline
was an experienced writer whose exciting life matched that of any
hero he created. Running off to sea at an early age, participating
in a series of adventurous military exploits, delivering temperance
lectures, campaigning for the Know-Nothing party, and surviving
six marriages, Buntline was an active man.[28]

In 1869, Buntline went west with the plan of making a dime
novel hero out of Major Frank North, commander of three companies
of Pawnee scouts engaged in fighting the Sioux. But when he sought
out North, the major declined the offer and suggested that Buntline
instead use the man "over there under the wagon."[29] The man
asleep under the wagon was William F. Cody, named "Buffalo Bill"
in honor of his previous exploits as a hunter killing buffalo for con-
struction crews of the Kansas Pacific Railroad. After talking with
Cody and accompanying him on several scouting missions, Buntline returned to New York to build a story around his newly-dis-
covered hero. *Buffalo Bill, the King of the Border Men* began as
a serial in the *New York Weekly* on December 23, 1869.[30]

By 1872, Cody's fame was such that a play, *Buffalo Bill, the
King of Bordermen*, written by Fred G. Maeder and based on Bunt-
line's story in the *New York Weekly*, opened at the Bowery Theater.
Cody, in New York at the time, was so impressed that he agreed to
act in a play which Buntline planned to write. On December 12, 1872,
Buntline wrote the script for "the Scouts of the Plains; or, Red Deviltry
As It Is," supposedly in four hours, and the play opened four days later.
Despite the fact that the two stars, Cody and Texas Jack Omohundro,
could not memorize their lines, the show was a popular success. The
critics, however, did not react to the gunplay and Indian killing so
favorably, as evidenced by a statement made by Cody: "Buntline,
as 'Cale Durg', was killed in the second act, after a long temperance
speech; and the *Inter-Ocean* said that it was to be regretted that he
had not been killed in the first act."[31] Nevertheless, the play went
on tour during the season of 1873-74, this time with an additional
western hero added to the cast—the famous Wild Bill Hickok. The
association with Wild Bill did not last long,[32] and finally, after three

years of working with Buntline, Cody and Texas Jack organized Buffalo Bill's Wild West, the show destined to win Cody immortality.

The importance of Buffalo Bill's theatrical career lies in the degree to which it influenced the dime novel, and ultimately the image of the western hero in general. Following the publicity surrounding his appearance on the New York stage in 1872, Buffalo Bill's name became magic in pulp literature. Not only was there suddenly an upsurge in the number of novels in which Buffalo Bill appeared, but in addition, Beadle and Adams began publishing many stories which were supposedly written by Cody. Although the famous scout may indeed have written a few, the evidence strongly suggests that the actual author was Prentiss Ingraham, an experienced dime novelist. A press agent for Cody's Wild West show, Ingraham was also, in terms of wordage, the most prolific writer of Buffalo Bill stories, a fact which again hints at the relationship between theatrical publicity and dime novel production.[33] Although Ingraham's contribution to the Cody canon is vastly exaggerated, it was considerable, especially in terms of the span of years during which his stories were in circulation.[34] About half a dozen dime novels, including those written by authors other than Ingraham, deal with the Wild West show, and two actually introduce cowboy stars of Cody's extravaganza, Buck Taylor and Nate Salsbury, to the public.[35] The exploitation of the dime novel as a means of publicizing the Wild West show helps to explain the aura of theatricality which surrounds the fictional character of Buffalo Bill, and which ultimately distorts the image of subsequent western heroes.

The changing fictional characterization of Buffalo Bill may easily be traced from 1869, when Buntline first introduced him to the public as *Buffalo Bill, King of Border Men*. In the illustration on the cover of the *New York Weekly* in which the story appeared, the great plainsman resembles the trapper heroes who preceded him; though he carries a pistol in his belt, he is still bearded, long haired, garbed in shaggily fringed buckskin, and he leans on a flintlock rifle. He does ride a horse in the story, but his morality remains that of the trapper, for he delivers temperance lectures to his occasionally intemperate companion, Wild Bill Hickok, and he shows no surprise when a gambler turns out to be a villain. However, despite his rugged demeanor and ungrammatical English, Buffalo Bill's noble thoughts allow him to win the lady of his heart, the exquisite Louisa La Valliere, whom he has rescued from a band of drunken soldiers. No doubt this is merely Buntline's attempt to account for the historical fact of Cody's marriage to Louisa Frederici, for the dime-novel hero of 1869 had not quite reached the social level at which he was permitted to marry a genteel heroine. As Buffalo Bill explains after rescuing Louisa, "If I see her anymore, I shall love her, and love above my station would be madness and folly."[36] This is probably the only story ever to appear in which Buffalo Bill is allowed a romantic attachment; throughout his subsequent dime-novel career he rescued countless heroines, winning their admiration but never their hands.

In Ingraham's novels, all written between 1879 and 1904, Buffalo Bill is portrayed in a manner which illustrates the changing stereotype of the western hero. No longer a crude trapper, he now gambles frequently and displays a flair for the theatrical, which finds expression in flamboyant dress and multiple costume changes. In addition, he speaks a kind of language which must have been Ingraham's conception of eloquence. Dialect and comic roles are assigned to Buffalo Bill's companions, especially to Wild Bill in the early novels. Following Ingraham's death in 1904, other dime novelists found it necessary to continue this practice. The anonymous author of *Buffalo Bill in the Land of Fire; or, Nick Nomad, the Mountain Wanderer* gave Buffalo Bill an associate named Nick Nomad, a dialect-speaking trapper used for comic purposes.[37] (Nomad's appearance here, as well as in a subsequent series of stories, testifies to the continued popularity of the trapper figure even into the twentieth century.) Occasionally, though, reversions occur in which the trapper actually becomes the central hero. For example, the action of an Ingraham novel written in 1893, *Buffalo Bill's Spy Shadower; or, The Masked Man of Grand Canyon*, is dominated by Old Huckleberry, an aged, buckskin-clad, dialect-speaking trapper out of the Leatherstocking tales. Only at the story's conclusion, after Old Huckleberry has disposed of a gang of road agents, does he remove his disguise and reveal himself to be none other than the great Buffalo Bill.[38] However, by this stage in the development of the dime novel, the trapper was rarely the central hero; as a vestige of an earlier era, his presence served merely to add another dimension to the story's appeal.

Through the efforts of Ingraham and other dime novelists (ex-

cluding Buntline), the fictional character of Buffalo Bill, in only
fifteen years, underwent a dramatic change. Whereas Buntline's
original had been in 1869 a crude plainsman delivering temperance
lectures, he was, by the middle of the 1880's a smooth-talking
"Prince of the Plains," a polished theatrical performer. But the
Western hero's acquisition of sophistication was accompanied by
a trend toward an increasingly questionable morality. Not only did
he gamble—a spicy pastime in the nineteenth century, and one which
no doubt contributed to his appeal—but he even dared at times to
take the law into his own hands. In Ingraham's *Buffalo Bill's Blind
Trail; or, Mustang Madge, the Daughter of the Regiment*, Buffalo
Bill skillfully captures a road agent. However, after learning that
the thief had taken to crime as a means of regaining gambling losses
which had placed the mortgage of his mother's home in jeopardy, the
prince of scouts chooses to ignore the social code and to conceal the
crime. Buffalo Bill tracks down the crafty gambler responsible for
swindling the road agent, and soon regains the lost money in an
honest game of cards.[39] The fact remains, of course, that Buffalo
Bill placed his individual concept of justice above that of the law,
substituting his personal moral code for society's, in a way that
would soon become characteristic to the Western hero.

The hero's increasing tendency to engage in amoral or extra-
legal activities is paralleled, and perhaps masked by, a growing emphasis upon social polish and courtly manners. Buffalo Bill treats
the gentler sex with infinite courtesy, and pauses in the midst of
even the most desperate situations to bury his dead. Duels, such
as the one fought in *Buffalo Bill's Double; or, the False Guide*, are
frequent, especially in later stories.[40] These activities are not unusual
for the prince of the plains, however, for the stories had by this time
assumed all the trappings of the medieval romance. Although Owen
Wister is commonly credited with introducing the chivalric element
into the serious western in *The Virginian*, his debt to the dime novel
is clearly indicated by such titles as *Buffalo Bill's Bonanza; or, the
Knights for the Silver Circle* and *Buffalo Bill and His Merry Men; or,
the Robin Hood Rivals*.[41] Buffalo Bill soon became a virtual knight-
errant dashing over the plains righting wrongs and aiding, or sometimes replacing, law enforcement, displaying the kind of mob psychology which demands that individual justice function when social
justice is thought to be inadequate. Like Don Quixote before him,

Buffalo Bill is, after 1906, accompanied by a faithful companion, "little Cayuse of the Piutes." Together, streaking across the plains, they bear a striking resemblance to the Lone Ranger and Tonto.[42]

With the appearance of Young Wild West, the Prince of the Saddle, in Frank Tousey's *Wild West Weekly* in 1902, the stereotype of the plainsman hero came full circle. Although Young Wild West was immensely popular (1924 numbers of *Wild West Weekly* appeared), his character shows little development beyond the prairie scout as knight-errant.[43] However, the movement of the dime-novel hero from crude plainsman to gallant knight was an important preliminary step, for the trend of the western hero toward extra-legal conduct, combined with an accompanying and perhaps compensatory emphasis upon courtly manners, set the stage for the cowboy—the next, and the most enduring, stereotype of the Western hero.

IV

"A Cavalier of Old: The Cowboy"

The role of the cowboy in the dime novel was relatively minor in comparison with other Western figures. Although he began to appear in pulp literature during the 1870's to provide additional color, it was not until 1887 that he finally reached heroic status. Even then, though, he did not attain the astounding and durable success achieved by the trapper, the plainsman, or the outlaw, evidently finding the competition provided by the other paper heroes too intense. However, despite his unimpressive record in the dime novel, he played a significant part in the evolution of the hero. Not only was the cowboy a logical outgrowth of the plainsman, but he proved to be, in addition, the most enduring stereotype of the Western hero. Outlasting the dime novel, populating the pages of countless serious westerns and pulp magazines, and riding desperately across millions of movie and television screens, the cowboy later attained international fame as the symbol of the American West.

Although he was an historical figure born of the cattle industry, the cowboy in the dime novel, as Henry Nash Smith comments, "apparently has nothing to do with cattle."[44] Instead, he usually fights Indians and chases lawbreakers, and his portrait in the dime novel is therefore tinged with the colors of all the previous heroes.

Most commonly, the cowboy is associated with the border ranger, that red-blooded plainsman determined to bring justice to the "rowdy border thugs" who terrorized the Southwest. Ten years before the cowboy became a hero in the dime novel, border rangers appeared in the novels of Major Sam S. Hall, the famous "Buckskin Sam" who had himself served six years with the Texas Rangers.[45] But Hall's realistic, if colorful, descriptions of the Texas Rangers were unusual, for the majority of Eastern dime novelists were unfamiliar with the West. More typically, Edward L. Wheeler contributed to the image of the Western hero by emphasizing the chivalric and theatrical aspects of Captain Chris Adams, a border ranger, in *Cloven Hoof, the Buffalo Demon; or, the Border Vultures, A Tale of the Southwest*: "The one was a tall muscular knight of the frontier, dressed in buckskin, with a face tanned to a nut brown hue from constant exposure to wind and sun; piercing gray eyes, dark curling hair, and a heavy brigandish mustache of like color. His form was of perfect mold, and he sat on his horse like a cavalier of old."[46] Thus, an established tradition of border rangers had been formulated long before the appearance of the dime novel cowboy. The border ranger was a variation of the buckskin-clad plainsman; he was usually a Texan who possessed all of the traits of the medieval knight. The pulp cowboy, initially a Texas product, and by vocation more a border ranger than a cowpuncher, was not surprisingly transformed in accordance with the established tradition.

Early in 1887, two pulp stories appeared in which the cowboy first assumed the role of hero: Leon Lewis's *Daredeath Dick, King of the Cowboys; or, In the Wild West with Buffalo Bill*, and Prentiss Ingraham's *Buck Taylor, King of the Cowboys*.[47] Although the fictitious Daredeath Dick appeared shortly before Buck Taylor, the former can hardly be said to be the first cowboy hero, for "Daredeath Dick is a character so weakly drawn, playing so minor a part in the story named for him, that any such claim is a technicality."[48] Instead, that honor is universally reserved for Ingraham's Buck Taylor, the character based upon the real life cowboy starring that year in Buffalo Bill's Wild West.

Ingraham's novel, purportedly an account of the "wild and thrilling" life of Buck Taylor, illustrates the fusion in the American mind of the cowboy with the pre-existent figure of the border ranger. The tale deals with Buck's attempt as a young man to enlist in Captain

McNally's Texas Rangers. Upon reporting to the Ranger camp, Buck is required to undergo a series of trials which includes boxing, wrestling, and bronc busting. He demonstrates his skill and courage at each of these tasks, and is therefore permitted to join the elite group and to wear the Ranger insignia. The remainder of the story relates the particulars of Buck's quest to save Captain McNally's daughter from the Indians.[49] In a later Ingraham novel, *Buck Taylor, the Saddle King; or, the Lasso Rangers' League, A Romance of Border Heroes of To-day*, his costume is described in detail:

> He was dressed in somewhat gaudy attire, wore a watch and chain, diamond pin in his black scarf, representing a miniature spur, and upon the small finger of his right hand there was a ring, the design being a horseshoe of rubies.
> About his broad-brimmed, dove-colored sombrero was coiled a miniature lariet [sic], so that the spur, horseshoe and lasso designated his calling.[50]

Both the adventures and the costume of Buck Taylor, the first cowboy hero, suggest the degree to which he was linked to the previous tradition of border rangers. Not only was he actually a Texas Ranger, but he also possessed the characteristics of the medieval knight. Discussing the similarities between the Buck Taylor stories and the medieval romance, Joseph Waldmeir calls attention to the fact that ". . . initiation into a band of the Chosen by passing tests of physical strength, the gaining of heraldic identification, the quest, courtesy to fallen or disarmed foe (one does not shoot one's enemy in the back), all are part and parcel of chivalric tradition."[51]

Divorced from his true vocation as a cattle herder, and arbitrarily endowed with the chivalric attributes of the border ranger, the cowboy hero as cowboy was doomed from the moment of his first appearance in the dime novel. First a victim of Ingraham's taste for flamboyant attire, and then a vehicle for Cody's Wild West show publicity, the cowboy entered into an irreversible spiral of deterioration in the dime novel. He was soon sensationalized almost beyond recognition. A number of dandies, direct descendants of the cowboy, populated the dime novel as early as 1891. The paragon of fop heroes, the cowboy-detective Dandy Dan of Deadwood, was the epitome of sartorial splendor even when tied to a column of stone in the midst of the dusty plains: "The prisoner was a young man, not above five and twenty years of age, and was dressed in a suit of neat black velvet, with patent leather boots on his feet. He wore a white shirt, the front of which was spotless, and in the center of the bosom blazed a magnificent diamond. His broad-brimmed sombrero at his side was gathered up at one corner by a rich cluster of diamonds."[52]

Although Ingraham's theatrical version of the cowboy dominated the dime novel and led to the cowboy's plunge into dandyism, Warren French discusses three other dime novelists who contributed to the image of the cowboy: Joseph Badger, Jr., Captain Frederick Whittaker, and William George "Gilbert" Patten (the author of the Frank Merriwell stories). In such stories as *Rob Roy Ranch; or, Imps of the Pan-Handle*, Badger shows a tendency to portray the cowboy realistically; however, the cowboy always remains a minor character in the novels.[54] Frederick Whittaker, on the other hand, depicted the cowboy as an ignorant, lawless ruffian, as indicated by titles like *Top-Notch Tom, the Cowboy Outlaw; or, The Satanstown Election,* and *The Marshal of Satanstown; or, The League of the Cattle-Lifters.*[55]

Only in the novels of William Patten did the cowboy appear as a naturally noble hero unspoiled by Ingraham's theatricality. Writing under his own name, or using the pseudonyms of William West Wiler or "Wyoming Will," Patten created courageous men of action: Hustler Harry, the Cowboy Sport; Prairie Paul; Hurricane Hal, the Cowboy Hotspur; Cowboy Steve, the Ranch Mascot; and, Cowboy Chris, the Vengeance Volunteer.[56] Patten's cowboys, however, were lost in the throng of dandies and detectives who dominated the dime novel trade in the 1890's. It was not until the publication of Wister's *The Virginian* that Patten's manly cowboy was resurrected and, tempered by a generous supply of Ingraham's medieval chivalry, cast by Wister into a mold capable of surviving the vicissitudes of popular taste.

The dime novel cowboy, although he did not reach the pinnacle of success attained by other western heroes, was quite popular, and his success can possibly be explained by his unique history and the character traits bred by that history. On the whole, it was not until the 1870's, when the burgeoning Texas cattle industry flowed over into the plains states, that the average Eastern reader heard of the cowboy at all, primarily through articles in popular periodicals. From the first, cowboys were associated with lawlessness; the *Washington Star*, for example, in 1878 called them "nomads . . . remote from the restraints of moral, civic, social and law enforcing life," who "journey with their herds . . ., loiter and dissipate, sometimes for months, and share the bought dalliances of fallen women."[57] Spreading this image of the cowboy as a lawless figure freed of social restraint, President Chester A. Arthur, in his First Annual Message to Congress in 1881, requested legislation that would enable the military to intervene in the activities of a roving gang of "armed desperadoes known as 'Cowboys' " who were at that time terrorizing the border region between Mexico and the Territory of Arizona.[58] Even as late as 1881, the American imagination conceived of the cowboy as an anti-social force.

However, a sudden reversal took place in the 1880's. The publication of Charles A. Siringo's *A Texas Cow Boy; or, Fifteen Years on the Hurricane Deck of a Spanish Pony* in 1885 did much to familiarize the public with the more humane traits of the cowboy; two years later Prentiss Ingraham was deifying Buck Taylor as a naturally noble, inherently superior hero. Ingraham's efforts to ennoble the cowboy are often quite frank. These men are wild, he explains in *The Cowboy Clan; or, The Tigress of Texas. A Romance of Buck Taylor and his Boys in Buckskin*, but they are also courageous and "noble in their treatment of a friend or a fallen foe." In *Buck Taylor, the Saddle King; or, the Lasso Rangers' League. A Romance of the Border Heroes of To-day*, Buck talks with a member of the army's Medical Corps, Surgeon Hassam, saying:

> I know well that a great many wicked men have crept into the ranks of our cowboy bands; but there are plenty of them who are true as steel and honest as they can be. We lead a wild life, get hard knocks, rough usage and our lives are in constant peril, and the settling of a difficulty is an appeal to revolver or knife; but after all we are not as black as we are painted.[59]

The rapid shift in the public mind from the cowboy as a lawless, anti-social figure to the concept of the cowboy as noble hero explains the ambivalent character of the fictional cowboy. He is a combination of both concepts, lawlessness and nobility—an amalgam which continues to appeal to audiences today. Like Buffalo Bill before him, the cowboy rides the range in search of lawbreakers, repeatedly taking the law into his own hands when he feels that justice has been thwarted. Following his own Western code of honor, and asserting his individual concept of justice when legal and political instruments are unable to function, the cowboy proved that violence worked when the established systems of society did not. This conflict between violence—the code of the West—and law, the cornerstone of middle class social values, reflected a profound ambiguity in the popular—not just American—imagination. Pondering the implications of the traditional theme of the western, John G. Cawelti explains that he is

. . . inclined to think that the conflict between the code of the West and the middle-class values of the East is a projection into fantasy of a reaction against the dominant middle-class values of our culture, a collective imagining of a way of life in which the individual is freed from the frustrating pressures of domesticity, steady employment, civic responsibility, and the other public virtues of modern middle-class life. In my view, the cowboy is an anti-hero to the successful law-abiding citizen, projected back into an eternalized moment of the past so that his essentially subversive message cannot seriously challenge our accepted values.[60]

Thus, the popularity of the cowboy, like that of the trapper and plainsman before him, was the result of his anarchic tendencies. To the reader frustrated by life in a rigid, controlled society, the cowboy was (and continues to be) a symbol of the final assertion of individual freedom, the ultimate expression of law-abiding rebellion against social restraint. It matters not that the cowboy is often a lawman—even when he wears a badge, he is portrayed by popular media as an individual, not as an arm of the law. For when the badge is removed from the heroic marshal's breast and worn by a lesser man, it is merely a tin star. When not upheld by the courageous, strong-willed individual, the law itself is as laughable as the good natured but bumbling deputy, Festus, of television's popular *Gunsmoke*.

V

"Magnificent Rogue: The Outlaw"

Contemporaneously with the development of the plainsman and the cowboy, another stereotype of the Western hero was also evolving in the American imagination: the outlaw. Appearing in the West almost immediately after the first discovery of gold, so-called "road agents" soon stirred up popular excitement that far outweighed their numbers—understandable, perhaps, considering that Wells Fargo alone lost nearly a million dollars in 313 stage robberies.[61] Dime novelists could scarcely overlook such daring deeds and clever escapes. At the same time, the choice of the outlaw as a fictional western hero was extremely fortuitous, for the popular mind had always been thrilled by the daring exploits of a long line of romantic pirates and European highwaymen. By placing Robin Hood in the costume of an American Western road agent, the dime novelist created a Western hero peculiarly American, yet imbued with all the color and reckless individualism of the magnificent rogues of the past. More importantly, the introduction of the outlaw hero introduced a new element into western pulp literature. Whereas the cowboy had been the ultimate expression of a law-abiding and perhaps justifiable rebellion against social restraint, the outlaw hero was an expression of open rebellion.

The first of the road agent heroes was created by Edward L. Wheeler, the flamboyant Philadelphian who wore a Stetson hat and is said to have saluted strangers as "Pard."[62] Wheeler produced the bandit hero Deadwood Dick, a character whose instant popularity stunned even the publishers. Released on October 15, 1877, *Deadwood Dick the Prince of the Road; or, the Black Rider of the Black Hills* contains a striking description of the outlaw-hero on horseback:

He was a youth of an age somewhere between sixteen and twenty, trim and compactly built with a preponderance of muscular development and animal spirits; broad and deep chest, with square, iron-cast shoulders; limbs small yet like bars of steel, and with a grace of position in the saddle rarely equaled, he made a fine picture for an artist's brush or a poet's pen. . . .

His form was clothed in a tight-fitting habit of buck-skin, which was colored a jetty black, and presented a striking contrast to anything one sees as a garment in the wild far West. . . . A broad black hat was slouched down over his eyes; he wore a thick black veil over the upper portion of his face, through the eyeholes of which there gleamed a pair of orbs of piercing intensity, and his hands, large and knotted, were hidden in a pair of kid gloves of light color.

The "Black Rider" he might have been justly termed, for his thoroughbred steed was as black as coal, but we have not seen fit to call him such—his name is Deadwood Dick. . . .[63]

Riding through a series of adventures in novel after novel, Deadwood Dick becomes the rebellious hero who embodies all of the attributes of preceding western heroes; even later, he retains the spicy flavor of criminality when he reforms and fights on the side of the law. A deadly shot and a master horseman, skilled in the art of disguise, he cleverly evades pursuit or tracks down villains—tasks facilitated by a guaranteed income of five thousand dollars a year from his own gold mine. Intelligent, handsome, and chivalrous, Deadwood Dick is decidedly potent when it comes to attracting the beautiful but sometimes tainted women who populate the novels. He usually resists their bashful advances, but he does on occasion succumb. Though married several times, Deadwood Dick continues to be a rootless hero, for Wheeler carefully disposes of the outlaw's past wives by unfaithfulness or death. Throughout the tales, Deadwood Dick and his lady bandit companion, Calamity Jane, exchange affection until, in *Deadwood Dick's Doom; or, Calamity Jane's Last Adventure. A Tale of Death Notch*, "they, the two wild spirits who had learned each other's faults and each other's worth in lives branded with commingled shame and honor," are joined in somewhat holy matrimony.[64]

Although Deadwood Dick is an appealing fictional character, his true source of popularity lies in his asocial status, his unrestrained individualism, and his total lack of moral or social restraint. Wheeler emphasizes this aspect of his hero's character from the beginning. In *Deadwood Dick, The Prince of the Road*, the hero, minus bandit costume and using his real name, Ned Harris, forces a tenderfoot, Redburn, to shoot a gambler. Redburn, who is naturally "averse to bloodshed," explains that he did not want to kill the gambler, and asks why Deadwood Dick forced him to do so. The hero turns to Redburn and replies that it was necessary to "salivate" the ruffian, for "You'll find before you're in the Hills long that it won't do to take lip or lead from anyone. A green pilgrim is the first to get salted. I illustrated how to serve 'em!" As he listened, "Redburn's eyes sparkled. He was just beginning to see into the different phases of this wild exciting life."[65] Devoid of moral restraint, the outlaw is a law unto himself; in the anarchic West, he is judge, jury, and executioner.

However, the outlaw's amorality is always masked by a thin veneer of respectability. Whereas the essentially subversive message of each of the other Western heroes was disguised by his more admirable attributes—the trapper by his innate virtue, the plainsman by social polish and chivalric customs, the cowboy by chivalry or a badge—the outlaw added to these elements a justification for his anti-social behavior. Society, he claimed, was to blame. In Wheeler's *The Phantom Miner; or, Deadwood Dick's Bonanza. A Tale of the Great Silver-Land of Idaho*, the "reformed" Deadwood Dick, after killing the last sheriff of Eureka for the latter's display of "rash hotheadedness," talks with the town's newly appointed sheriff. The sheriff remarks, ". . . you recognize no law, young man," and Deadwood Dick, answering in a manner which suggests that he has reformed in name only, says: "No more I don't. But didn't I offer to make amends, and become an honest, loyal citizen, if the people of Eureka would accept of me? Yes, you know I did, and they chose my hate rather than my friendship. They shall have all they want of it." Accepting the sheriff's offer of friendship, but refusing his aid, Deadwood Dick speaks the classic lines of the western hero: "I ask no one to fight my battles. . . . All my life I have had to depend upon my own muscle. I can fight the battle on alone."[66] Throughout pulp fiction, the bandit vindicates his illegal behavior on the basis that he has been denied a respectable place in society, and that he has, as a result, been forced to rely entirely upon his own "muscle."

As the ancestor of numerous noble outlaws who soon would become dominant in the dime novel and eternal in the popular imagination, Deadwood Dick achieved almost literal apotheosis in *Deadwood Dick's Dream; or, The Rivals of the Road. A Mining Tale of Tombstone.* After being captured and hanged as an outlaw, the noble hero explains, "I was cut down and resuscitated by a friend, and thus, while I hung and paid my debt to nature and justice, I came back to life a free man whom no law in the universe could molest for past offenses."[67] Resurrected, eminently free, eternally divorced from the laws of man and God, Deadwood Dick provided an ideal model for subsequent dime-novel outlaws.

Later novels penned by Wheeler illustrate his awareness of the fact that Deadwood Dick's true source of popular appeal lay in his defensible rebellion against society. As a result, justification for the hero's death as a social being, and his rebirth as a free individual immune to law, appears so often that it becomes a fictional cliché. Fred Brayton, the hero of *The Detective Road-Agent; or, The Miners of Sassafras City,* formerly a detective, takes to the road as a result of a false conviction of murder.[68] In *Solid Sam, The Boy Road-Agent; or, The Branded Brows. A Tale of Wild Wyoming,* Solid Sam turns to a life of crime because a group of ruffians (true villains are differentiated from noble outlaws by their lack of polished manners) has appropriated his gold mine. He plans to waylay them individually and collect the gold which is rightfully his. Finding this impossible, the hero instead demands that the innocent citizens of Placer City restore his gold and pay him protection money. When they refuse, the noble outlaw strikes a powerful blow against organized society—he and his band "justifiably" reduce the town to a "series of heaps of smoking ashes and charred embers, to tell of the vengeance of Solid Sam."[69]

However, the clearest example of the noble outlaw's vindication appears in Wheeler's *Dick Drew, the Miner's Son; or, Apollo Bill, the Road-Agent.* Approaching the problem laterally, Wheeler discusses road agents in general:

> As a rule, this class is only a few degrees less rough and to be feared, than the typical border ruffian; but, circumstances have been chronicled of a brave and gallant man, with a spice of nobility in his heart, who has taken to the profession of stage robbery, more on account of some secret life trouble, than taste for the business itself.

Thus prepared for the admittedly atypical situation, the reader eagerly awaits the appearance of a "brave and gallant" road agent. All desire is soon sated, though, for when Apollo Bill makes his entrance one readily perceives the "spice of nobility in his heart"; he wears a scarlet buckskin suit and a plumed sombrero, and leads a band of cohorts dressed in crepe masks and red flannel costumes. The "secret life trouble" which has caused law-abiding citizen Bill Blake to be reborn as the dashing Apollo Bill is immediately revealed. Illogically, he has become a bandit because his home and family were destroyed by border ruffians. Since this is not justification enough, he must be the victim of an injustice perpetrated by society as a whole; the reader later finds that while seeking to avenge the murder of his family, Bill has accidentally shot and killed an innocent man. Pursued thereafter by the untiring

> minions of the law, . . . hunted down to the last resort, he rallied around him a band of fellows and took to the mountains. They were discovered in their first retreat and branded road-agents ere they had earned the right to such a calling. Assailed by despondency and anger at this injustice, Apollo Bill fled to this fastness and organized his men into what is known as Apollo Bill's road-agents.[70]

Apollo Bill, like so many other fictional outlaw heroes, has been falsely accused by a society ignorant of the nature of "true" justice; he is given no choice but to rebel.

The outlaw, like the trapper, the plainsman, and the cowboy, became a hero in the dime novel primarily as a result of his anarchic tendencies. In an age of alienation and widespread discontent, he mirrored the fears and frustrations of the ordinary reader. By identifying with the magnificent rogue, and by vicariously participating in his justifiable rebellion, the reader was able to purge his feelings of alienation and anxiety. Even today, though television and movies have supplanted the dime novel, a basically adult audience continues to deify its rebels. Whether the hero be the dashing Deadwood Dick or the charming bandits of the screen's *Butch Cassidy and the Sundance Kid*, the principle remains unchanged. It is likely, then, that the trend of the dime novel western hero toward increasing rebelliousness was the result of the growing anxieties of modern life—anxieties which grew in response to the corresponding increase of industrialization, urbanization, and societal restraint upon individual freedom in the years following the Civil War.

NOTES

[1] G. Edward White, *The Eastern Establishment and the Western Experience: The West of Frederic Remington, Theodore Roosevelt, and Owen Wister* (New Haven and London, 1968), 31.

[2] James Fenimore Cooper, *The Pioneers* (New York, 1962), 422, 421, 424.

[3] White, 32-33.

[4] Edmund Pearson, *Dime Novels; or, Following an Old Trail in Popular Literature* (Boston, 1929), 99.

[5] (New York, 1950), Chapter IX, "The Western Hero in the Dime Novel," 99-125, and Chapter X, "The Dime Novel Heroine," 126-135.

[6] 134.

[7] 134-135.

[8] 101.

[9] Marvin Fisher, *Workshops in the Wilderness: The European Response to American Industrialization, 1830-1860* (New York, 1967), and Leo Marx, *The Machine in the Garden: Technology and the Pastoral Ideal in America* (New York, 1964).

[10] Ray Allen Billington, *The Far Western Frontier, 1830-1860* (New York, 1956), 41-42, and Russell B. Nye, "Cops and Cowboys" (Chapter VI of work in progress), MSS 70-71.

[11] Nye, 78.

[12] This tale, Beadle's Boys' Library of Sport, Story, and Adventure, No. 144 (1887), is discussed by Smith, 103.

[13] Street & Smith's Buffalo Bill Stories, No. 100 (1903?), (Gold Star Books Collector's Edition [IL7033]).

[14] Beadle's Frontier Series, No. 23 (1908), 95.

[15] Smith, 104.

[16] Captain Comstock [Charles Dudley Warren?], Frank Starr's American

Novels, No. 18 (1869), 9, 51.

17Beadle's Half Dime Library, No. 8 (1877), 1.

18Edward L. Wheeler, *Old Avalanche, the Great Annihilator; or, Wild Edna, the Girl Brigand*, The Deadwood Dick Library, No. 8 (1900), and *Deadwood Dick on Deck; or, Calamity Jane, the Heroine of Whoop-Up*, The Deadwood Dick Library, No. 15 (1900).

19J. Milton Hoffman, *Gunpowder Jim; or, The Mystery of Demon Hollow*, Beadle's Frontier Series, No. 37 (1908), 12, and "An Old Scout," *Young Wild West Running the Gauntlet; or, The Pawnee Chief's Last Shot*, Frank Tousey's Wild West Weekly, No. 37 (1903).

20Smith, 102.

21Hoffman, *Gunpowder Jim*, 18, 98.

22This tale, Beadle's Dime Novels, No. 18, is discussed by Smith, 106-107.

23Harry Hazard [Joseph E. Badger, Jr.], Frank Starr's America Novels, No. 118, and Harry St. George [Harry St. George Rathborne], Beadle's Half Dime Library, No. 108.

24Smith, 108, discusses this aspect of Beadle's New Dime Novels, New Series, No. 133; Old Series, No. 454.

25Smith, 108-109, makes this point about Beadle's Pocket Novels, No. 140 (1872).

26Edward S. Ellis, *Viola Vennond; or Life on the Border, Philadelphia Dollar Newspaper* (XX, July 2, 1862 and following five issues); Latham C. Carleton [pseud.], *The Hunters; or, Life on the Mountain and Prairie*, Irwin P. Beadle's Ten Cent Novels, No. 1 (1863); anon., *The Fighting Trapper; or, Kit Carson to the Rescue*, American News Company (1874).

27"Buckskin Sam" [Major Sam S. Hall], Beadle's New York Dime Library, No. 3 (1873).

28Albert Johannsen, *The House of Beadle and Adams* (Norman, 1950), II, 167-176, and Sam Henderson, "Love, War, Liquor, and Rebellion," *Pioneer West*, IV (Apr., 1970), 38-43.

29Smith, 115.

30*New York Weekly* (XXV, No. 6, Dec. 23, 1869 - XXV, No. 17, Mar. 10, 1870).

31Colonel William F. Cody, *Life and Adventures of Buffalo Bill* (Chicago, 1917), 265.

1   32267.

33Smith, 119, 124, and Don Russell,
    (Norman, 1960), 388.

34Russell, 387-388.

35Russell, 389, 392, makes this point about Prentiss Ingraham's *Buck Taylor, King of the Cowboys; or, The Raiders and the Rangers. A Story of the Wild and Thrilling Life of William L. Taylor*, Beadle's Half Dime Library, No. 497 (Feb. 1, 1887), and Leon [Julius Warren] Lewis' *Daredeath Dick, The King of the Cowboys; or, In the Wild West with Buffalo Bill*, Beadle's Banner Weekly (Nov. 6, 1886 - Jan. 15, 1887); Beadle's Dime Library, No. 629 (Nov. 12, 1890).

36Smith, 117, as quoted from an exact reprint of Buntline's first Buffalo Bill story entitled *Buffalo Bill* (New York: International Publishers, n.d.), 183.

37"by the author of Buffalo Bill," Street & Smith's Buffalo Bill Stories, No. 196 (1950?).

38Beadle's Dime Library, No. 777 (1893).

39Russell, 403, makes this point about Beadle's Dime Library, No. 691 (1892).

40"by the author of Buffalo Bill," Street & Smith's Buffalo Bill Stories, No. 128 (1903?).

41Prentiss Ingraham, *Buffalo Bill's Bonanza; or, The Knights of the Silver Circle*, Beadle's Dime Library, No. 644 (1891). *Buffalo Bill and His Merry Men; or, The Robin Hood Rivals*, Beadle's Dime Library, No. 735 (1892).

42Russell, 498-409.

43Charles Bragin, *Bibliography: Dime Novels 1860-1964* (Brooklyn, N.Y., 1964), 7.

44Smith, 124.

45*Kit Carson Jr., the Crack Shot of the West. A Wild Life Romance*, Frank Starr's New York Library, No. 3 (1877), 2.

46Beadle's Half Dime Library, No. 26 (1878); *The Buffalo Demon; or, The Border Vultures. A Tale of the Southwest*, Beadle's Pocket Library, No. 7 (1884); The Deadwood Dick Library, No. 3, (1900), 3.

47See n. 35.

48Russell, 392.

49Joseph J. Waldmeir, "The Cowboy, the Knight, and Popular Taste," *Southern Folklore Quarterly*, XXII (Sept., 1958), 115-116.

50Beadle's Dime Library, No. 649 (1891), 2, in Smith, 124.

51Waldmeir, 116.

52"Noname," *Dandy Dan of Deadwood and His Big Bonanza*, Frank Tousey's Five Cent Wide Awake Library, No. ? (1891?), (Gold Star Books Collector's Edition [IL7-37]), 73.

53Warren French, "The Cowboy in the Dime Novel," *Texas Studies in English*, XXX (1951), 219-234.

54Beadle's Dime Library, No. 409 (1886).

55Beadle's Dime Library, No. 303 (1884), and Beadle's Dime Library, No. 310 (1884).

56William G. Patten, *Hustler Harry, the Cowboy Sport; or, Daring Dan Shark's General Delivery*, Beadle's Dime Library, No. 545 (1889). *Wild Vulcan, the Lone Range-rider; or, The Rustlers of the Bad Lands. A Romance of Northwest Nebraska*, Beadle's Half Dime Library, No. 682 (1890). *Hurricane Hal, the Cowboy Hotspur; or, Old True Blue's Pilgrimage in Satan's Section. A Romance of the Red Spur Ranch*, Beadle's Dime Library, No. 676 (1891). *Cowboy Steve, the Ranch Mascot; or, The Bond of Blood*, Beadle's Half Dime Library, No. 806 (1893). Wm. West Wilder—"Wyoming Will" [Pseud.], *Cowboy Chris, the Vengeance Volunteer; or, the Death-Hunt Pards*, Beadle's Popular Library, No. 30 (1891); Beadle's Half Dime Library, No. 1075 (1898).

[57]Douglas Branch, *The Cowboy and His Interpreters* (New York, 1961), 189.

[58]Smith, 122-133.

[59]Smith, 124, makes this point about *The Cowboy Clan*, Beadle's Dime Library, No. 658 (1891), 7, and *Buck Taylor, the Saddle King*, Beadle's Dime Library, No. 649 (1891), 21.

[60]John G. Cawelti, "Cowboys, Indians, Outlaws," *The American West*, I (Spring, 1964), 35, 77.

[61]Earl Pell, "When Road Agents Ruled the Roost," *Real Frontier*, I (Apr., 1970), 10.

[62]Johannsen, II, 296.

[63]Beadle's Half Dime Library, No. 1 (1877); The Deadwood Dick Library, No. 1 (1900), 4-5.

[64]The Deadwood Dick Library, No. 39 (1900), 28.

[65]*Deadwood Dick, the Prince of the Road*, 9.

[66]The Deadwood Dick Library, No. 7 (1900), 7.

[67]Smith, 111-112, remarks on this passage from Beadle's Half Dime Library, No. 195 (1881), 8.

[68]The Deadwood Dick Library, No. 63 (1900).

[69]The Deadwood Dick Library, No. 32 (1900), 31.

[70]The Deadwood Dick Library, No. 48 (1900), 4-5, 17

TURN-OF-THE-CENTURY COUNTRY-LIFE NOVELS

Charles W. Scheef

The pastoral ideal has been a literary theme at least since Theocritus, 300 years before Christ, and has probably been present in the Western imagination since the formation of the first "urban" centers in ancient Mesopotamia and Greece. Throughout history the ideal is dependent upon the presence of cities, in one form or another, against which is contrasted the image of an untainted, idyllic country landscape. Long ago something of a myth in man's collective unconscious, this idea persists today in the lyrics of popular country and western music, and in such diverse manifestations as advertising ("country soft, country fresh Salem cigarettes") and the mid-twentieth century rush from the cities toward the suburbs. The country novels to be discussed here play a definite role in this pervasive tradition.

In America the pastoral ideal begins with the view many settlers bring with them of the New World as a vast, untouched Garden of Eden. Here is a lush, unspoiled land where any man may begin his life anew in almost literal emulation of Adam. Some indeed saw the new land as treacherous and fraught with deadly perils for the body and soul, but many more view America as a pastoral dream world, the ideal spot for the hordes of mankind too long pent up in European ghettos. But the dream of Jefferson and Crevecoeur was soon challenged by those, such as the Jacksonian Democrats, who recognized the benefits to be reaped from the new scientific and technological knowledge. By 1900, a spokesman for country life such as Liberty Hyde Bailey, although still proposing farming as "the primitive and underlying business of

135

mankind," is reduced to admitting the necessity for outright "conquest" of the land, using every modern method science can offer.[1] The Jeffersonian ideal has by this time been greatly revised to accommodate a thriving industrialism.

But in the popular imagination and in literature the tendency becomes not to incorporate industry and technology into the picture of the country, but rather to view these influences as a threat and to reaffirm the eighteenth-century agrarian dream. Cooper's stories of Natty Bumppo are an early example: the natural man in a natural setting, Natty is pushed further and further westward as civilized society expands and threatens to make his life uncomfortable. Emerson too recognized not only the beauty and healthfulness of a natural life in the country, but its valuable therapy for modern man's spirit:

The land is the appointed remedy for whatever is false and fantastic in our culture. The continent we inhabit is to be physic and food for our mind, as well as our body. The land, with its tranquilizing, sanative influences, is to repair the errors of scholastic education, and bring us into just relations with men and things.

Little more than fifty years later these sentiments are repeated almost verbatim by fictional country folk such as Eben Holden and Silas Strong.

With the swift and tremendous growth of cities after 1890 and beyond into the twentieth century, it was only natural that as urban life became crowded, complex, and problem-ridden, the older ideal of the pleasures and virtues of country life would reappear in American writing with renewed energy. The move to the city almost literally depopulated much of the countryside; people thronged to the cities looking for economic advancement, a richer and more exciting life, and if they found them, also found thousands of others looking for the same things in an environment of crowded, dirty slums and crowd-packed stifling streets. For many, disillusionment with city life followed, one result of which is the "outdoor movement," a rise in the popularity of such country pastimes as hunting, fishing, and camping. "Recreation,' says Foster Rhea Dulles, becomes "a primary concern of the twentieth century social movement to reform the evils of urban life."[2] But for those who could not afford a camping trip or a resort vacation to escape the city, the country novels around 1900 provided a worthy substitute. Through them one could leave the impersonal, complex city and return to a peacefully simple, rural world where every new acquaintance was soon a friendly neighbor.

Such is the ideological tradition of the main theme in the country novels, and such the sociological impetus for their popularity. From a literary standpoint, these works are difficult to classify, for they made up no school of writing as identifiable as the local colorists. F. Hopkinson Smith and Irving Bacheller both had many volumes of sentimental family-life stories with little or no hint of the country about them. Historical novels, such as Maurice Thompson's *Alice of Old Vincennes*, contained rural themes, and the country novels often relied on historical elements. Many of the novels contained distinctly non-country ingredients, particularly the romantic love interest that often appeared as a minor strand of the plot. In twenty-two novels considered, twenty concluded with marriages or engagements. Two novels had double marriages, one (James Lane Allen's *The Mettle of the Pasture* (1903)) has a triple.

The country-life novels also included elements of local color and regional interest, and occasionally attempts at literary realism. Like the local colorists, the novelists stressed characterization of regional types, attempting to reproduce dialects indigenous to a particular area. The broad range of country novels contained characters from the Kentucky mountains, the New England sea coast, upstate New York, and Southern plantations. All these characters emerged with similar values and ideals, but the novels took some care in careful descriptions of the features of the surroundings. James Lane Allen and John Fox, Jr., for example, were particularly skilled at evoking the rugged beauty of the Kentucky mountains. Fox, especially, included touches of realism that rival the local colorists'. More often than any other country novelist, Fox described the harsher side of rural life as well as its earthy beauty:

Until a man has lived a year at a time in the mountains he doesn't know what a thin veneer civilization is. It goes on and off like a glove, especially off. Put twenty *average* blue-grass families down in the mountains half a dozen miles from one another, take away their books, keep them there, with no schools and no churches, for a hundred years, and they will be as ignorant and lawless as the nountaineer.

Fox drew the bitter, violent mountain feuds with authority, for, born and reared in Kentucky, he knew at first hand the conflicts of which he wrote. Allen, too, utilized scenes from his childhood in Kentucky; Edward Westcott similarly based much of *David Harum*

(1898) on his own years as a bank clerk in Syracuse. But despite their attention to realistic detail, none of these authors, except Fox, let authentic description determine his point of view; all at composite, idealized versions of life in rural America that affirmed the traditional pastoral dream. (One unusual minor exception is Irving Bacheller's gory account of young Willie Brower's Civil War experiences in *Eben Holden* (1900).)

The country novels, however, cannot be blamed for lack of realism; to draw an authentic picture of life was not their intent, nor did they intend to be Stephen Cranes or Frank Norrises. In fact, James Lane Allen, in his "Preface" to *Summer in Arcady* (1896) attacked the "invasion from the literature of the mother-country" which "has spread abroad as the old and evil and ever-hated darkness." Allen assailed the dark-visioned novels of George Meredith and Thomas Hardy as

. . . black, chaotic books of the new fiction . . . what unhealthy suggestions they have courted, what exposures of the eternally hidden they have coarsely made, what ideals of personal depravity they have scattered broadcast, what principles of social order they have attacked, what bases of universal decency they have been resolute to undermine.

One important function of the country-life novel, as Allen and others conceived it, was to counteract this "downward-moving fiction of manifold disorder." Authors should, Allen felt, "wrest a moral victory for each of the characters," instead, as Irving Bacheller wrote, of "turning people into animals and animals into people" in the manner of Zola and the naturalists. Rather than delve into the complex human psyche, or brood over man's struggles with fate and his fellows, they gave their reader tales to please and reassure, instead of disturb and confuse him. As Joseph C. Lincoln said,[3]

It would be very hard for me to write a long story which should end dismally. It is only too true that stories in real life frequently end that way, but I don't like my yarns to do so. . . .

Thomas Nelson Page, in his introduction to F. Hopkinson Smith's *Felix O'Day* (1915), bestowed on him the highest praise he could:[4]

The prevailing mark of his work was his abounding and unconquerable optimism, of which the cherriness of his nature speaks in every page he ever wrote. It proclaims itself in every character he ever portrayed. He lived in a world of cheer and he increased the sum of cheer in it.

What the country-life novelists did, then, through the settings and characters of a quiet, rural world, was to provide consolation and temporary escape for the harried reader. Refusing to mirror the disorientation around them, they concentrated instead on creating a simple, coherent, human vision.

In the country novels characterization always predominates over theme. Two of the most popular books in this genre are cases in point; Bacheller's *Eben Holden* and Westcott's *David Harum* center on an eccentric, colorful country type. The same is true of Smith's Colonel Carter, Read's Major Cranceford, and Lincoln's Cap'n Eri, to cite three more examples. With these and other simple and honest characters, the authors seek to teach by example, to show their reader the effects of country living by emphasizing the easy, comfortable life-styles of their bucolic heroes. Even in a book like Bacheller's *Silas Strong* (1906), in which the author is deeply concerned with the lumber industry's mutilation of the countryside, Strong's character dominates. A spokesman for the beauties of the wilderness in its natural state, he charms the reader into seeing things his way rather than being bombarded with overt propaganda. Likewise in all the other novels: the inherent nobility and uprightness of the country characters illustrate the desirable qualities of a rural society, so that the authors seldom rely on key thematic passages to convey their message.

In the same way the delineation of simple country characters takes precedence over plot, except for the love interest. Even the most common element used to unify these plots, romantic love, is usually handled as a minor strand of the story. In *David Harum*, John K. Lenox, the young visitor to the country, is in love with Mary Blake. But the love story is dropped after chapter ten, to reappear in the final episodes, forty-five through forty-eight, when the two are married. In the thirty-five chapters between the main focus of attention is on David Harum and his horse trading yarns. Similarly, in John Fox's stories of the Kentucky mountaineers, a love story or a clan feud might provide moments of tension and conflict, but neither furnishes the main plot. In *The Kentuckians* (1897), Boone Stallard, a congressman from the mountains is temporarily involved in a feud with the rival Keaton clan and in the end of the book wins the hand of the Governor's daughter, Anne Bruce. But both the feud and the love story arouse less interest and take up less space than Fox's use of Stallard as a representative of "a people who had drifted back towards barbarism through no fault of their own." In most of the novels, complicated or tightly knit plot structures are sacrificed in favor of leisurely and often disorganized, haphazard portraits of picturesque country types in their natural settings.

But despite their emphasis on characterization, few of the country novels develop their characters with the skill or depth of the better local colorists and regionalists, as in novelists such as Mary N. Murfree or Sarah Orne Jewett. It is difficult, in reading the country novels, to distinguish one character from another. They all have in common simple philosophies, homely outlooks on life, and humorous characteristics; a very few have personal idiosyncrasies that set them apart from the type. The outstanding distinction, for example, between F. Hopkinson Smith's Colonel Carter and Joseph Lincoln's Cap'n Eri is that the former is a Southern gentleman, the latter a Cape Cod seaman; otherwise, they are both retired, benevolent old men, known for their sincerity, sense of humor, and down-to-earth appreciation of the simple things in life. The majority of the other philosopher-figures are the same. Even when one seems to differ, like David Harum, the sharp-trading Yankee, he turns out by the book's end to be a kindly old country fellow after all, who was simply testing the sincerity of his young assistant, John Lenox. The only way in which many of these central characters in the country novel can be distinguished from one another is usually by where he lives (in the woods, on the seacoast, in the north country, on a backwoods farm, in the South). But while such stereotyping provides a major reason why these books could never become first-rate novels, it no doubt at the same time helps to explain their popularity. Few Southern gentlemen were ever so winning as Smith's Colonel Carter of Cartersville, and few backwoodsmen as quaint and colorful as Bacheller's Silas Strong, but they combined all the traits of the type into a composite, idealized version that appealed to the reading public as something that must be true. Even a downeast character like David Harum, who was based on a real-life original, must have gone through a number of adjustments before he became the embodiment of the "cute" Yankee horse-trader. The same stereotypes that kept these novels in the second rank of fiction, to the mass read-

ing public seemed wholly satisfactory characters who matched perfectly preconceived notions of what a wise old country philosopher
ought to be.

One of the earliest of these earthy, country philosophers is
Colonel Carter, a fifty-year old Virginian, first introduced by F.
Hopkinson Smith in *Colonel Carter and Other Tales of the South*
(1891). The narrator of "Colonel Carter of Cartersville" describes
this quaint figure as

. . . a frank, generous, tender-hearted fellow . . . happy as a boy; hospitable
to the verge of beggary; enthusiastic as he is visionary; simple as he is genuine!
A Virginian of the good birth, fair education, and limited knowledge of the
world and of men, proud of his ancestry, proud of his State, and proud of
himself; believing in States' rights, slavery, and the Confederacy.

But Carter is not a master of a thriving antebellum plantation; the
story takes place after the Civil War and is set in New York City,
where the Colonel is trying to find backers for his wildly idealistic
"Cartersville and Warrentown Air Line Railroad." In the process
Colonel Carter takes on as much complexity and ambiguity as any
of these country characters ever do. He is not entirely an idealized
Southern gentleman, for he is possessed with the unromantic notion
of bringing, though his proposed railroad, industrialization to his
corner of Virginia. This dream and his attempts to interest city
financiers in it, make him at once a representative of a rural society
and a naive, somewhat comical figure. Most of the country philosophers oppose commercialism and hope to keep industry out of their
quiet, pastoral worlds. But the Colonel is saved from being a traitor
to country ideals by the impracticality of his plans for Cartersville.
Fitzpatrick, the Colonel's financial advisor in the city, humors Carter
by trying to push his railroad proposal, but he knows it will never find
support; since his schemes are unreal, the Colonel is turned into a gentle,
harmless, slightly eccentric old man. But the charm of his dream and
the lost way of life he represents still has much appeal. Behind his
impractical plan there is still the old agrarian vision:

The old manor house restored and the barns rebuilt, the gates rehung, the old
quarters repaired, the little negroes again around the doors; and he once more
catching the sound of the yellow-painted coach on the gravel, with Chad helping the dear old Aunt down the porch steps. This, deep down in the bottom of
his soul, was really the dream and purpose of his life.

This ideal has a strong hold on the city-bound stockbroker Fitzpatrick, in the first story, as well as the sequel, *Colonel Carter's Christmas* (1903). What the Colonel means to Fitz is further brought out in the latter's criticism of Wall Street:

> Down here in the Street we've got to put things down on paper and we don't trust anybody. We don't understand the kind of man whose word is literally as good as his bond, and who, to help any man he calls his friend, would spend his last cent and go hungry the balance of his life.

Another character who very nearly escapes from the stereotype is Edward Noyes Westcott's David Harum, from the novel of that name, published in 1898. Harum's motto is "Do unto the other feller the way he'd like to do unto you, an' do it fust," and he plays the role of the shrewd Yankee trickster to the hilt. The story opens with a horse trade in which Harum pays $125 for a nag he soon learns is lame. Then, through a series of re-sales and re-purchases, he finally makes up for all but $35 of his loss and moves on to foreclosing a mortgage on a helpless widow on Christmas morning. But in the nick of time he reveals, to the surprise of the widow and his new assistant, John Lenox, that since the widow's husband was the first person who ever treated him "human," Harum will tear up the mortgage and invite the widow to Christmas dinner. Throughout the book he delights in pretending to be a heartless villain, then suddenly revealing his true feelings, which, of course, are inevitably wise and kindly. But Harum's cunning soon becomes predictable, and the reader takes it no more seriously than he does Carter's grandiose schemes. At heart David Harum is a lovable man who appeals to the reader because his roguery is fake, and because under this façade lies a warm human being whose homespun philosophy and quaint expressions like "Scat my ———!" are amusing and good-natured. Like Carter, Harum's most winning basic characteristic is his simplicity:

> A good fair roadgait's good enough fer me; three square meals, a small portion of the 'filthy weed,' as it's called in po'try, a hoss 'r two, a ten dollar note where you c'n lay your hand on't, an' once in a while, when your conscience pricks ye, a little somethin' to permote the cause o' temp'rence, an' make the inward moniter quit jerkin' the reins—wa'al, I guess I c'n git along, heh?

Irving Bacheller, one of the most popular of the country novelists, wrote four novels centered on the homely philosopher figure. None had comic overtones, but were all serious, simple heroes with explicitly optimistic philosophies derived from their rural environments. The most successfully drawn was the central character of *Eben Holden: A Tale of the North Country* (1900) and *Eben Holden's Last Day A-Fishing* (1907). As Willie Brower, the young narrator says, "We all loved him for his kindness and his knack of story-telling." Even though Holden plays only a minor part in the first novel, which is largely devoted to Willie's experiences in the Civil War and job-hunting in New York City, his uncomplicated country beliefs hover over the book and influence Willie in whatever he does. Even after Willie goes to work for Horace Greeley in New York and becomes a city man, kindly old Eben remains Willie's ideal of humanity. The best summary of what Eben Holden's life and values represent is found in the book's closing lines, his last words:

I ain't afraid.
'Shamed o' nuthin' I ever done.
Alwuss kep' my tugs tight,
Never swore 'less 'twas nec'sary,
Never ketched a fish bigger'n't was
Er lied 'n a hoss trade
Er shed a tear I did n't hev to.
Never cheated anybody but Eben Holden.
Goin' off somewheres, Bill—dunno the way nuther—
Dunno 'f it's east er west er north er south,
Er road er trail;
But I ain't afraid.

All of Holden's sayings have what Willie calls "a cheerful temper." His picture of heaven is a place with

No bull thistles, no hard winter, no narrer contracted fools; no long faces, an' plenty o' work. Folks sayin' 'How d'y do' 'stid o' 'good-by,' all the while—comin' 'stid o' goin'. There's goin' t' be some kind o' fun there.

This hopefulness that things will always turn out for the best is an attitude Holden shares with rural types in all these novels. They are seldom depressed by the hard work or dullness of country life; adversity is only a temporary irritation that can be overcome by the assumption of a cherry outlook. As the hero says in *Eben Holden's Last Day A-Fishing*, a sequel to the very popular first book:

Sometimes I think they must 'a' lost one commandment, an' that is: Be happy.

Ye can't be happy an' be bad. I never see a bad man in my life that was hevin' fun.

Bacheller's other two country heroes, Silas Strong and Darius Olin, share, to a large extent, this genial faith. *Silas Strong: Emperor of the Woods* (1906), even though he is continually threatened by the lumber industry and is, indeed, finally pushed from the woods, remains amazingly placid in the face of his doom. True, he is depressed but seldom bitter and never despairing. Rather, he looks back to a day when the woods were free and pure and finds consolation in the ideal of the past. Strong's motto is "old-fashioned ways is best," and while he is not so happy as Eben Holden, he has Holden's simple optimism. But Bacheller suggests this rosy outlook can be challenged in ways Eb only vaguely fathomed; in Silas Strong the threat of the twentieth century to country life is most clearly apparent.

Darius Olin, in the novel *D'ri and I* (1901), is an inferior reflection of Eben Holden and Silas Strong. D'ri is a "slow and sober" hired hand who joins the narrator, Ray Bell, in fighting the British in 1812. He is a humble and steadfast country figure, who, when he receives a medal for bravery, calls the symbol "reedic'lous," for "they don't no man deserve nuthin' fer doin' what he'd orter."

Other country types, since they all more or less mirror the five characters discussed, can be briefly summarized. The hero of Joseph C. Lincoln's *Cap'n Eri: A Story of the Coast* (1904), the most popular of his many Cap Cod mariners, is an Eben Holden removed from the "North Country" to the bucolic world of "Orham on the Cape." John Fox, Jr.'s Major Buford in *The Little Shepherd of Kingdom Come* (1903), and Opie Read's Colonel Remington Osbury ("a true Kentuckian with a sort of miscellaneous and unanalytical courtesy") in *A Kentucky Colonel* (1890) and Major John Cranceford in *An Arkansas Planter* (1896), are among other gentlemanly shadows of Smith's Colonel Carter. In the last of these, the Major's loyalty to Southern principles is tested realistically by a race riot taking up nearly half the book, stirred up by a malcontent Northern white man. References to racial matters, however, are few in the country novels. James Lane Allen's Judge Morris, in *The Mettle of the Pasture,* or F. Hopkinson Smith's Judge Counton in *The Romance of an Old-Fashioned Gentleman* (1903) and true Southern gentlemen in "a land where hospitality was a religion."

As a foil to the country philosopher, the other typical figure in the country-life novels is the city visitor, often the narrator, who serves as guide and commentator for the reader. Bucolic characters by themselves might prove to the urban reader to be only amusing "specimens" in something of a rural zoo; but if a character resembling the reader is present to point out the refreshing virtues of the pastoral people, the author's point cannot be missed.

A perfect example of this type is the Wall Street broker Fitzpatrick in F. Hopkinson Smith's Colonel Carter stories. His interest in the Colonel is based on the contrast between Carter's way of life and his own. Throughout these stories Fitzpatrick takes pains to convince his city friends that Carter is not merely an amusing anachronism, but that he represents a more leisurely and humane life style that city folk would do well to imitate. Another example of the type is Phil Stoneman in Thomas Dixon's *The Clansman.* Phil is a young Northerner fighting in the Civil War; but when he is wounded in the South and then nursed back to health by the Southern belle, Margaret Cameron, he slowly gives up his prejudices against the South and is converted to its viewpoint. Near the novel's end he tells Margaret,

I love the old-fashioned dream of the South. Maybe you have enchanted me, but I love these green hills and mountains, these rivers musical with cascade and fall, these solemn forests—but for the Black Curse, the South would be to-day the garden of the world.

Most "straight" characters who extol the country point of view, like Fitzpatrick and Stoneman, end as true believers in country ways. In the novels of John Fox, Jr., however, the non-country types recognize the problems of a rural setting, as well as the many advantages, somewhat more realistically. Jack Hale, who comes to the mountains in *The Trail of the Lonesome Pine* (1908) to make them "the iron centre of the world," is the only non-country figure in a novel populated by characters with names like Devil Judd Tolliver and The Red Fox. To these people Hale is a "furriner," but Hale becomes so involved with the mountain folk that he turns into one himself. Fox is not entirely certain this is a good thing, for while Hale is becoming "countrified," the mountain girl he loves, June Tolliver, is going to school in the Blue-grass and losing touch with her environment. In all Fox's novels there is an uneasy ambivalence about the contrasting values of civilization and mountains. His city characters are not unreserved admirers of rural life. Hale's experience in the mountains

. . . hardened and strengthened his mouth, steeled his eyes and made him more masterful in manner, speech and point of view, and naturally had added nothing to his gentleness, his unselfishness, his refinement or the nice consideration of little things on which women lay such stress.

But Fox resolves the conflict in favor of the virtues of mountain life; June returns to take her place beside him and Hale gives up his plans to industrialize the area. "I'll plant young poplars," he tells June

to cover the sight of every bit of uptorn earth along the mountain there. I'll bury every bottle and tin can in the Cove. I'll take away every sign of civilization, every sign of the outside world.

"And leave old Mother Nature to cover up the scars," said June.

"So that Lonesome Cove will be just as it was."

"Just as it was in the beginning," echoed June.

"And shall be to the end," said Hale.

In Fox's *The Heart of the Hills* (1912), the non-country characters are cousins, Gray and Marjorie Pendleton, who become involved with two young people from the mountains, also cousins, Jason and Mavis Hawn. Even though boy and girl in each couple have always assumed they would eventually marry, Gray finds himself attracted to Mavis' simple country beauty, and Marjorie to Jason's rough, unsophisticated nature. For a while it appears there may be two marriages of mountain and civilized society, but in the end the twain cannot meet. Marjorie says

There was never a time that I did not feel in both a mysterious something that always baffled me—a barrier that I couldn't pass, and knew I could never pass.

And Gray guesses at the nature of this "barrier":

. . . it's a reserve, a reticence that all primitive people have, especially mountaineers; a sort of Indian-like stoicism, but less than the Indian's because the influences that produce it—isolation, loneliness, companionship with primitive wilds, have been a shorter while at work.

"That's what attracted me," said Marjorie frankly, "and I couldn't help always trying to break it down—but I never did."

In addition to his role as guide and commentator, the city character in the country-life novel serves to provide the reader with a character with whom he can identify. Through him he can return to a peaceful, simpler rural world that he either once knew or dreamed about. He can return to the country with Adam Moss in James Lane Allen's *A Kentucky Cardinal* (1895), in the same manner he follows Melville's Ishmael to sea:

At times the needle of my nature points towards the country. On that side everything is poetry. I wander over field and forest, and through me runs a glad current of feeling that is like a clear brook across the meadows of May. At others the needle veers round, and I go to town—to massed haunts of the highest animal and cannibal. That way nearly everything is prose.

These characters, who learn about country life from the rural people, are thus in the best position to extol its virtues to the reader by contrasting the city's worst with the country's best. Philip Burwood, in Opie Read's *A Kentucky Colonel,* takes a job helping the Colonel write his "History of Shellcut Country" and ends by marrying the Colonel's daughter. John Lenox, in *David Harum,* at first contemptuous of Homeville's rustic ways, returns after a European trip with his new wife, settles down, and names his first child David. Willie Brower, in *Eben Holden,* through he makes a success of life in the city, never loses his countrified clarity of vision, and never forgets the contrast of city and country ways; for him the city will always be filled with

. . . men licking the hand of riches with the tongue of flattery; men so stricken with the itch of vanity that they groveled for the touch of praise; men even who would do perjury for applause. I do not say that most of the men I saw were of that ilk, but enough to show the tendency of life in a great town.

Besides the country philosopher and the involved or uninvolved "straight" character, these novels contain a few other types. There are often young country lovers, especially in Fox's mountaineer stories and Allen's pastoral idylls, such as *Summer in Arcady,* which lacks a strong central figure such as Eben Holden or David Harum, and is concerned almost exclusively with the romance of two simple country youngsters, Daphne and Hilary. Another common type is the kindly, elderly aunt or grandmother such as Colonel Carter's Aunt Nancy ("A true Southern lady"); the housekeeper for the three

retired seamen in *Cap'n Eri,* Martha Snow; David Harum's Aunt
Polly Bixbee; and Silas Strong's sister, "Sinth" Strong.

Surprisingly few comic characters appear in these novels, perhaps because the authors are so sincere about their country heroes
that they fear strong humorous characters may divert attention from
them. Then again, it may also be that the reader will be sufficiently
amused by their heroes. Such is the case with Smith's Colonel Carter
and Westcott's David Harum—their own eccentricities provide enough
humor for the story. Only Opie Read, among the better-known
country-life writers, deliberately created minor comic characters.
Gideon Batts in *An Arkansas Planter,* is a debt-ridden loafer who
serves as court jester to the novel's main figure, Major John Cranceford; in *A Kentucky Colonel,* old Buck Hineman not only provides
humor but drives all the characters to distraction with his poor flute
playing.

The theme in these novels that unites them all is the idea,
exemplified in the main characters, that the simple life, lived in a
natural, rural setting, is morally uplifting. From this pastoral
generalization the novels draw a number of corollaries. First, if the
unspoiled landscape kept as it was in the past, is morally beneficial,
then the past itself, kept alive in the rural tradition, is undoubtedly
morally better than the present is or the future will be. If the
"good old days" were good, then the new days, to be good, must
preserve the values of the past or lose them. Second, country life
leads one to view the world with a cheery optimism, supported by
an abiding faith that everything is for the best, or will turn out to be.
The rural character, built on personal honesty and moral integrity,
make things that way; hard work, perseverance, and goodwill bring
the happy ending. Third, and most important, if the country, past
and present, does have a salutary effect on man, then urbanization
and industrialization have just the opposite. The country is a place
of peace and plenty, while the city is a spawning ground for all that
is false and treacherous; the country builds men's minds, characters,
and bodies, the city destroys them. In the novels, the country is a
place where traditions are preserved and honored; where men can
fulfill their potential for healthy, happy minds and bodies; and
where the corrupt artificiality of urban society does not intrude on
the pastoral dream.

Behind the plots and messages of these novels, of course, lies

Nature itself, the source of beauty, strength and morality. The novels are loaded with descriptions of field and farm, mountain and valley, the seasonal passage of time, and the effects of the natural world on its human inhabitants. James Lane Allen, especially, creates in his Kentucky country a magic world almost entirely set apart from civilization; his characters walk through enchanted scenes and feel closer to trees, birds, and animals than those of any other novelist. The conflict in *Aftermath* (1895), a sequel to *A Kentucky Cardinal*, is between the narrator, Adam Moss, and his new wife Georgiana, who attempts to pull Moss away from nature and toward herself. But at the end she realizes that while she grows old, nature for Moss will be new each spring. And resigned to her husband's bond with nature, she tells him:

I am not deceived, you have not forgotten nature. It draws you more power-fully than anything else in the world. Whenever you speak of it, you say the right thing, you find the right word, you get the right meaning. With nature alone you are perfectly natural. Towards society you show your shabby, awk-ward, trivial, uncomfortable side.

But not all of Allen's characters have such ethereal rapport with nature. The schoolmaster, John Gray, in *The Choir Invisible* (1897), for example, finds the Kentucky wilderness meaningful not only because of the natural beauty of the seasons pulsing through it, but rather because it shapes human character. Honor, courage, and "the burning spiritual heroism" of the pioneers are qualities fostered by contact with nature, which is not so important to man for simply *being* what it is, but rather for what it *does* to him.

Characters in John Fox, Jr., recognize the harsh effects of mountain life, yet with all its crudities, they usually prefer the mountains to "the smoke and steam and bustle and greed of the Twentieth Century" city. The mountain girl, June Tolliver, is thrilled by the pace of life in the city but her first visit

. . . was enough and too much for June. Her head buzzed continuously and she could hardly sleep, and she was glad when one afternoon they took her into the country again.

At the end of the story, though June has been polished and refined by city life, she decides to return to the mountains.

They were not to blame—her people, they but did as their fathers had done before them. They had their own code and they lived up to it as best they could, and they had no chance to learn another.

Such is the attitude of most of Fox's characters. The mountains breed roughness and vulgarity as well as simple, honest virtues; but mountain people are nevertheless bound to the land and the past. Though it may be harsh and uncouth, it is also "a land of peace and of a plenty that was close to easy luxury." The children of the mountains may lead barbaric lives, but they are blessed with nature's abundance, which makes them strong, self-reliant people.

Irving Bacheller's Silas Strong also finds the country as man's most natural home. Even the small city of Ogdensburg repels him and after being robbed of his watch, he beats a hasty retreat to the wilderness:

His conclusions regarding the city were now fully formed. He broke with it suddenly, and struck out across country and tramped sixty miles without a rest. Ever after the thought of Ogdensburg revived memories of confusion, headache, and irreparable loss.

City folks, he concludes, live in a kind of hell; they

live under a sky two feet above their heads an take their air secont handed and drink at the bar instead of the spring an eat more than what they earn an travel on wheels an think so much of their own helth they ain't got no time to think of their countrys.

When the rapacious lumber interests threaten his beloved woods, Silas, in an eloquent passage, tells his reader (as Bryant and Emerson had in different language) what Nature means to man:

They's m-medicine here t' cure all the sickness in a hundred cities; they's f-fur 'nough here t' c-cover their naked—they's f-food 'nough t' feed their hungry— an' they's w-wood 'nough t' keep 'em w-warm. . . . Ye r-rob the world when ye take the tree-tops out o' the sky. Ye might as well take the clouds out of it. God has gi'n us g-good air an' the woods an' the w-wild cattle, an' it's free—an' you—you're g-goin' t' turn ev'rybody out o' here an' seize the g-gift an' trade it fer d-dollars.

If there is an over-all message in these books, this is it: the country is a sacred gift from God that can heal any of the anxieties and ills modern man suffers, and provide him with a pure, perfect world where the best in him can thrive.

This same theme is also explicit in Bacheller's *Eben Holden,* in which the hero's simple ideals are reinforced by a long speech by Horace Greeley on the city's vanity and corruption:

Here the lie has many forms—unique, varied, ingenious. The rouge and powder on the lady's cheek—they are lies, both of them; . . . the many who imagine a vain thing and pretend to be what they are not—liars every one of them. It is bound to be so in the great cities, and it is a mark of decay. . . . For truth you've got to get back into the woods. You can find men there a good deal as God made them—genuine, strong, and simple.

The central message of the country-life novels is not always so explicitly stated as it is in *Silas Strong* and *Eben Holden,* but it is always there. Beyond this theme, which ties together the novels as a type, the authors of course included other elements of the popular contemporary novel calculated to interest the reader even though they might have no direct relation to the message. As in the historical romances of the period, these novels often included actual historical personages—Daniel Boone, George Washington, James Audubon, Commodore Perry, Horace Greeley. The love plots derive directly from the sentimental romance; the regional elements from the local color, regional novel. But the country-life novels, as Bacheller explained in the preface to *Silas Strong,* were really not intended to be "literary performances." They were, he said, simply stories which move "with a leisurely pace, like that of the woods lover on the trail," a place "to forget the calendar and measure time on the dial of the heavens." They were written to present a relaxed, rural dream world that might serve Americans as an alternative to the frantic escalation of industrialization and urbanization that the nineties and early twentieth century was going through. Their simplicity of message is matched by their simplicity of plot and characterization, but what they had to say provided reassurance and consolation to those disturbed by the changes and complexities of turn-of-the-century life. It is even more difficult today than in 1900 to take their idealized view of country life seriously, but what a pleasure to imagine that it could be that way!

THE NOVELS

Allen, James Lane. *Aftermath: Part Second of "A Kentucky Cardinal."* New

York: Harper and Brothers, 1895.

_____. *The Choir Invisible.* New York: Grosset and Dunlap, 1897.

_____. *A Kentucky Cardinal.* New York: Harper and Brothers, 1895.

_____. *The Mettle of the Pasture.* New York: Macmillan Company, 1903.

_____. *Summer in Arcady, A Tale of Nature.* New York: Macmillan Company, 1896.

Bacheller, Irving. *D'ri and I.* New York: Grosset and Dunlap, 1901.

_____. *Eben Holden: A Tale of the North Country.* Boston: Lothrop Publishing Company, 1900.

_____. *Eben Holden's Last Day A-Fishing.* New York: Harper and Brothers, 1907.

_____. *Silas Strong: Emperor of the Woods.* New York: Harper and Brothers, 1906.

Dixon, Thomas. *The Clansman: An Historical Romance of the Ku Klux Klan.* New York: Grosset and Dunlap, 1905.

Fox, John, Jr. *The Heart of the Hills.* New York: Charles Scribner's Sons, 1912.

_____. *The Kentuckians.* New York: Harper and Brothers, 1897.

_____. *A Knight of the Cumberland.* New York: Charles Scribner's Sons, 1906.

_____. *The Little Shepherd of Kingdom Come.* New York: Grosset and Dunlap, 1903.

_____. *The Trail of the Lonesome Pine.* New York: Charles Scribner's Sons, 1908.

Lincoln, Joseph C. *Cap'n Eri: A Story of the Coast.* New York: Grosset and Dunlap, 1904.

Read, Opie. *An Arkansas Planter.* Chicago: Rand McNally and Company, 1896.

_____. *A Kentucky Colonel.* Chicago: F. J. Schulte and Company, 1890.

Smith, F. Hopkinson. *Colonel Carter and Other Tales of the South.* New York: Charles Scribner's Sons, 1908.

_____. *Colonel Carter's Christmas.* New York: Charles Scribner's Sons, 1903.

_____. *Felix O'Day.* New York: Charles Scribner's Sons, 1915.

_____. *The Romance of an Old-Fashioned Gentleman.* New York: Charles Scribner's Sons, 1907.

NOTES

[1] Liberty Hyde Bailey, *The Country Life Movement in The United States* (New York, 1911), 14.

[2] Foster Rhea Dulles, *A History of Recreation: America Learns to Play* (New York, 1965), 211-12, 229.

[3] Stanley Kunitz and Howard Haycraft, eds., *Twentieth Century Authors* (New York, 1942), 828.

[4] F. Hopkinson Smith, *Felix O'Day* (New York, 1915), xii.

SOCIAL HISTORY AND THE CRIME FICTION
OF MARY ROBERTS RINEHART

Arnold R. Hoffman

Twenty-five years ago Edmund Wilson asked "Who Cares Who Killed Roger Ackroyd?" and stated that for his own part he certainly did not.[1] The importance of Wilson's aversion to "detective stories"— as he narrowly termed what is indeed a broad variety of fiction—lies not only in his essaying the matter from his position as a recognized literary critic, but also in the fact that mysteries, detective novels, crime stories, thrillers—indeed, the whole spectrum—had marshaled by 1945 an immense public constituted from all strata of society. As Wilson himself noted in an essay the previous year, some strong devotees of the form were to be found among "the most serious public figures of our time": Woodrow Wilson, W. B. Yeats, T. S. Eliot, and Paul Elmer More, to cite only those named specifically by Wilson.[2] Further, there had been on both sides of the Atlantic a number of competent book-length studies of "mysteries," among them H. Douglas Thomson's 1931 *Masters of Mystery* and Howard Haycraft's 1941 *Murder for Pleasure*.[3] In their seriousness, books like Thomson's and Haycraft's are only a partial answer to Wilson, for they take as an unsubstantiated premise that mysteries *are* "popular."

The other aspect to the complete answer lies in the consideration of *how many* people are concerned about the fate of whoever did in Mr. Ackroyd. In 1947 Frank Luther Mott, in his statistical commentary on best selling books in America, demonstrated conclusively that a great many people have cared enough to place several

153

mysteries on the annual best seller lists.[4] To explain precisely what
they care about and why they respond with money and reading time
to particular authors and books is quite another matter, ultimately
founded on as subjective a basis as Edmund Wilson's declination.
In *Golden Multitudes*, Mott asks rhetorically his own question, "What
makes a best seller?" and concedes "[t] here is no formula which may
be depended upon,"[5] in mystery fiction or any other genre, to explain
the phenomenon of authors and books becoming aspects of what this
age is attempting to identify as popular culture.

In whatever way popular literature, as one segment of that popular
culture (or mass culture, as Messrs. Rosenberg and White would have
it[6]), may in the end be defined by its many analysts—and in all like-
lihood the definitions will be nearly as diverse and divergent as the
number of definers—if some account is taken of the author's term of
production, the number of works published, and the number of sales
tallied for those works, Mary Roberts Rinehart will be a major figure
in American popular literature, and, thereby, in America's popular
culture. The point of especial importance to this paper is that a major
portion of her literary reputation rests on her mystery fiction.

Considering Mrs. Rinehart's "crime stories," as she preferred to
call them,[7] or indeed any aspect of her career in letters, with an intent
and organization even approaching the conduct of historical or critical
scholarship is really a new venture, one offering both the rewards and
pitfalls of fresh research. It is surprising to this writer that, considering
the general reputation of Mrs. Rinehart, very few commentators have
noticed her and even fewer have given her more than cursory attention.[8]
One can be done very quickly with a recall of the commentary on her
work, crime fiction or otherwise.

Apparently the earliest document is the slight monograph of 1924,
from the company of George H. Doran, Mrs. Rinehart's publisher from
1915 to 1929. In addition to two articles by Mrs. Rinehart herself,
Mary Roberts Rinehart: A Sketch of the Woman and Her Work contains an opening, sugary advertisement by Grant Overton and an insipid
embarrassing sketch by Robert H. Davis.[9] A long stretch of time ensues
but in 1941 Howard Haycraft's *Murder for Pleasure* redeems the time b
setting forth in five rather astute pages a simple outline of the virtues
and vices of Mrs. Rinehart's mystery fiction.[10] A much more representative treatment of Mary Roberts Rinehart is W. B. Mowery's *Professional Short-Story Writing*, in which Mrs. Rinehart is merely named

in a sentence with three other authors as one who writes "detective fiction . . . as genuinely emotional as straight fiction."[11] *Golden Multitudes* of 1947 has been mentioned; it devotes two paragraphs of of text to Mrs. Rinehart, but largely to the publishing success of *The Circular Staircase*.[12] John Tebbel's *George Horace Lorimer and The Saturday Evening Post* of 1948 is interesting, not as criticism but as a glimpse of Mary Roberts Rinehart as public and private personality.[13] Being an interesting person outside of her books, Mrs. Rinehart—and I think Matthew Arnold would applaud my inability to call her merely "Rinehart"—was particularly appealing to interviewers. Two records of visits with her, the former more revelatory than the latter, are Robert van Gelder's and Harvey Breit's.[14] Sutherland Scott's *Blood in Their Ink* (1953) becomes at times a bit histrionic in its rhetoric, as much mystery "criticism" seems to, but through the several pages devoted to Mary Roberts Rinehart, one does perceive Scott's insight into atmosphere and motivation in her crime stories.[15] Insight in a much briefer compass is the case with A. E. Murch's 1958 *The Development of the Detective Novel*. He gives Mrs. Rinehart two paragraphs. I have saved for the last what is perhaps the most prestigious of all the references to Mary Roberts Rinehart, slight as it is: that of Cleanth Brooks in *The Well Wrought Urn*. And, quite succinctly, Brooks speaks to the point dealt with by everyone interested in popular culture.[16]

For what is the sensibility of our age? Is there any one sensibility? Do we respond to T. S. Eliot, Dashiell Hammett, Mary Roberts Rinehart, or Tiffany Thayer? The objective answer must be that some of us respond to one and some to another.

From the foregoing it should be clear that, as I have said, this essay undertakes, even in its rather limited scope, to discuss what is virtually unresearched work.

Mary Roberts was born at Pittsburgh, Pennsylvania, in 1876 to a poor sewing machine maker and part-time inventor, whose veins flowed with, in his daughter's phrase, strict "Covenanter blood."[17]

Her beginning in fiction was humble and honest enough. In 1896, while a student at the Pittsburgh Training School for Nurses, she married Dr. Stanley Marshall Rinehart. In a few years she was busily rearing three sons, who were later to distinguish themselves in the publishing industry. But as Haycraft records the fact,

A stock-market slump in 1903 wiped out the Rinehart's small savings and left them $12,000 in debt. In a vague hope of contributing to the family support, Mrs. Rinehart began to write short stories in the intervals of bringing up her family of growing boys. Considerably to her surprise, her first story sold to *Munsey's Magazine* for thirty-four dollars. . . . While convalescing from an operation she wrote her first long story, and her first crime story, *The Man in Lower Ten*, which was published serially in 1907 but not in book form until 1909. Her first work to appear between covers was *The Circular Staircase* (1908). . . .[18]

From that point—or, really, from the *Munsey's* story—Mrs. Rinehart's writing success closely imitated the proverbial snowball.

She wrote and published successfully for almost fifty years; as Haycraft notes, her first fiction was sold to *Munsey's Magazine* in 1903, and her last new novel was published in 1952. (The "new" is important, for three other books, collections of previous work, were to be published before her death in 1957.) Admittedly not to be compared with the prolific Erle Stanley Gardner, Mrs. Rinehart did produce an extraordinary amount of work, and in the final result, a very broad canon: crime fiction, humorous fiction, romances, travelogues, war reportage, commentary on writing (nothing that one could call literary criticism), an autobiography (updated once), plays, articles, and sketches. By 1933, forty-six books (including omnibuses) carried her name. In 1952, with the publication of her final novel, a mystery, Mrs. Rinehart's name stood below sixty-one book titles. The slackened pace in the years since 1938, necessitated by impaired health, hurt her average, but in 1952 it still stood at slightly over one book a year for forty-four years—an impressive output by almost any reckoning.

Indeed, in the quantitative terms of reception alone, she must be accounted a "popular" writer. In *60 Years of Best Sellers: 1895-1955*, Alice Payne Hackett asserts that Mrs. Rinehart is one of those writers with the most titles—eleven in her case—on the sixty annual lists by specific publishers. Too, she is among those enduring longest on the lists: from 1909 to 1936.[19] *The Circular Staircase*, her first novel published as a book—by Bobbs-Merrill in 1908—sold in the regular edition 300,000 copies. Through the three Grosset & Dunlap reprint editions, sales reached nearly 250 thousand copies. Then, by way of a Triangle Books hardcover edition, a Pocket Books paper edition, and two Dell paperback issuings (the latter currently available in the paperbound racks), the novel's sales have gone substantially higher. In 1947 Mott cited the figure 750,000.[20] By Mrs. Hackett's 1956 computation, the figure had climbed to 800,000, and the Dell publications follow that. The *Newsweek* review of her 1950 *Episode of the Wandering Knife* submitted that her books had sold "some 10,000,000" copies.[21] Her crime story of 1909, *The Man in Lower Ten*, was the first American detective novel to make the annual best seller list.[22]

Mrs. Rinehart's other books subsequently to make the list were: *The Window at the White Cat* (1910), *When a Man Marries* (1910), *K* (1915), *Amazing Interlude* (1918), *Dangerous Days* (1919), *Poor Wise Man* (1921), *The Breaking Point* (1922 and 1923), *Lost Ecstasy* (1927), *The Door* (1930), and *The Doctor* (1936).[23] Of course, what such figures never reflect, and what it is impossible to know, is the number of *Saturday Evening Posts*, *Ladies Home Journals*, *Good Housekeepings*, and other periodicals that were bought just for the serializations of these and other Mary Roberts Rinehart books. At any rate, Mrs. Rinehart's best sellers alone are a qualitatively impressive production, even had she written no other books. And of those eleven best sellers, seven were crime stories.

Mary Roberts Rinehart's books were not only sold—they were read, by an immense and heterogeneous public. Among her high-placed or famous admirers, Mrs. Rinehart counted Herbert Hoover ("thirty years of continuous esteem"[24]) and Gertrude Stein. She endeared herself to masses of readers by a warm and personal response to all kinds of appeals, the answers to which made her address the public in print. After reaching an early fame substantial enough to occasion an influx of correspondence, Mrs. Rinehart chose Saturday as her weekly time for reading letters and dictating and signing answers to admiring fans, aspiring writers, and even distraught mothers and lonely wives, particularly during the two world wars.

An example of Mrs. Rinehart's public response—and not really as much of a footnote as it might seem—is her May Day, 1943 article for the *Saturday Review*: "To Mother, with Love. Some Thoughts About Books on Mother's Day."[25] She wisely proposes different books for different mothers, depending upon the extent of their personal relation to the war; books on the war and foreign countries will not do for everyone, but she subtly suggests that crime fiction as escapism is suitable. She concludes:

. . . I am a woman and a mother. Every book I have listed I have read and cared for. And a book lasts, especially if on the fly-leaf it says, "To Mother, with love."

The obvious sentimentalism of the whole article has its reflections in her mysteries.

The remainder of this essay attempts to examine a major portion of the crime stories of Mary Roberts Rinehart as they reflect or comment upon the social mores of the United States. In *The Development of the Detective Novel*, A. E. Murch says,[26]

her first crime novels are particularly interesting because they owe nothing to French or English influences, and represent the emergence of a new vein of purely American detective fiction, *with an authentic background of characteristically American social conditions.* (my italics)

It must, of course, be remembered at all times that Mrs. Rinehart is the author, and, like other writers, even the most aesthetically polished, she selects and chooses from the background Murch observes.

From a survey of twenty-one of Mrs. Rinehart's books, the most coherent discussion of society in her crime fiction should begin according to categories. Therefore, I've chosen to isolate *swearing, drinking, smoking, attitudes toward race, violence, psychology, social classes,* and *sex.* For commentary upon both the validity of these categories and the representative quality of the mysteries, I have chosen also occasionally to glance at some of the immensely popular Tish stories, her humorous tales of three old maids' picaresque adventures. The stories about Miss Letitia Carberry and her cronies, first born in 1910 to a long run in the *Saturday Evening Post*, reflect all of the categories I have enumerated.

From the proposed list, the category that most clearly reflects an alteration in social attitude through the years is swearing, including both profanity and milder expletives. From *The Circular Staircase* of 1908 through *The Frightened Wife and Other Murder Stories* of 1953, one may observe an increasing use of profanity, qualified only in the first and middle years if the narrator is female. In the last books, the sex of the story's teller seems irrelevant.

In that first novel, the narrator is Miss Rachel Innes, a middle-aged spinster given once only in a rare outburst of emotion to ejaculate "fiddlesticks." (This is Tish's best exclamation, too, in the early stories.) In speaking to Miss Innes, another character once has occasion for using "damned" and the phrase "I'll see him in hell," but in the manner of Chaucer's apology, the man emphasizes his wrestling with the morality of repeating these words that had been spoken by a third person. Once a strange man in a crowd, never to be identified or seen again, is heard to exclaim "What the hell!" but that suffices for the gratuitous profanity.

In *The Man in Lower Ten* (serial 1907, book 1909) the narrator is a young attorney, but not given to profanity. However, his somewhat wild-living law partner, McKnight, *is* given to colorful expressions like "Jove," "make an ass of oneself," "what in blazes," or "the blanketyblank thing." The narrator, apparently because he is our hero and must maintain an aura of gentility, utters only one "darned," all in all quite an example of self-restraint.

A particularly interesting development comes in 1910 with *The Window at the White Cat*. A variety of phrases entirely new to Mary Roberts Rinehart are introduced, e.g., "who in the devil's name," "Good God," "I'll be damned," "God only knows," and "for God's sake." The striking point is this: Mrs. Rinehart has the central crime and a great deal of the action take place in an urban men's club, devoted to heavy drinking, smoking, and much gambling. Yet in that atmosphere there is virtually no hard profanity; nor is there more in *The Case of Jennie Brice* (1913), *The After House* (1914), or two short novels published together in 1921, *The Confession* and *Sight Unseen*. The first, narrated by a young nurse, contains almost no profanity; only an unsavory character says "Hell." The second, important for its treatment of alcoholism, uses "damn" and "damned" frequently, but there is no swearing by the narrator-hero, an exemplary young medical school graduate.

The Breaking Point of 1922 really marks Mary Roberts Rinehart's emergence into the Twenties, if we think of that decade in the stereotype of freer language. The novel is only tangentially a mystery; there was a murder out West years before the novel opens, but the hero's amnesia and certain machinations by other principals have obscured the details of the homicide and the identity of the murderer. But for the first time in Mary Roberts Rinehart's crime fiction, the hero, a young man, regularly uses "damn" and "damned," for example, "I don't give a damn about it" and "I know damned well." Yet true to the established form, the strongest profanity is reserved for a "villain." The suspiciously foreign-looking character who wants to revenge himself upon the hero says at one point, for the expression's first time in

Mrs. Rinehart's books, "I don't give a God-damn."

By 1930 and *The Door*, profanity and even the mild expressions, what Tish's maidenly, matronly friends would call "indecorous speech," are part and parcel of the narrative. No one is a foul mouth, but "damn" and "hell" are frequent; most importantly, when the men swear, they do so directly in front of women. In this pre-Depression world no one is struck by violated proprieties.

The State vs. Elinor Norton of 1934 is in many ways Mrs. Rinehart's most violent novel. Even more than *The Breaking Point*, this novel details the torture of a soul. Here a woman is psychologically racked through years of contest with a tyrannical mother embittered by poverty, an insensitive husband, and an immoral, belligerent lover. Of course, all comes right in the denouement, but until then her life is one torment. An objective correlative of that is the virtual ubiquity of "hell"—"the hell of a time," "the hell of a way," "giving it hell," "raise a merry little hell"—phrases all saying that circumstances have, in another of the book's phrases, "made her life actual hell." In 1938 with *The Wall*, Mrs. Rinehart achieves her most natural spectrum of swearing, traversing the range from the at once contemptible and pitiable Juliette's affectation of high-society in her "Thank God" and "God" every other word to the kindly old sheriff's "by the great horn spoon."

The Yellow Room of 1945 mirrors the general lessening of social restrictions that had followed with the exigencies of the war and the consequent general inattention to decorum. So, for the first time "bastard" appears in a book of Mrs. Rinehart's, although it is used in an innocuous phrase: "this house is an architectural bastard." For the first time someone, and not a ruffian says "God-dammitt," but at the same time, Mary Roberts Rinehart's third person narrator can write "here his language became unprintable. He used a few army words not common in polite society, and added some of his own invention." The observation to be made is that the words alluded to here are, on the evidence of what *is* printed in the novel, the four-letter Anglo-Saxon terms and some Freudian derivations. In surveying these and other novels, one sees Mary Roberts Rinehart moving through the years toward a more realistic, less forced use of profanity, no matter the sex of the narrator. There are dramatic shifts toward a wider usage at the opening of the Twenties and at the end of War War II. Her first heroes are generally restrained, especially before women, but by the time of *The Frightened Wife*, the hero is the roughest talking of all. In fifty years, Mary Roberts Rinehart shifts from the decorum of Wilkie Collins toward (but not too far) the colorful diction of Mickey Spillane.

Another aspect of Mary Roberts Rinehart's crime fiction that mirrors society's trends is drinking. It is, however, handled as a social amenity, not for its own sake, but because it reflects the behavioral attitudes of different generations in different periods. Observant to the fact that *anything* may have a point of interest or humor—compare the myriad repetitions of "by the great horn spoon"—Mrs. Rinehart provides oddity in the imbibing of various characters. Miss Innes, narrator of *The Circular Staircase* and a middle-aged spinster, finds her refuge in the teapot, although she does accept a sociable glass of elderberry wine during one calling visit. Tish's blackberry cordial is ubiquitous, always held in readiness as a restorative, even on a camping trip to the Rocky Mountains! An equally striking eccentric drinker is McKnight of *The Man in Lower Ten* who has already been observed as the narrator's sidekick, the scapegoat, the one upon whom a multitude of venial but lively sins can be cast. Accordingly, McKnight twice, in apparently typical actions, drinks a concoction of everything that's available to hand.

However, throughout the crime novels and the Tish stories, it is only those who are of the lower classes and of the theatre crowd who get drunk. Dramatic instances of the latter appear in *The Case of Jennie Brice* and *The Breaking Point*. (The single exception occurs in *The After House* (1914), a novel which deals with alcoholism as much as it can while its main business is being a mystery.) Yet Mrs. Rinehart was not unequivocally opposed to alcohol, for in the post-World War II novels, "cocktails" or "highballs" are an ordinary part of the characters' lives. On the other hand, Mrs. Rinehart can be ironic. In *The Swimming Pool* of 1952 there is an almost juvenile fascination with serving high-balls—constantly. But again, as with the swearing, the issue revolves upon the hero or heroine. From main characters who generally eschew liquor or take it only in extreme moderation, Mrs. Rinehart ends by developing principal figures who drink as a matter of course.

There is relatively little to say about smoking in Mary Roberts Rinehart's novels. Generally, the heroes smoke, but sometimes only cigars. And in *The Man in Lower Ten* the gentlemen make a point

of asking the lady or ladies if they may smoke. In the Twenties—
and dramatically in *The Door* of 1930—one suddenly finds young
ladies of good family smoking, usually as acts of overt defiance.
Throughout Mrs. Rinehart's mysteries, smoking, of whatever kind
and even after it is quite acceptable, is used extensively as a narrative crutch: to show nervousness, in the shaky match; to show
regained calm, in the steady match or smooth inhalation; to show
deliberation, in the careful lighting; and to show poor taste or defiance, as in the case of the liberated young woman of *The Wall* (1938).
Moreover, smoking plays its role in the detection of crimes: in *The
Album* a cigar stub gives the lead to a certain person's presence, and
in *The Wall*, a lipstick-stained cigarette butt is a major clue.

In the matter of reflected social attitudes toward race, there
seems to be no pattern, no progression as one might from these other
subjects expect to find, from a somewhat narrow prejudice to an enlightened liberalism or at least open-mindedness. In fact, the social
critic inclined to accusation would probably find racism in the novels.
The Circular Staircase has a real Uncle Tom, Thomas Johnson, a
servant. (Blacks are seen in Mrs. Rinehart's fiction only as servants,
and faithful ones at that.) Miss Innes "watched Thomas shuffle along"
and later remarks that "Thomas shuffled out." Her servant Beulah is
"coal-black." Believing the nature of Negroes to be distinct in all
regards, one man observes "those darkies seldom have a penny;"
similarly, *The Case of Jennie Brice* uses the archetypal loyal Negro
retainer, given to shuffling and a softly muttered "praise Gawd."
Again in *The Man in Lower Ten*, there is a "colored housemaid,"
this time named "Euphemia." Mrs. Rinehart attempts a Negro dialect
for a porter on the train, but she fails so miserably and the porter is
such a pitiful man that he is past all convincing and comes off merely
ludicrous. *The Door* (1930) has an Amos, a superstitious and plainly
devious servant whose presence and behavior prompt such statements
as these: "There are some people to whom all Negroes look alike"
(from the narrator); "Show a Negro a police badge and he'll come
clean" (this from a stalwart, representative police officer); "his
color was the peculiar gray of the terrified Negro" (this from a friend
of the narrator).

However brief these stereotyped treatments of Blacks, other
races are even more quickly dismissed and in clichés no less unkind.
For a servant, McKnight has a "Jap," and McKnight's friend observes

"it would take a Turk to feel at home in red and yellow pajamas."
In *The Window at the White Cat*, "German cupidity" is assumed;
and at a Chinese restaurant the diners get "a slanteyed welcome."
Twenty-four years after McKnight's "Jap," the hero's maid in *The
State vs. Elinor Norton* (1924) does not trust "Japs" or "them
Orientals." From all of this in the pre-World War II decades, one
might expect real enmity to develop after the war. But in the post-
war novels "krauts" and "Japs" are mentioned, even in recollection
of the war, without any vindictiveness beyond that in the slang. Only
in *The State vs. Elinor Norton* is any kind of objectivity or sensitivity
evident, and this after those references to "Japs." In Wyoming, one
local character thinks of Indians as "lazy devils" and "shiftless cattle
thieves"; but the narrator thinks to himself, "Our Indians are what
we have made them."

In short, Mary Roberts Rinehart adheres to stereotyped, flat
characterizations for non-Anglo-Saxon ethnic groups. The characterizations are so short, really, as to seem most of the time to be
supercilious dismissals, nor does the picture become brighter as
Mary Roberts Rinehart moves through her career. If one were to
say that in the mysteries there simply is not time for full, sympathetic character development, one might turn to the Tish story
"Like a Wolf on the Fold" (1913) for an illustrative comparison.
This story is built entirely on the episode of Tish's good nature being
imposed upon, and finally defrauded, by a "dratted Syrian." The
attitude of the story's Anglo-Saxon principals, an attitude Mrs. Rinehart's tone never denies, can be summed up in two words: dirty
foreigners.

However underplayed the racial element is in Mrs. Rinehart's
crime fiction, the same cannot be said for violence. However, only
a few generalizations on violence can be drawn with regard to Mrs.
Rinehart's mysteries, and those are far more relevant to her brand
of story than to her fiction as a social mirror. Usually, one murder
precipitates, directly or obliquely, one to three others. Those killed
subsequent to the principal murder know something about it, either
the killer or his motivation. Again in general, Mrs. Rinehart is pre-
disposed toward having the gore take place offstage. Often we learn
of a person being struck on the head and then pushed downstairs in
an always unsuccessful attempt to disguise the true mode of attack.
Why that should be necessary is never clear. But with equal frequency,

neither the blow nor the fall kills the person. People are shot at close range and from afar, stabbed to death while asleep, and killed with golf clubs and hypodermic injections of lethal drugs or air. But as these illustrations indicate, the means of death is never imaginative. The only deaths that stand apart are those in *The After House* (1914), in which the deceptively gentle old salt—patterned strongly in respect to his apparent wisdom on Melville's Old Dansker of *Billy Budd*— turns out to be a religious fanatic who "though himself a priest of heaven, appointed to make ghastly sacrifices at certain signals from on high." He dismembers three sleeping victims with an ax.

The problem of the old sailor is clearly a psychological one, and psychology as a broad area of interests and effects is a category of some importance in Mary Roberts Rinehart's mysteries. One might remember that Freud's first major works were published in translation in the first decade of this century and the ideas were immediately picked up, often at second and third hand, by a large American public. Mary Roberts Rinehart's *Window at the White Cat* (1910) is important for its incorporation of some instruments of experimental and diagnostic psychology. One chief suspect for the crime is put through a lengthy word association test. During the testing, the examining doctor asserts that "psychology is as exact a science as mathematics." (However, true to Mrs. Rinehart's code of reliance on detective intuition, the test does not reveal the true criminal.)

The Breaking Point of 1922 comes at the beginning of a decade and a half of intense interest in the possibilities of psychoanalysis and psychotherapy. *The Breaking Point* is a long novel for Mary Roberts Rinehart, and it hangs on the point that a traumatic experience can make a man forget a former existence, i.e., suffer amnesia. Suspicion arises that the young hero, Dr. Dick, was mixed up in some unlawful deed in a prior life that he cannot remember. To find out who he is, Dick Livingstone throws off his present existence and travels west to the place of his reputed trouble. By absolutely rejecting his life back East, he does regain his former identity and a partial knowledge of the murder in which he had been implicated. Then, to go back to those he has loved, he must throw off that regained life, which has become a slovenly existence; and through the sympathy of his foster-father, he succeeds in coming back. This is handled quite well, however vague its scientific aspects may seem, and at no time are the technicalities really more clear than when Dr. Dick's foster-father goes into the big city to see a "psycho-analyst," about his boy's troubles and is told "We've only commenced to dig into the mind."

After *The Breaking Point*, Mary Roberts Rinehart pays very little attention to psychology until the 1945 and post-war stories, when battle-fatigue and shell-shock—in short, war trauma—become frequent subjects. In *The Yellow Room* the hero is a veteran disabled by both physical and mental wounds. A principal figure of "The Burned Chair" (included in *The Frightened Wife and Other Murder Stories*) is a still-suffering victim of Korea. Another story of that volume, "If It Were Only Yesterday," is a third person narrative, but the center of consciousness is the mind of the murderer, an insane young woman, obviously unbalanced by an automobile accident. A psychiatrist is briefly introduced, probing into her resentment toward the invalid sister whom she murders before committing suicide.

In addition to a concern with psychology and its intricacies, Mrs. Rinehart's crime fiction also manifests her and the public's interest in psychic phenomena. In her own life, she believed that she had twice received communication from Dr. Rinehart shortly after his death. Unsure of the outcome of such experiences if continued, she never again tried for contact.[27] In the crime fiction, this first-hand communication with the spirit world is reflected a number of times in unexplained phenomena, such as the autonomous glowing of *The Red Lamp* (1925), and in incidental allusions to seances. Much of the action in *Sight Unseen* of 1921 takes place during seances when knowledge about certain crimes is cryptically transmitted through the medium. At the conclusion, there is no rational explanation offered for the supersensory knowledge which revealed the information. Interest in the unexplainable grew to a fad in the Twenties, but apparently was still relevant in 1938. *The Wall* of that year introduces sympathetically a secondary figure who is a regular seance participant and believer.

Being without effort very much an American, and having been born into and come to live in two strikingly different social classes, Mary Roberts Rinehart could be expected to be class conscious, and also conscious that class differences in America were at the best very shaky. Her early crime fiction, even through *The Wall* of 1938, is

often told by a narrator whose position makes requisite the introduction of grand old homes (sometimes seemingly haunted), summer
resorts, town cars, and servants of all types. Mrs. Rinehart never
explicitly says that the good old days of dignified affluence are gone
for America, but again and again her narrators or other major characters are now the genteel poor. Very clearly she caters to America's
nostalgia for a time when large fortunes and *grande dames* ruled
society. In the Twenties and Thirties there was a sharp awareness
that the Gilded Age was only a memory, to be clung to by the few
of that generation remaining. Finally, in Mrs. Rinehart's mysteries
after 1945, there is no longer a concentration upon the details of
managing inheritances, houses, and wild children.

Importantly, the wild children of Mrs. Rinehart's fiction in
the first half of her career are not the sex-ridden creatures of today's
hard-boiled fiction. Yet Mary Roberts Rinehart's crime fiction really
is not of "another time"; it is of several times, through which decorous
young ladies who might be kissed on the first anniversary of their "affairs" (*K*, 1915) have metamorphosed into witty females who can
balance a cigarette, cocktail, and tennis racket all at once.

In the process of this radical change—and the men are a part
of it, too—Mary Roberts Rinehart never plays for sensationalism.
In only one of the mysteries is there anything other than a conventional marriage or romance (allowed its obstacles of money,
position, and distance). And that is *The State vs. Elinor Norton*
of 1934. A major portion of the story is involved first with Blair
Leighton's attempts to get Elinor away from her husband and his
rather offhand dalliance with a sluttish country girl while he maneu-
vers, and then with Elinor's agony after her husband has been killed
and Blair begins sleeping with her, holding out the promise that he
will marry her. There are no bedroom scenes, but at one point
Elinor appears before the men in lounging pajamas, and it is clear
later that adultery is taking place. However, it is the conclusion
to the novel that is most important. The narrator, whom one
hesitates to call the "hero," for his physical role in the story is
severely limited, finally persuades Elinor to marry him, just before
she is to enter an Episcopal convent. For the first time, a Mary
Roberts Rinehart hero takes a sullied woman to wife.

In an essay on "The Simple Art of Murder,"[28] Raymond
Chandler refers to Robert Graves' and Alan Hodge's *The Long*

Week End, a study of English life and manners after World War I which gives some attention to detective stories. Their observation is that mysteries do not reflect what is going on in the world, because only writers without vision or ability write mysteries, a kind of unreal fiction.[29] This essay differs with that point of view.

A reading of Mrs. Rinehart's "crime stories" and research into her life and the publication history of her books, indicates that there are two views under which her mysteries may be examined: as craft or art, and as a record of social thought and behavior across some fifty years. As a literary craftsman, Mary Roberts Rinehart worked imaginative variations on "mystery formulas" that are partly stock and partly germane to her own work. She was not the first to use notes behind baseboards or re-papered walls, but she often thought to use an old roll of the original paper for the job. And, although it is hardly to her credit, she is generally recognized as the founder of the "Had-I-But-Known" (or HIBK) school. Under the aspect of an artist, she was, in her own words, "primarily interested in people and their motivations,"[30] and at times—very irregularly— she does achieve finely drawn, absorbing characterizations. That of Rachel Innes is one.

However, instead of looking at aesthetic issues, this essay has dealt with Mrs. Rinehart's sensitivity to and portrayal of cultural shifts during her long career. In the mysteries the narrators often survey the world of a waning—or better, moribund—Victorian upper class, sometimes from within, sometimes from the viewpoint of the genteel poor, and sometimes through the eyes of the middle class. In an aura of nostalgia that ebbs and flows, one sees old fortunes dwindling through too many heirs, no heirs at all, or mere waste. One sees social refinements, the proprieties, being stubbornly maintained by one generation and glaringly ignored by its successor. The generation gap is never more strikingly evident or more sensitively depicted than in *The Breaking Point* where the old man looks to God and trusts and the young man acknowledge a vague Providence but insists on searching. In a succession of images generally so deftly executed that they complement rather than obscure a good story— and Mrs. Rinehart always thought of herself as a storyteller, not as a literary figure[31]—we watch the quickening pace of the workaday world and leisure life bring in cigarettes to replace pipes and cigars, fast driving to replace a walk on a picnic, and fifteen minutes alone for a young couple instead of five (*The Case of Jennie Brice*).

Significantly, Mrs. Rinehart avoided a hard didactic line on any of the social issues. In 1908 she was *not* a young rebel advocating social upheaval. In 1934 she was *not* a middle-aged law giver. And in 1952 she was *not* an entrenched old woman railing against the encroachments of the young and the new. Rather, from the outset of her career Mrs. Rinehart manifested a feeling for both sides of the issue. Her detractors might say she simply knew what would sell to most people, but at the end of this research I would say she observed and recorded the topical with an objective sensibility.

MARY ROBERTS RINEHART'S BOOKS AND PLAYS

The following chronological listing of Mrs. Rinehart's books and plays is an effort at collecting in one place the titles of her major works, a task never before accomplished. The 1960 *Who Was Who in America* is the most complete list before this compilation, but it omits three books.

Those titles preceded by asterisks are currently available in paperback editions.

1908	*	*The Circular Staircase*
1909	*	*The Man in Lower Ten*
		When a Man Marries
1910		*The Window at the White Cat*
1911		*Amazing Adventures of Letitia Carberry*
1914	*	*The Case of Jennie Brice*
		Where There's a Will
	*	*The After House*
	*	*The Street of Seven Stars*
1915		*K*
		Kings, Queens and Pawns
1916		*Tish*
		Through Glacier Park: Seeing America First (with Howard Eaton)
1917		*Bab: A Sub-Deb*
		Long Live the King
		Tenting Tonight
		The Amazing Interlude
		The Altar of Freedom
1920		*The Truce of God*
1921		*Love Stories*
	*	*Dangerous Days*
		A Poor Wise Man
		Isn't That Just Like a Man? (with Irwin S. Cobb)

1922		*Twenty-three and One Half Hours' Leave*
	*	*Sight Unseen and The Confession*
		Affinities and Other Stories
		More Tish
	*	*The Breaking Point*
		The Truce of God
1923		*The Out Trail*
1924		*Temperamental People*
1925		*The Red Lamp*
1926		*Nomad's Land*
		Tish Plays the Game
1927	*	*Lost Ecstasy*
1928		*Two Flights Up*
1929	*	*This Strange Adventure*
		The Romantics
1930	*	*The Door*
		Mary Roberts Rinehart's Mystery Book
1931		*My Story*
		Rinehart's Romance Book
		Book of Tish
1932	*	*Miss Pinkerton*
1933		*The Album*
		Crime Book
1934	*	*The State Versus Elinor Norton*
1936	*	*The Doctor*
1937	*	*Married People*
		Tish Marches On
1938	*	*The Wall*
1939		*Writing Is Work*
1940		*The Great Mistake*
1941		*Familiar Faces*
1942		*Haunted Lady*
1944	*	*Alibi for Isabel*
1945		*The Yellow Room*
1948		*A Light in the Window*
1950		*Episode of the Wandering Knife*
1952		*The Swimming Pool*
1953	*	*The Frightened Wife*
1955		*The Best of Tish*
1957		*The Mary Roberts Rinehart Crime Book*

PLAYS

1908	*Double Life*
1908	*The Avenger* (with Mr. Rinehart)
1909	*Seven Days* (with Avery Hopwood)

1913	*Cheer Up*
1919	*Tish*
1920	*Bab*
1920	*Spanish Love* (with Avery Hopwood)
1920	*The Bat* (with Avery Hopwood)
1923	*The Breaking Point*

NOTES

[1] Collected in *A Literary Chronicle: 1920-1950*. Anchor Books (New York): Doubleday, 1952, pp. 338-345.

[2] "Why Do People Read Detective Stories?" in *A Literary Chronicle: 1920-1950*, pp. 323, 327.

[3] *Masters of Mystery: A Study of the Detective Story* (London: Wm. Collins Sons, 1931); *Murder for Pleasure: The Life and Times of the Detective Story* (New York: Appleton-Century, 1941).

[4] *Golden Multitudes: The Story of Best Sellers in the United States* (New York: Macmillan, 1947), pp. 262-268, 303-331, *passim*.

[5] *Ibid.*, p. 285.

[6] Bernard Rosenberg and David Manning White, eds., *Mass Culture: The Popular Arts in America* (New York: The Free Press, 1957). See especially the first two essays by Rosenberg and White, respectively.

[7] "Mary Roberts Rinehart," an interview by Harvey Breit for *The New York Times Book Review*, February 3, 1952. Collected in Harvey Breit, *The Writer Observed* (New York: World, 1956), p. 228.

[8] For a bibliography on detective fiction, see Haycraft, *Murder for Pleasure*, pp. 279-297.

[9] Robert H. Davis, ed. (New York: George H. Doran, 1924).

[10] Pages 87-91.

[11] (New York: Thomas Y. Crowell, 1953), p. 18.

[12] Page 265.

[13] (Garden City, New York: Doubleday, 1948), pp. 55-63.

[14] Robert van Gelder, "An Interview With Mary Roberts Rinehart," *Writers and Writing* (New York: Scribner's 1946), pp. 145-148. The interview was done December 15, 1940; Breit, *The Writer Observed*.

[15] (London: Stanley Paul, 1953), pp. 22-25.

[16] (London: Dennis Dobson, 1949), p. 210.

[17] Mary Roberts Rinehart, *My Story: A New Edition and Seventeen New Years* (New York: Rinehart, 1948), p. 4.

[18] *Murder for Pleasure*, pp. 87-88.

[19] (New York: R. R. Bowker, 1956), pp. 7-8.

[20] *Golden Multitudes*, p. 312.

[21] "Rinehart's 60th," *Newsweek*, XXXVI (July 17, 1950), 82. Although 10,000,000 is an impressive figure, it pales beside the 167 million sales claimed for Erle Stanley Gardner by his publisher at the time of his death. (Detroit *Free Press*, March 12, 1970, p. 5-B).

[22]Hackett, p. 110.

[23]Hackett, pp. 112-161, *passim*.

[24]Breit, p. 229.

[25]*Saturday Review*, XXVI (May 1, 1943), p. 11.

[26](New York: Philosophical Library, 1958), p. 213.

[27]Mary Roberts Rinehart, "Things I Can't Explain," *Reader's Digest*, LVI (April, 1950), 5-6. I cite the *Reader's Digest*, although the article is condensed from *My Story*, because the periodical is much more easily obtainable.

[28]*Atlantic Monthly*, CLXXIV (December, 1944), 57.

[29]*Ibid.*

[30]Breit, p. 228.

[31]van Gelder, p. 146.

THE CHARACTER AND FUNCTION OF POPULAR RELIGIOUS POETRY 1820-1860

Delwyn L. Sneller

What precisely is meant by popular American nineteenth-century religious poetry? Religious poetry, in this study, means Christian poetry (Catholic and Protestant) which centers itself around the Bible and Christ, calls its readers to thankfully and humbly worship the Creator, assures all of God's loving Providence, comforts believers who mourn, provides instruction in the ways of piety, calls attention to heavenly themes, and enumerates Christian virtues, duties, affections, and trials. Poems which sing of Law, Beauty, Duty, Nature, or Virtue are uplifting and moral but are not religious according to this Christian definition.

Since hundreds of American newspapers, almanacs, magazines, periodicals, and journals published thousands and thousands of religious poems, I chose to examine only those which were printed before the Civil War in *Godey's Lady's Book* and *The Christian Examiner And Theological Review*. Because these two were indeed popular and are typical of the others, they represent them well. To complement and explain the excellent variety of religious verse they contain, both magazines (especially *The Examiner*) provided lengthy and valuable articles concerning the nature of poetry and its relation to faith and the nineteenth-century way of life.

Religious verses were by far the most popular art form of this age, because they grew out of and enhanced the nineteenth century's preoccupation with revival meetings, hymn sings, Sabbath schools, and churches. Churches were so numerous in 1850 that they could accommodate 70% of the total white population. Needless to say,

172

ministers, Sunday school teachers, and revival leaders, as well as editors of popular magazines, sought and deeply appreciated the labors of hymn writers and devotional poets. Let him who would begin to understand nineteenth-century popular poetry study first the Christian muse. Hymns and meditative lyrics were as much a part of nineteenth-century life as no-deposit Coke bottles and paperbacks are of our age.

Aside from content, Christian poetry lies near the heart of popular literature in another significant way. Stylistically, religious verse closely resembles other popular types of poetry: love poems (verses wept over by young virgins trembling like winter-stricken birds), patriotic poems, legendary or narrative verse, laments over the loss of youth, nature lyrics, and translations ("The Moon," an Icelandic Song, literally translated). Even the most irreligious, epicurean, or transcendental poem could be identical to a Christian lyric in metre, in nature of imagery, and in function of rhyme. The following poem, for example, though thematically non-Christian, is written in a common hymn metre, Eight and Sevens:

Cui Bono?

What is Hope? a smiling rainbow
   Children follow thro' the wet;
'Tis not here, still yonder, yonder—
   Never urchin found it yet.

What is Life? a thawing iceboard
   On a sea with sunny shore.
Gay we sail—it melts beneath us—
   We are sunk, and seen no more.

What is Man? a foolish baby,
   Fighting fierce for hollow nuts;
Demanding all, deserving nothing—
   One small grave is what he gets.

Unfortunately, much nineteenth-century literature seems ridiculous or at best dull to us now, even though it was reverently read by its first audience. But now who would not laugh at a poem describing the marriage of a mute gentleman and a deaf lady which ends this way:

> No word! No sound! and yet a solemn rite
> Proceedeth 'mid the festive lighted hall.

Or at "To Melancholy," by Maria to Edwin, which is prefaced by this pointed apology:

The following stanzas were written by a young Woman, who, when composing them, was labouring under a very considerable degree of active mania.

But if popular poets like Francis S. L. Osgood, J. H. Kimball, Laetitia Elizabeth Landon, Rev. Hobart Caunter, James Montgomery, T. A. Worrall, W. Gilmore Simms, Bayard Taylor, M. E. MacMichael, Horatio E. Hale, H. T. Tuckerman, Leman Grimstone, Miss E. Gooch, Seba Smith, N. P. Willis, and N. C. Brooks wrote unfortunate poems sometimes, they also wrote superb religious poems sometimes. John Ross Dix's description of heaven is still touching:

> a noble band,
> Redeemed from every tribe, from every land
> Shall walk with us by overflowing streams,
> And hold high converse on immortal themes.
> What bliss to roam those radiant fields among,
> And hear of Abraham's faith from Abraham's tongue;
> Mark rapt Isaiah's look of holy fire,
> Or list to melodies from David's lyre—
> Converse with him whose voice delayed the sun—
> Learn wisdom from the lips of Solomon,
> And him of Patmos see, to whom 'twas given,
> On earth, to lift the veils of Hell and Heaven.

Shocking realism veins the blank verse "Scripture Anthologies," composed by N. C. Brooks. The following passage, which describes the beheading of John The Baptist, is powerful and vivid.

> The man of blood bore in the gory head
> On reeking platter, while the pallid lips
> With life still quivered, and the blanching cheek,
> Like faded violets. In the gasp of death,
> In all its lividness, in all its writhe
> Of mortal agony, with gouts of blood
> Stiffening the beard, clotting the mangled locks—
> The youthful maiden, with complacent smile
> And step of triumph, bore the bleeding head
> Unto her mother.

But what lies between the poems twentieth-century readers laugh at and those which seem modern and strong? Sheer boredom—at first reading. The following example, typical of nineteenth-century religious verse, is composed of vague phrases and worn out imagery.

The Sermon on the Mount

> He [Christ] points them to the red cloud's wings
> Above the radiant east unfurl'd;
> And lo! the sun majestic springs
> In gladness on the waking world.
> The rock and hill—the wave and shore—
> The field and forest are all bright,
> And Nature's thousand voices pour
> Her full heart-breathings of delight.
> 'Tis like your God! his gentle rain,
> His liberal sunshine widely falls
> Alike upon the desert plain,
> And yonder city's towering walls.
> The undeserving of his care,
> And they whose thoughts are all above,
> The guilty and the grateful share
> A Father's never-weary love.
> . . . . . .
> Be like thy God—be like the sun—
> And where thy healing power extends,
> Let willing deeds of love be done
> Alike to enemies and friends;

How should one approach such poetry? Clarence A. F. gives this advice in the *Lady's Book* of 1847:[1]

When a critic cannot get out of himself to comprehend life different than his own, and read another's work in the very atmosphere where it was written, he will not show us the truth, though he may think he has the voice of an oracle.

The truth of his suggestion cannot be overemphasized—especially in studying the popular poetry (religious or otherwise) of his time. Getting "in the very atmosphere where it was written," though nearly impossible to do, is absolutely essential, because the verse was written to satisfy definite needs of nineteenth-century American society. Poems were not merely enjoyed during this period; they were used.

How were poems used, or what were their functions? First, popular poets fashioned poems specifically to muffle the worries, sooth the tensions, and relax the minds of their readers. The nineteenth century found its respite from perplexing cares in melodic stanzas which portrayed life's "highest, clearest, calmest, best hours."[2] Longfellow's "The Day is Done" describes, and is itself precisely this kind of poem:

> The day is done, and the darkness
> Falls from the wings of Night,
> As a feather is wafted downward
> From an eagle in his flight.
>
> I see the lights of the village
> Gleam through the rain and the mist.
> And a feeling of sadness comes o'er me.
> That my soul cannot resist.
>
> A feeling of sadness and longing,
> That is not akin to pain,
> And resembles sorrow only,
> As the mist resembles the rain.
>
> Come read to me some poem,
> Some simple and heartfelt lay,
> That shall soothe this restless feeling,
> And banish the thoughts of Day. . . .

This excerpt from a review of the 1833 edition of Miss Gould's *Poems* emphasizes the public's need and respect for after-hours poetry:[3]

It is impossible to find fault with Miss Gould's poetry. It is so sweet and unpretending, so pure in purpose and so gentle in expression, that criticism is disarmed of all severity, and engaged to say nothing of it but good. It is poetry for a sober, quiet, kindly-affectioned, Christian heart. It is poetry for a united family circle, in their hours of peace and leisure. For such a companionship it was made, and into such it will find, and has found, its way.

As this passage indicates, the reverent optimism and gentle assurance of Christian poetry (which suited Miss Gould's talents exactly) made hearth-side hours entertaining, satisfying, and comforting.

According to nineteenth-century literary criticism, popular poetry, besides evoking restful and hypnotic magic, also possessed evangelical powers. It was seen as the "Priestess of Religion," because it shed "a rosy light upon the path of duty" and presented "Images of what is lovely, affecting, and glorious in human character." Thus, poetry

could serve as a "source of much pleasure as well as improvement."[4]
This produced lines like the following, which are soothing and yet
didactic.

> Let me my weary mind recline
> On that eternal love of Thine,
>   And human thoughts forget;
> Childlike attend what thou wilt say;
> Go forth and do it while 'tis day,
>   Yet never leave my sweet retreat.

These comments, published in 1826, reveal the tone and heart of
popular literary theories.[5]

We . . . believe that poetry, far from injuring society, is one of the great instruments of its refinement and exaltation. It lifts the mind above ordinary life,
. . . and awakens the consciousness of its affinity with what is pure and noble.
In its legitimate and highest efforts, it has the same tendency and aim with
Christianity; that is to spiritualize our nature. . . . Poetry has a natural alli-
ance with our best affections. It delights in the beauty and sublimity of outward nature and of the soul. . . . Its great tendency and purpose is, to carry
the mind beyond and above the beaten, dusty, waery walks of ordinary life;—
to lift it into a purer element, and to breathe into it more profound and generous
emotion. It . . . strengthens our interest in human nature by vivid delineations
of its tenderest and loftiest feelings, spreads our sympathies over all classes of
society, knits us by new ties with universal being, and through the brightness
of its prophetic visions helps faith to lay hold on the future life.

Clearly, then, poems were expected to tranquilize their readers
and bring them the gospel of salvation and Christian duty—sometimes
both at once. A third function is closely related to the second; if
poetry showed man that he is more than dust, it also showed him
that nature is more than granite and dew.[6]

Who has not seen a leaf whirled about by the wind, and then lodged in the hollow
of a tree? but who except a poet would have recalled the circumstance? who but
a poet would have found in it an analogy to any thing in the moral world? This is
to look upon nature with a poet's eye, and to interpret nature with a poet's sense.

In order to fashion nature "into a thousand emblems of spiritual
things," the poet was expected to use his imagination as a *"medi-
ator between the senses and the soul."*[7] "The Sermon On The Mount"
(quoted above) obviously moves from nature description to divine
teaching. Similarly, a good many Christian hymns, usually grouped

in a section called "The Seasons," also bridge or link natural revelation and divine revelation, sea shores and the Scriptures, enjoyment and emblem, senses and soul.

Fourthly, popular religious poetry was intended to comfort families mourning the death of a friend or relative. Death, during the nineteenth century, formed a trinity with birth and marriage, as sacred as that of the Divine Trinity. The death bed summoned family reverence and prayerful silence. During this wait, simply-worded lyrics about heaven and Jesus were read aloud or sung. And they gave comfort.

> But to that bright land of love I go,
> With the fountain clear of ceaseless flow,
> Where Sharon's rose and lily grow,
>   And the balm of life perfumes the air;
> While drop no tears—no grave is seen
> To mar the fields of living green;
> No storms obscure the sky serene;
>   No piercing thorn can wound me there.

Closely related to the consoling function of popular religious poetry is the fact that a great many poets tried to make their readers weep. Why? Because many families found it not only enjoyable but sincerely necessary to weep over poems such as this:

LINES ON THE DEATH OF LITTLE CHILDREN

> I came where, in its snow-white shroud,
>   The form of little Willie lay;—
> How my heart ached! I wept aloud—
>   For anguish I could scarcely pray.
>
> "Oh God! and is this all," I cried,
>   "That's left of little Willie now?"
> And bending down by his bedside,
>   I kissed that cold and stony brow.
>   . . . . . .
> Dear Willie! what a weight of grief,
>   What agony I've borne for thee!
> But oh, unspeakable relief!
>   To feel, thy spirit now is free:—
>
> To feel that thou art safe and well
>   From pangs that rend mortality;

> That thou art gone, sweet lamb! to dwell
> 'Mid the pure pasture of the sky.

The reason why such an astonishing number of "Little Willie" poems appear in popular literature and why they were appreciated and even demanded by their audience remains a mystery until one examines the mortality figures for nineteenth-century America. Of the approximately 250,000 whites who died in the United States during 1850, well over 100,000 were children under ten years old. And of the 100,000, nearly 97,000 were children under five. In other words, in 1850 almost 40% of all deaths occurred to children under five years old. Baffling illnesses and farm accidents stole many children away from their families during the nineteenth century. Writing and crying over "little Willie" poems was not a fad, but a common, tragic necessity.

> 'Twas in the time of early spring,
>   When the small rain falls soft and fast,
> When the first vernal warblers sing,
>   In hope that winter's hour is past;—
>
> 'Twas then our darling's grave we made,
>   Where earth was moist with Nature's tears;
> And there, in silent sorrow, laid
>   The blighted hope of future years.

There are two misconceptions concerning the sentimental poetic experience (crying over a poem) which must be corrected. First of all, this experience was by no means spontaneous or chaotic; it was carefully anticipated by poets and thoughtfully prepared for by readers. Moreover, its effect was both refreshing and profound. Secondly, there really is no such thing as a sentimental poem—only a sentimental experience which demanded more of the reader than of the poem. To be sure, the poet went to great pains to prepare a special type of poem which would help the sentimental experience to occur (as will be shown later), but the poem, through its style and description, served only as a catalyst to sentimental ecstasy. Thus, the poem was secondary, and the reader's preparation primary. Before a poem could encourage sentimental ecstasy to take place, the reader needed four elements. If any one of the four was missing from the reader's being, the ecstasy would never occur. Besides having a sentimental death-poem before

her, the soon-to-weep reader 1) had to have experienced a loss similar
to that described in the poem, 2) had to still be sorrowful over the
loss, 3) had to know that others had also experienced similar sorrow
(weeping alone was sadness not sentimental release), and 4) had to be
religious enough to believe in the soul's immortality and salvation.
Perhaps the third and fourth necessities do not seem to fit, but they
were definitely essential, for only when individual sadness was seen
to be part of cursed mankind's sorrow, and contrasted with God's
eternal love, could the full power of the sentimental ecstasy be enjoyed.[8]

Expressions and descriptions of human suffering, instead of depressing us with
melancholy, become sublime or touching, when that suffering is brought into
direct or indirect contrast with man's nature and hopes as an immortal being,
or is represented as calling into exercise those virtues which can exist in such
a being alone. There is no pathos in the mere lamentations of an individual
over his own peculiar lot, or over the condition of a race to which he feels it
an unhappiness to belong.

Biographical fact, memory, sensitivity to the sufferings of all men, and
faith in Christ's loving providence fused around even the vaguest and
simplest of poems, giving them splendor and depth enough "to bid
the big tear start, / Unchallenged, from its shrine, / And thrill the
quivering heart / With pity's voice."

Sentimental rapture which crystallized around nature poetry also
depended upon the same types of necessities. Before one could weep
over a nature poem he 1) had to have seen a lake similar to the one
described by the poem, 2) had to remember the sight vividly (the
reader's memories—not the poet's trite images—summoned tears),
3) had to know that others had also witnessed similar natural grandeur
and 4) had to be religious enough to believe that nature contains moral
lessons and teaches eternal promises.

A sixth (and final) service popular poets rendered their readers
is easy to recognize but difficult to describe or explain. Magazine
verse (especially religious) attempted to instill the public with child-
like virtues. In nineteenth-century eyes, children instinctively adored
natural beauty, were blessed with Christian innocence and humility,
and were free of the hypocrisy, passions, and obsessions which ruined
the sensitivity of adults. Literary critics argued that such child-like
virtues enabled one to properly understand nature.[9]

May it not be assumed that a warm perception, and high enjoyment of what is beautiful in creation proves some degree of virtue? Can the feelings which are not in harmony with themselves, respond to the melodies of nature? Do not the corrosions of hatred, the festerings of remorse, pour a poison-cup over her purest charms? Can the heart which is a prey to the grosser passions, inflated by ambition or seared with the love of gain, humble itself to the simplicity of the lessons, which the flowers and the fields teach? Do not even the artificial customs of society impair the relish for rural pleasures, and tempt the spirit away from the trustful childlike adoration of the Supreme?

These same endowments, according to the critics, also enabled poets to write poetry. Childhood and poetic genius are consistently equated.[10]

There was a time when poetry was created every day, and that was a time when the grown-up were children.

We believe there is poetry, eloquence, genius in every child that is born; but early education (and that, to be sure, is a very comprehensive cause), the influence of artificial, conventional life, and the world's delusions quench the heaven-kindled spark, or so encrust the soul that the fire cannot find its way outward. . . . As a child grows up, he is ashamed to be a poet.

Adult poets, then, either had never lost their childhood naturalness, or had rediscovered it by reading poems describing and praising child-like virtues and genius.

And what did such spiritually child-like poets do? They wrote child-like poems (humble, harmonious, pious, natural) to help their readers become child-like again. Here, of course, the circle takes shape. No poet or poem could properly interpret or transfer to others the Bible's message of humility or nature's message of pure harmony, unless both poet and poem first became their message— became child-like.

The popular religious verse of the nineteenth century was never purely utilitarian and stylistically shoddy. It was artless, perhaps, and naive, but rarely careless or obtuse. The author knew precisely why he wrote clear, plain, quiet poems. Undoubtedly, complicated metres and surprising language would obliterate a sentimental experience by drawing the reader's attention away from his own background, memories, and faith, and too much towards the poem's artistic structure. What the reader brought to the poem was far more important than any stylistic brilliance and freshness displayed in the poem. In fact, nineteenth-century readers distrusted poetry which *displayed* feelings. What they sought instead was[11]

the presence without the display, of a tenderness and pathos, an elegant simplicity and devotional feeling, which win upon the heart, and sometimes touch it as with strains from unearthly worlds.

A display of artistic language would only "caricature sentiments, and present the most grotesque images to fancy." One critic, who praised Bryant's *Poems* (1836), claimed that "he breathes a calm and quiet strain that harmonizes well with the gentle excitement awakened by contemplating the beauties of Nature."[12]

Secondly, religious poets purposely filled their stanzas with "easy transitions," "natural associations," and "the free, simple, unaffected language of the heart,"[13] because complexity would quickly garble the spiritual lessons they meant to teach. The popular poet's audience, while literate, was hardly sophisticated or educated beyond practical skills. The majority of adults and children demanded simple poetry, and those poets who put Christ's humility first in their thoughts and who sincerely intended their lyrics to spread the gospel avoided writing anything new, rare, or complex.

Christ did, after all, stress charity and simplicity rather than wit. Should not Christian poets follow Christ's example? While composing religious verse, should they forget this advice?[14]

Religion ought to be left in her native simplicity, rather than hang her ears with counterfeit pearls.

That only is devotional poetry, which is the utterance of devout feeling in the forms of the imagination. It is the soul that gives its life to such poetry. . . .

Of course, popular poets sometimes forgot their pride and wrote embarrassing stanzas; for this they were often chided:[15]

We always regret to find dull, prosy, unmeaning stories and poems palmed off under the title of "moral and religious," as though nothing could be pious that was not stupid.

A hollow or awkwardly trite poem would seem as irreverent at a death-bed scene as would a too-clever poem. Both would be insulting and insincere; simplicity, tenderness, and imagery had to blend silently.

Come to the bed of death!
Step lightly—check that rising sigh;
Behold the parting of the breath,
    Without an agony;
Behold how softly fades
    The light and glory in that eye.
As gently as the twilight shades
    The azure sky;
Come and bow in thankfulness
To Him who life's last hour can bless!

In many ways the religious and the sentimental, as they were blended in popular verse, were similar. Both demanded poems sufficiently vague and simple for the reader to identify with easily, and both required more of him than of the poem. Poets were faced with creating verses which were graceful enough to hold the reader's attention, but not so stunning as to make him forget *himself*:

Some humble door among Thy many mansions,
Some sheltering shade where sin and striving cease,
And flows forever through heaven's green expansions
The river of Thy peace.

There, from the music round about me stealing,
I fain would learn the new and holy song,
And find at last, beneath Thy trees of healing,
The life for which I long.

Another reason why nineteenth-century religious poets wrote sweetly quiet poetry derived from the belief, emphasized by romantic reviewers, that truth was sweet and calm. Therefore, poems consisting of "language and imagery offensive to good taste" embodied no truth:

Especially in a community like ours, where so many harsh and excited voices are sounding, we gladly hear the gentler accents of the bard. At a time when truth and conscience themselves are made not seldom to speak in a tone of severity borrowed from the passions, we are glad to have their own proper sweetness restored to them in the numbers of the Muse.

Since truth was sweet and quiet, slavery and other disturbing topics were unsuited to poetry. L. A. Godey and Sarah Hale, who scarcely dared whisper about women's rights, kept all mention of slavery out of their magazine. Even kindly Whittier, who called Thoreau a pagan and who cast Whitman's *Leaves of Grass* into the fireplace, was sharply criticized by subscribers of the *Lady's Book* for being "too sectarian." *The Christian Examiner*, which discussed such topics as capital punishment and the American Indian problem, at first refused to "support . . . any particular theory upon a subject so embarrassing" as slavery.[17] Later, however, it published descriptive articles about it. Popular taste made one thing powerfully clear; the horror which Garrison battled with his cleaver-edged eccentricity was hardly a fit subject for prose, and never one for poetry. Paradoxically, the age which idolized Milton as "the sublimest of men"[18] feared to praise the blazing reform poetry written by its own small remnant of prophets.

A fourth advantage afforded by the humbleness and vagueness of popular verse is analogous to the virtues of a treasured tobacco pipe, which reminds the smoker of many other relaxing smokes he enjoyed and the happy occasions surrounding them. So too with the poetry. Since uniqueness was discouraged, these poems commonly resembled one another. One poem could, therefore, bring to the reader's mind several other poems he had enjoyed, and one peaceful reading hour could recall the comfort of previous reading sessions. Thus the popular poem heightened its effect not by displaying its own peculiar beauties but by calling upon the reader's memory.

The popular poet's avoidance of earthy or robust imagery stemmed from the common belief that poetry should extract and concentrate "life's ethereal essence," arrest its "volatile fragrance," and prolong its "more refined but evanescent joys." Moreover, popular religious verse fitted the nineteenth century's definition of meditation; "pausing on truth already discovered."[19] Because poets were expected to spiritualize society, and not to present new theological truths, they relied heavily upon traditional and biblical imagery. Never-changing truths were expressed in never-changing words. Popular taste dictated that God, salvation, and eternal rewards were subjects best described through abstraction and understatement, which did not mean that the result need be ineffective. An example of tastefully restrained understatement is this brief description of a saved soul meeting Jesus in heaven:

> And away through their midst came the
> Saviour of men.
> And my heart he engraved with his love-
> writing pen,

> And he gave me the crown which the
> Cherubim wore,
> And he whispered, "Go forth, thou art
> mortal no more."

The nineteenth century demanded what critics called a "truly American" literature, constructed out of the vocabulary of everyday American speech and from images of familiar American landscapes and home life. As early as 1832, Henry Wadsworth Longfellow described and dignified such poetry in his "Defense of Poetry," printed in the *North American Review* July of that year. So too the *Christian Examiner* in 1845 expressed the same concern for verse couched in the language of ordinary men, avoiding a false poetic diction":[20]

The truth, we believe, is, that if a man has the spirit of poetry in him, he will be more apt to utter it in the strong, simple speech of everyday, homely life, especially if he be dealing with subjects familiar to every eye and heart, than to resort to that hereditary stock of phrases called "poetic diction."

Popular poetry of this character attempted to unite people—to give the nation coherence. Bryant, for instance, was deeply respected because he did exactly this; said one reviewer:[21]

He deals not in those obscure thoughts and images which present themselves to a small class only of thinkers, but pours the soft light of his genius over the common path on which the great multitude is moving. His poetry is simple and unaffected, beautiful without being overloaded with ornament, inspired by quiet communion with nature, not a transcript from the writings of others.

Another reason why popular religious poets kept their stanzas clean and clear is a result of the belief that poetry and music had much in common. The most captivating poems, critics believed, were those which could be set to music, or which were intrinsically melodic in metre and rhyme. Bryant's "Death of The Flowers" enchanted its readers with musical charms:[22]

Here is description, here is feeling, and here is music too, music of the most tender soul-subduing kind.

As the adjective "soul-subduing" hints, critics realized that poetry's musical qualities, like music itself, possessed powers beyond those which merely gave pleasure:[23]

Music is one of the fairest and most glorious gifts of God, to which Satan is a bitter enemy; for it removes from the heart the weight of sorrows and the fascination of evil thoughts. Music is a kind and gentle sort of discipline: it refines the passion and improves the understanding. Those who love music are gentle and honest in their tempers.

Similarly, rhyme, while adding grace to verse, strengthened the moral thrust of poetry:[24]

Rhyme has a nobler mission than merely to tickle the ear and please children. Perhaps the pleasure derived from it is akin to that which comes from listening to the echo in fields. Two lines ending harmoniously seem like the mouths of two witnesses establishing and enforcing the thought expressed.

Given the nineteenth century's moral tone, the communal vigor of music, and the plain strengths of popular verse, probably the most effective religious poetry written during this time was the hymn, which combined music and religion with poetry. Seemingly simple and artless, the hymn-poem was anything but that. They lacked acrobatic metrical contortions and stayed with the traditional forms, but a great deal of skill and art went into their lyrics, which were often printed as religious poems. Yet a listing of the different hymn metres understood and recognized by average nineteenth-century churchgoers cannot help but impress modern readers. A knowledge of hymn metres enables one to appreciate the artfulness of poems which at first appear as simple as nursery rhymes. Those who read the poems which appeared in the journals, and who sang the hymns whose lyrics the popular poets composed, knew the skillful from awkward, and appreciated the competence of the skilled. Those bards who ignored hymn metrics and/or rhyme schemes soon lost popularity. N. C. Brooks for example, composed over twenty-four blank verse "Scripture Antholo gies" bewteen 1840 and 1847, but his poetic retellings of biblical history were never popular for long. He and his imitators faded into obscurity, while less-profound and less-erudite but more musical poets grew in fam

A few disturbing questions remain (and probably always will remai unanswered about nineteenth-century poetic theory. Is it true, as roma tic readers assumed, that a selfish man could never write poetry and that an evil man could neither create nor understand religious poems? And how valuable to society is intellectual genius which is void of "*Moral beauty*"? Should "Moral Excellence . . . be estimated far above Intellectual superiority, because of its purifying effect on the heart"?

Do humble religious poets help mankind more than authors such as "Byron, and Voltaire, and Rousseau" who "were almost gods" in understanding but who "destroyed every virtuous principle and feeling" of their readers?[25]

> The soul's divine whom God employs
> To comfort humankind—rejoice,
> While Falsehood groans, to hear they voice
>   So clear and true,
> Whose swelling music drowns the noise
>   Of Folly's crew.
>
>   . . . . .
>
> Oh! ye self-honoring bards and sages,
> Whom busy vanity engages
> In making names for coming ages,
>   Yet little feel
> That God will criticize your pages
>   Without appeal.

NOTES

[1] Clarence A. F., "Editors' Table," *Godey's Lady's Book*, 34 (1847), p. 52.

[2] Anonymous, "Article VI (Poetry)," *The Christian Examiner and Theological Review*, 38 (1845), p. 221.

[3] Anonymous, "Article IV (Poetry)," *The Christian Examiner*, 14 (1833), pp. 320-321.

[4] B. B. Thatcher, "Religious Character of the Poetry of Mrs. Hemans," *Godey's Lady's Book*, 21 (1840), p. 166; Anonymous, "Article V (Bryant)," *The Christian Examiner*, 22 (1837), p. 66; Anonymous, "Review (of Mrs. Hemans' *The Forest Sanctuary; And Other Poems*)," *The Christian Examiner*, 3 (1826), p. 411; Sarah J. Hale, "The 'Conversazione,' " *Godey's Lady's Book*, 14 (1837), p. 3.

[5] Anonymous, "Article I (Milton)," *The Christian Examiner*, 3 (1826), pp. 33-34.

[6] Anonymous, "Article VII (Coleridge)," *The Christian Examiner*, 14 (1833), p. 113, R. 451.

[7] Anonymous, "Article VII—Poetry And Imagination," *The Christian Examiner*, 42 (1847), pp. 263-264, R. 455.

[8] Anonymous, "Article V (Poetry of Mrs. Hemans)," *The Christian Examiner*, 19 (1836), p. 347, R. 451.

[9] Mrs. L. H. Sigourney, "The Perception of the Beautiful," *Godey's Lady's Book*, 20 (1840), p. 10.

[10] Anonymous, "Article V (Children's Poetry)," *The Christian Examiner*, 13 (1833), p. 332; Anonymous, "Article VI—Poetry," *The Christian Examiner*, 38 (1845), p. 225.

[11] Anonymous, "Article XVIII (Bowring's poems)," *The Christian Examiner*, 4 (1827), p. 525.

12 Anonymous, "Article V (Bryant)," *The Christian Examiner*, 22 (1837), p. 67; *Ibid.*, p. 63.

13 Anonymous, "Article V (Bryant)," *The Christian Examiner*, 22 (1837), p. 63.

14 Anonymous, from "The Gatherer," *Godey's Lady's Book*, 3 (1831), p. 183; Anonymous, "Article II (Lays of the Gospel)," *The Christian Examiner*, 38 (1845), p. 318.

15 Sarah J. Hale, "Editors' Book Table," *Godey's Lady's Book*, 20 (1840), p. 45.

16 Anonymous, "Article IV (Mason)," *The Christian Examiner*, 4 (1827), pp. 67-68; Anonymous, "Article VII—Poetry And Imagination," *The Christian Examiner*, 42 (1847), p. 251.

17 Sarah J. Hale, "Editors' Book Table," *Godey's Lady's Book*, 38 (1849), p. 297; Anonymous, "Miscellany: On Slavery In The United States," *The Christian Examiner*, 4 (1827), p. 201.

18 Anonymous, "Article I (Milton)," *The Christian Examiner*, 3 (1826), p. 31, R. 449. The metaphysical poets were also highly regarded during this period.

19 *Ibid.*, p. 35; Anonymous, "Article II (Bulfinch's poetry)," *The Christian Examiner*, 38 (1845), p. 316.

20 Anonymous, "Article VI—Poetry," *The Christian Examiner*, 38 (1845), pp. 217-218.

21 Anonymous, "Article V (Bryant)," *The Christian Examiner*, 22 (1837), p. 67.

22 Anonymous, "Article III (Commonplace Book)," *The Christian Examiner*, 12 (1832), p. 95.

23 Anonymous, from "The Gatherer," *Godey's Lady's Book*, 5 (1832), p. 168.

24 Anonymous, "Article VI—Poetry," *The Christian Examiner*, 38 (1845), p. 213.

25 Anonymous, "Is Genius Desirable?" *Godey's Lady's Book*, 14 (1837), p. 162.

FOUR POPULAR POETS: A CENTURY OF TASTE

Wilma Clark

Poetry, in our day, is not a popular art. Books of poems are not found on best seller lists (or not until Rod McKuen). As Carl Bode writes, "Americans now in the Age of Prose eye a poet suspiciously, dismissing his poems as either too difficult or too easy."[1] This is an effort to understand why certain poets, over a span of four distinctly different and succeeding historical periods in American literary history, have been able to attract large numbers of readers: Lydia Huntley Sigourney (1791-1865), Ella Wheeler Wilcox (1855-1919), Edgar A. Guest (1881-1959) and Rod McKuen (1933-   ).* My purpose is to discover, insofar as possible, the sources of their popular appeal, and to expose the dichotomy that exists between popular and elite poetry. Certain generalizations about them can be made at the beginning. All four poets lived lives which were variations on the American rags-to-riches theme; all had humble beginnings, yet gathered substantial incomes from their works. All seemed to have a deep and uncanny understanding of the beliefs, values, and needs of the great mass of ordinary people undoubtedly stemming from their own backgrounds. All possessed powerful personal magnetism that attracted attention and admiration; people bought their poems out of interest in—and even love for—the poet himself.

Lydia Huntley, the daughter of a gardener in Norwich, Connecticut, at twenty-three moved to Hartford to open a school for

---

*Because of limitations of space, however, this paper is limited to examination of two, Ella Wheeler Wilcox and Rod McKuen, and brief mention of Mrs. Sigourney and Edgar Guest.

girls and to publish her first book *Moral Pieces in Prose and Verse* in 1815. In 1819 she married Charles Sigourney, an educated, successful merchant in Hartford. She then published books and articles for the next fifty years; as "the sweet singer of Hartford" she dominated American popular poetry for the first half of the nineteenth century.

In 1828 she and N. P. Willis shared a $100 prize offered by *The Token*, the first successful American annual. It was through the elegantly bound annuals of the 1830's that she became most widely known. By the forties she had transferred her attention to the magazines which began appearing everywhere and which supported her reputation until her death in 1865. Before then she published 69 books and contributed over two thousand articles to nearly three hundred periodicals. Her *Letters to Young Ladies* appeared in twenty American and five English editions, and *Letters to Mothers* in eighteen American and four English editions. Throughout her career she was besieged with requests for poems; by churches for hymns to be sung at consecrations, ordinations, installations; by charitable societies for anniversaries; by academies and schools for exhibitions; by readers wanting anything from elegies and epitaphs to an ode for a lover to his mistress. Her heavy correspondence was an indication of the sensitive rapport between Mrs. Sigourney and her audience. She was personally admired, many women feeling that they could become more like the pure, holy, virtuous Mrs. Sigourney by reading her poems.

After 1890 American popular verse was dominated by the "newspaper poets," of whom Mrs. Ella Wheeler Wilcox was by far the most successful. Ella Wheeler was born in Johnstown, Wisconsin, one year after her parents had migrated from Vermont. At 15 her first "effusion" was published in the New York *Mercury* and at 16 she entered newspaper work when Frank Leslie sent her ten dollars for a poem. Her big "break" came in 1883 when Jansen and McClurg in Chicago refused to publish her *Poems of Passion* on the grounds that they were "immoral"; newspaper headlines in Milwaukee and Chicago did the rest, and her popularity zoomed:

TOO LOUD FOR CHICAGO
THE SCARLET CITY BY THE LAKE SHOCKED BY BADGER
GIRL, WHOSE VERSES OUT-SWINBURNE SWINBURNE AND
OUT-WHITMAN WHITMAN

In 1884 she married Robert Wilcox, an Eastern businessman and a gentleman who enjoyed fine foods, gracious living, the arts, world travel. The couple moved to Connecticut where Mrs. Wilcox lived until her death in 1919. She continued writing for syndicated distribution as well as for books of her own. She had reached such a wide audience during the nineties through her syndicated articles in the Hearst newspapers, that in 1901 the New York *American* commissioned her to go to England to write an American poet's impression of Queen Victoria's funeral.

In addition to love lyrics in Mrs. Wilcox's work, there are long narrative poems idealizing women, hortatory poems encouraging other "barefoot" boys and girls to raise themselves up as she had done, philosophical works exploring the nature of happiness, life, death, and the "spiritual worlds beyond." *The Beautiful Land of Nod* was a delicately illustrated collection of poems, songs, and stories for children.

Like Mrs. Sigourney, Mrs. Wilcox participated in a lively interaction with her readers. Her New York newspaper column (an Ann Landers prototype) made people feel as though they knew her personally. During World War I Mrs. Wilcox wrote poetry for American soldiers, and at the age of 62, embarked upon a visit to the war zone for a reading tour. In defending her work against severe criticism, Mrs. Wilcox once wrote: "If I chance to be a popular poet it is because I have loved God and life and people, and expressed sentiments and emotions which found echoes in other hearts."

Edgar A. Guest, another newspaper poet, was a self-made man in the pattern of a Horatio Alger novel. He started his newspaper career as an office boy for the Detroit *Free Press* in 1895 and remained on the *Free Press* payroll until his death in 1959. As assistant to an exchange editor, Guest clipped and pasted verse from other newspapers for filler, which gave him the idea of trying some verse on his own. His first poem appeared in the *Free Press* on December 11, 1898; in 1904 he began writing a verse a day.

After his brother published his first three books of poems, Edgar Guest caught the eye of syndicates and book publishers. In 1916 he met Frank Reilly who afterwards published all Guest's books. Reilly printed 3,500 copies of *A Heap O' Livin'*, then 25,000 copies in the second printing, and 100,000 copies in each additional printing. Over a seventy-year period Guest wrote some 11,000 poems which were periodically collected; the *Collected Verse* of 937 pages, which was first issued in 1934, is now in its twentieth printing.

Guest never missed a deadline, and for years his verses appeared daily in three hundred newspapers with a circulation of about ten million. He enjoyed national fame, was a platform speaker in great demand; in 1952 the Michigan Legislature named him state poet laureate, declaring that people found in his poems "moral support in times of stress and have enjoyed his subtle humor and homespun philosophy." Guest never claimed to be a poet. He was a "newspaper man who writes verses" or "rhymes, doggerel, anything you want to call it. I just take the simple everyday things that happen to me and figure out that they probably happen to a lot of other people, and then I make simple rhymes out of 'em and people seem to like 'em."[2]

The best-selling poet of modern times—and perhaps of all time—is Rod McKuen, a musician, arranger, and singer. McKuen too began in obscurity, growing up in San Francisco as a product of a broken home. Like Edgar Guest, Rod McKuen had little formal schooling and spent his youth at odd jobs: herding cattle, punching out cookies in a Nabisco factory, lumber-jacking and breaking horses, selling shoes, writing a newspaper column, working as a disc jockey. Drafted in 1953, discharged and back in San Francisco in 1955, he sang folk songs, then tackled New York and almost starved as a rock singer. In the early 1960's he had a hit record and promoted it on an eight-week, eighty-performance tour of America's bowling alleys. The strain on his vocal cords resulted in the loss of his voice and gave him the rasping whisper which sounds "as though he gargles with Dutch Cleanser," as one critic put it.

Then suddenly he was a phenomenal success. In the spring of 1969, *Publisher's Weekly* noted that for the first time in seventy years of record-keeping, McKuen was the only author to have three books in the top ten best-sellers within one year: his first three books of poems. The Academy of Recording Arts and Sciences presented the Grammy Award to McKuen for the best spoken word album of 1968, *Lonesome Cities.* (Defeated nominees were the Kennedy-Nixon debates, Martin Luther King's *I Have a Dream*, and Paul Schofield's *A Man for All Seasons.*) Since Random House began publishing his poems, McKuen has produced a new book each year and has sold over two million copies: *Stanyan Street and Other Sorrows,* 1966;

Listen to the Warm, 1967; *Lonesome Cities*, 1968; *In Someone's Shadow*, 1969. The dust jacket on the latest book claims more than forty albums of McKuen recording his own songs and more than nine hundred compositions performed by other artists, having sold a total of fifty million records. McKuen too has developed a sensitive rapport with his audience. In fact, public interest in McKuen as a person approaches adulation; he has, on occasion, been forced to leave a public appearance in an armored car.

THE CONSOLER
MRS. LYDIA HUNTLEY SIGOURNEY (1791-1865)

In Mrs. Sigourney's day death was the overriding fact of life at the height of her career, between 1840 and 1846 in Boston 46% of all deaths were of persons under five; even by 1892 the average age in the United States was thirty-three, and only six out of one hundred persons lived to be sixty-five years old. Three of Mrs. Sigourney's own babies died, and her only son died at the age of nineteen. Mrs. Sigourney wrote whereof she knew. A formula evolved in her poetry: no matter what earthly complexity or disappointment had been experienced, the subject of the poem was able to discover perfect happiness in heaven. As Gordon Haight has put it, "The spirit floating skyward became the favorite ending for all her poems."

Mrs. Sigourney wrote for an audience who lived a hard and uncertain life. She had the technical skill that enabled her to express routine pieties in the form of sweetly melodious verse in such a way that great numbers of people were consoled, pleased, and uplifted.

THE ENERGIZER
MRS. ELLA WHEELER WILCOX (1855-1919)

Appearing a half century after Mrs. Sigourney's work, the poetry of Ella Wheeler Wilcox was similarly hortatory and didactic. Yet there were certain shifts in popular sentiment apparent in Mrs. Wilcox's poems. Most obvious was that sexual passion was recognized as a subject for popular poetry. Some writers date the close of the Victorian age as 1901, the year of Queen Victoria's death, but the heart-wails in Mrs. Wilcox's *Poems of Passion* in 1883 anticipated it.

In a later edition of *Poems of Passion* Mrs. Wilcox explained in a "Preface" how the collection had come about. She claimed to have written about 1200 poems, only forty or fifty of which treated "entirely of that emotion which has been denominated the 'grand passion'—love," and pointed out that only a few of the poems were "of an extremely fiery character." Yet her poems were likened to "songs of half-tipsy wantons"; the Chicago *Herald* hoped that Miss Wheeler would write some *Poems of Decency*, and another reviewer called her a distributor of "poisoned candy." Her new publishers judged the moment shrewdly, and capitalizing on the publicity, sold 60,000 copies of the book in two years. The theme of passionate love is stated in the opening poem of the volume, which begins by asking, "How does Love speak?" and answers:[3]

> in the warm,
> Impassioned tide that sweeps through throbbing veins,
> Between the shores of keen delights and pains;
> In the embrace where madness melts in bliss,
> And in the convulsive rapture of a kiss—
> Thus doth Love speak.

In "Delilah" the dying Samson is tormented by visions of his early love.

> She touches my cheek, and I quiver—
> I tremble with exquisite pains;
> She sighs—like an overcharged river
> My blood rushes on through my veins;
> She smiles—and in mad-tiger fashion,
> As a she-tiger fondles her own,
> I clasp her with fierceness and passion,
> And kiss her with shudder and groan.

The poem, she explained, was "meant to be an expression of the powerful fascination of such a woman upon the memory of a man, even as he neared the hour of death." If the poem was immoral, the Biblical story inspiring it was immoral. She stubbornly claimed it her "finest effort." The volume closes with "The Farewell of Clarimonde." The passionate Clarimonde admonishes her lover Romauld, who is now entering the priesthood, that none of his rites, duties, fears of Hell, or hopes of Heaven will be able to erase the memory of her love from his soul.

> Before the Cross shall rise my fair form's beauties—
> The lips, the limbs, the eyes of Clarimonde.

She adds that holy joys will never compare with the joys he experienced with her in sexual love.

> Like gall the wine sipped from the sacred chalice
> Shall taste to one who knew my red mouth's bliss.
> . . . .
> Think not in all his Kingdom to discover
> Such joys, Romauld, as ours, when fierce yet fond
> I clasped thee—kissed thee—crowned thee my one lover.

Although it was only a few poems which created the scandal, the scandal was itself significant in helping to understand the direction of the poetess's career thereafter. First, critics were led astray in the excitement. Jenny Ballou points out that many of the poems in the early volume were "lovely in their lilt, overbrimming with an authentic freshness of emotion." "Impatience" is cited as an example:

> How can I wait? The nights alone are kind;
>   They reach forth to a future day, and bring
> Sweet dreams of you to people all my mind:
>   And time speeds by on light and airy wing.
>   I feast upon your face, I no more sing.
>   How can I wait?

Yet critics consistently read double meanings into such poems, and were tempted into the biographical fallacy. Had Miss Wheeler actually experienced the thrills described in "Farewell of Clarimonde" or was the poem chiefly, as she explained, an imitation of Theophile Gautier?

Second, scandal seemed to give Mrs. Wilcox a taste for sensationalism. The critics responded to the *Poems of Passion* with mid-Victorian horror, but the book sold widely and natives of Wisconsin proudly hailed Ella Wheeler as their "talented, hard-working, cheerful little song-bird." Ella Wheeler enjoyed the role immensely and played it the rest of her life. In fact, her role of popular poetess became more important to her than her poetry. She gloried in her humble origins and took the role of "barefoot-girl-made-good" seriously; she loved perfume and color, wore a large ring on her thumb, and always some chiffon around her neck; she continued to wear her hair in bangs, and couldn't resist carrying her bright red parasol to attract attention. She grew to need public adulation, and never had the patience or desire to discipline her work.

Like Rod McKuen nearly a century later, Ella Wilcox wrote about the vicissitudes of love. Love, she knows, will not always last.

> I am oppressed with this great sense of loving;
> . . . .
> Too deep the language which the spirit utters;
>   Too vast the knowledge which my soul hath stirred.
> Send some white ship across the Sea of Silence,
>   And interrupt its utterance with a word.

In "Perfectness" (*Poems of Passion*) the pathos of perfection is revealed: the supreme moment of love "when the soul unchecked / Soars high as heaven, and its best rapture knows"—contains "a deeper pathos than our woes" because "Resistless change, when powerless to improve / Can only mar." "What Shall We Do?" probes the subject of how to dispose of old love. Shall we hide it? Shall we drown it? Shall we burn it? The only answer is to starve it, to deprive it of all food—glance, word, sigh, memory, vain regret. Only then will it die. In several poems the lovers regretfully anticipate the end of love and separation: "Not Quite the Same," "You Will Forget Me," "Friendship After Love."

In a large group of poems lovers look back wistfully on affairs long finished. In "But One," for example, the year has but one perfect month, one June. When it is finished the robin's song never seems in tune again. The theme is quite skillfully developed in "Queries." "Time the Jew" is a rag-buyer who bargained for the "tattered remains of a threadbare bliss, / And the worn out shreds of a joy divine" to stuff into his "ragbag of the Past."

> Since Time, the rag-buyer, hurried away
>   With a chuckle of glee at the bargain made,
> Did you discover, like me, one day,
>   That hid in the folds of those garments frayed,
> Were priceless jewels and diadems—
> The soul's best treasures, the heart's best gems?

Another group of love poems dealt with the injustices suffered by women who have been used and cast aside. An innocent young maid in "The Change" (*Collected Poems*) is "in earnest" but he "is feigning" as they walk through the garden.

> A young life crushed, and a young heart broken,
>   A bleak wind blows through the lovely bower,
> And all that remains of the love vows spoken—
>   Is the trampled leaf of a faded flower.

In one famous poem, "The Birth of the Opal," Mrs. Wilcox dealt figuratively with the subject of sexual intercourse and conception. With her special gift for creating scandal, Mrs. Wilcox recited the poem publicly while pregnant herself. Ironically, her first and only baby died soon after birth, and she discovered later that the opal was a gem of ill omen. In another poem, "The Creed," she argued that the true legitimacy of a child is determined not by the parents' wedlock, but rather by the reality of their love, an idea repeated in "Three Women":

> The child
> Not conceived in true love leaves the mother defiled.
> Though an army of clergymen sanction her vows,
> God sees "illegitimate" stamped on the brows
> Of her offspring. Love only can legalize birth
> In His eyes—all the rest is but spawn of the earth.

Although Mrs. Wilcox displayed unique audacity in treating sexual desire and the intimacies of marriage rather frankly in her verse, she followed the pattern of the sentimental novelists in glorifying woman as noble, motherhood as a sacred function, and the wife as spiritual model for husbands.[4] *Maurine*, her long narrative poem, was accurately advertised as "an ideal poem about a perfect woman," who through a somewhat stormy emotional career, illustrated female perfection in all her sacred offices, as friend, sweetheart, wife, and mother. Mrs. Wilcox made an interesting confession several years after she'd written this poem:

I wrote *Maurine* from pure *Imagination*. It proves I think that I knew more of *friendship* than of *love* when I wrote it. I am sure I would have allowed all my girl friends and their families to have pined away and died before I would have given up Mr. Wilcox to them, after I met him and loved him!

But the point is that much of the philosophy on womanhood appearing in Mrs. Wilcox's poems—and in her Ann Landers-like prose

articles in the New York *Journal*—deviates not at all from the contemporary conservative views of proper womanhood. In spite of
enthusiastic movements for the emancipation of women, Mrs. Wilcox
was equivocal on the subject. When French feminist leader termed
her "Battle Hymn of Women" the "Marseillaise" of womanhood,
Mrs. Wilcox reminded readers of her *Journal* column that although
"brains are sometimes an assistance to woman in the right use of
her affections," nevertheless, "a great deal of the love element had
better be interfused with common sense." She assured her readers
that "to be a gifted poet is a glory; to be a worthwhile woman is a
greater glory."

All of this is reinforced in the long narrative poem *Three Women*
(1897) advertised as a study of the "lives of three good and beautiful
women in every phase of weakness, passion, pride, love, sympathy,
tenderness." The three women are contenders for the love of Roger
Montrose, an attractive but world-weary man for whom life has
grown stale. The poem begins with a friendly debate: Maurice
Somerville has great faith in the basic nobility of women, but his
cynical friend Roger Montrose is a well-seasoned world traveler who
has discovered that each woman, if tempted in the proper way, will
fall.

Mabel Lee is greatly admired in the town as the "public bene-
factress," but only her closest friends can see that her good works
are balanced by her failures in the privacy of home. Mabel Lee's
mother is "maid to her daughter"; the father and brother are "slaves
at her bidding"; "an excellent plan / To make a tyrannical wife for
some man." Mabel Lee is guilty of pride; when Roger Montrose
falls in love with her, he finds her frigid, incapable of personal affection. Her interest is aroused in her husband only when he becomes
a drunkard and a vagrant, which gives her a chance to control him
by working to save his soul, in short to *reform* him.

Ruth Somerville, the second woman, is an old-fashioned house-
wifely type who would have been completely satisfied as wife and
mother. Bitter when Roger is deluded by the attractiveness of a
worldly woman, she speaks:

> The man whom I worshipped ignored
> The love and *comfort* my woman's heart stored
> In its depths for his taking, and sought Mabel Lee.

> Well, I'm done with the role of the housewife. I see
> There is nothing in being domestic. The part
> Is unpicturesque, and at war with all art.

With stubborn determination Ruth enters medical school and becomes a successful doctor with the understanding that her career will be dropped instantly when she marries:

> Once a wife, I will drop from my name the M.D.
> I hold it the truth that no woman can be
> An excellent wife and an excellent mother. . . .
> The world needs wise mothers, the world needs good wives,
> The world needs good homes, and yet woman strives
> To be everything else but domestic. God's plan
> Was for woman to rule the whole world, *through* a man.

The third woman in the poem is Zoe Travers, a young widow emerging from grief and realizing the need for a man again. A foil to Mabel Lee, in whom intellect ruled over heart, Zoe Travers is a warm, passionate woman who yields to the temptation of an affair with Roger Montrose. The affair ends when Roger tires of her and the tormented woman shoots him and kills herself. The two corpses turn up at Ruth Somerville's medical school, where the young lady doctor feels compassion for the "lovely sinner" Zoe Travers, in whom the lightning-passions of Love could have been "like a current of life giving joys" instead of the "death dealing bolt which destroys."

Mrs. Wilcox's handling of the subjects of love and women seemed to have a dual appeal to her readers: her poems countered the avantgarde movement for women's rights and reinforced instead the widespread and commonly held views that women were ideally noble in character and belonged in the home; at the same time, many of her poems offered a more overt treatment of sexual love than could be found in other popular literature.

Mrs. Wilcox was quite clear about the functions of popular poetry, and was occasionally quite explicit about the duties and obligations of a poet. Her purpose, plainly, was to comfort the reader, to brighten his world. In the poem, "Contentment" (*Collected Poems*, p. 236), she writes that her labors will have been rewarded

> If any line that I ever penned
> Or any word I have spoken

> Has comforted heart of foe or friend—
> . . . .
> If in any way I have helped a soul,
>   Or given a spirit pleasure.

In *Three Women* Maurice Somerville, who turned to helping the poor and to writing poetry as therapy for a broken heart, summarized the poetic creed of Mrs. Wilcox:

> The souls whom the gods bless at birth
> With the great gift of song, have been sent to the earth
> To better and brighten it.

The great sin for a poet was to add in any way to the despair of his reader:

> The sin unforgiven
> I hold by the Cherubim chanting in heaven
> Is the sin of the poet who dares sing a strain
> Which adds to the world's awful chorus of pain
> And repinings.

The foundation of the optimism that pervaded Ella Wheeler Wilcox's poetry was her faith in the goodness and order of God's plan. In *Three Women* Maurice Somerville found consolation in the over-all goodness of Providence, and learned that the "true secret of living" was to "accept what Fate sends" and to grow "out of self, back to him—the First Cause." (p. 191)

This faith in the Plan appears in several of the shorter poems. In "Presumption" (*Collected Poems*) we read

> Whenever I am prone to doubt or wonder—
> I check myself, and say, "That mighty One
> Who made the solar system cannot blunder—
> And for the best all things are being done."

Especially reminiscent of Pope's *Essay on Man* is the poem "Whatever Is—Is Best" (*Poems of Pleasure*).

Besides teaching her readers to accept suffering as a part of a bigger, perfect plan, Mrs. Wilcox also offered them the consolation (as Edgar Guest did later) that pain and suffering improve character. All people suffer at some time; "God pity those who cannot say, / 'Not mind, but thine,' who only pray, / 'Let this cup pass,' and cannot see / The *purpose* in Gethsemane." ("Gethsemane," *Collected Poems*) In "The Musicians" (*Collected Poems*) Pain, the musician, is the "soul-refiner"; it restrings the strings of the "quivering heart." Suffering binds men together: "And I held all men to be my brothers, Linked by the chastening rod."

In contrast to the heaven-pointing Mrs. Sigourney, Mrs. Wilcox's gaze was usually directed steadily at the good earth. If acceptance of suffering and faith in God's plan helped to make life endurable, then the other chief ingredient of the Wilcox philosophy was the importance of love for others, a point stressed later by Edgar Guest.

> So many Gods, so many creeds,
> So many paths that wind and wind,
> When just the art of being kind
> Is all this sad world needs.

"When I Am Dead" (*Collected Poems*) treats the idea extensively: better than a marble monument will be words of some who will be able to say "I've helped them," given a "refreshing draught," spoken "words of comfort like oil and balm." "True Culture" (*Collected Poems*), in the poems of both Mrs. Wilcox and Edgar Guest, is "to speak no ill," "to see beauty and all worth," to keep one's own life discreet and well-ordered, and to avoid causing pain to others.

Mrs. Wilcox reflects a shift in popular sentiment about religion. In her verse there is a definite move away from the dogma of Mrs. Sigourney's poetry. In "God's Measure" (*Collected Poems*, p. 313) she explains that a man may stand near God even though "he dwells / Outside the pale of churches, and knows not / A feast-day from a fast-day, or a line / Of scripture even."[5]

For her the religious experience often assumed the form of mystical union with the All, a central experience in much of the nineteenth century Romantic poetry. Yearning for such mystical union is described in "Searching" (*Collected Poems*):

> These quiet Autumn days,
> My soul, like Noah's dove, on airy wings
> Goes out and searches for the hidden things
> Beyond the hills of haze.
>
> With mournful, pleading cries
> Above the waters of the voiceless sea

> That laps the shore of broad Eternity,
> Day after day, it flies.

But the search is in vain, and the narrator admonishes her soul to "wait" and "rest." In several poems, however, the mystical union is accomplished. In "Life" (*Collected Poems*) the moment of penetrating insight is described:

> As when a mighty forest, whose green leaves
> Have shut it in, and made it seem a bower
> For lovers' secrets, or for children's sports,
> Casts all its clustering foliage to the winds,
>
> And lets the eye behold it, limitless,
> And full of winding mysteries of ways:
> So now with life that reaches out before,
> And borders on the unexplained Beyond
> I hear the awful language of all Spaces;
> I feel the distant surging of great seas,
> That hide the secrets of the Universe
> In their eternal bosoms; and I know
> That I am but an atom of the Whole.

Large numbers of readers were attracted to her poetry by this element of mysticism in her work, which increased over the years and became especially strong after she and her husband were converted to theosophy.

Ella Wheeler Wilcox wrote poetry that appealed to her readers because it performed several important functions—it bolstered their faith, encouraged them against adversity and sorrow, energized their hopes and ideals. Her own simple, fundamentalist faith enabled her to write verse that was convincing and encouraging, that engendered in her public the same strong, certain faith she herself possessed. Echoing Emerson, she told her readers that within each man there is a "best self, that pure atom of God / Which lies deep within each heart like a seed in the sod." (*Three Women*). In "Achievement" she wrote "Trust in thine own untried capacity / As thou wouldst trust in God Himself. Thy soul / Is but an emanation from the whole." With such power lying hidden in every personality, human potential seemed "Limitless" (*Collected Poems*):

> There is nothing, I hold, in the way of work,
> That a human being may not achieve
> If he does not falter, or shrink or shirk,

And more than all, if he will *believe*.
. . . .
When the motive is right and the will is strong
There are no limits to human power.

Coupled with this belief in the possibilities of individual achievement was Mrs. Wilcox's profound faith in the American way. Herself a rags-to-riches product of it, she sincerely believed in the virtues of work, thrift, and democratic equality. She continually exhorted her readers to try, try again, to avoid idleness. "Oh, idle heart, beware! / On, to the field of strife, / On, to the valley there, / And live a useful life." If they stumbled, she encouraged them to rise up; no force could keep down a person who continued the struggle. She was herself always their shining example, a "pure phenomenon of democracy."

Ella Wheeler Wilcox did not produce what even the most generous critics would call "good" poetry. She wrote instead what came naturally to her; she reflected, and wrote for, the average mind. She wrote to encourage people, to brighten the world for them; to her, she said, "*heart* was more important than *art*," and she explained it in a poem:

Though critics may bow to art, and I am
  its own true lover,
It is not art, but *heart*, which wins
  the wide world over.

Though smooth be the heartless prayer,
  no ear in heaven will mind it.
And the finest phrase falls dead,
  if there is no feeling behind it. . . .

THE HOMESPUN PHILOSOPHER
EDGAR A. GUEST (1881-1959)

The verses of Edgar A. Guest reflected and reaffirmed those middle class values commonly accepted by Americans in the first half of the twentieth century: Home, Work, Country, Faith in God, and Brotherhood. When Guest died in 1959 these values were accepted by most Americans. But the decade since Guest's death has seen a cataclysmic reevaluation of everything that his generation took for granted. The change is clearly recorded in the contrast between the verse of Edgar Guest and Rod McKuen, whose points of view and attitudes reflect the startlingly sudden breakdown in the 1960's of belief-system held solidly by middle class Americans for decades. Of the values treated in Guest's verse, Brotherhood is the only one not seriously challenged today. McKuen's poems, written in the late 1960's and reflecting the times, assert the values of love and communication, but the traditional themes of Home, Work, God, and Country receive cursory treatment or none at all. The value of human love—Brotherhood—is the only major theme emphasized consistently throughout the four popular poets studied in this paper.

FRIEND AND LOVER
ROD McKUEN (1933-

The first three books of Rod McKuen's poems have sold more than the combined works of T. S. Eliot, Robert Frost, and Edna St. Vincent Millay. Just before Christmas, 1969, the first printing of *In Someone's Shadow* was the largest of *any* book, poetry or otherwise, in the history of Random House, and just after Christmas the bookstores were out of it.

The contrast in values between Guest and McKuen is a direct reflection of the contrast between the values of the current generations in America. In one poem McKuen mentions the generation gap (*Shad.*, pp. 43-44).[6] A young couple see themselves growing older, voting conservative, trying to force their children into "the world / [they've] just come through." The children will protest, just as the parents have done, for freedom to form their own lives:

> But every generation gap
> should have some kind of bridge
> even if it's only made of love.

In McKuen Home has disappeared from the central position it held in the society represented by all three of the other poets discussed: Sigourney, Wilcox, Guest. There are biographical reasons for the poet's disinclination to envision Marriage and Home. McKuen himself had little homelife during childhood, and in his first poem in *Stanyan Street and Other Sorrows* remembers the painful absence of a father.

Then, too, McKuen is a drifter, by nature and by choice. He lives with two sheepdogs, two Siamese cats, and no wife. Several of the poems reflect his preference for drifting instead of marrying.

Sometimes he distinguishes between living alone and being lonely.

> It's not the same thing, you know. . . .
>
> Mostly it's letting yourself come first for a while.
> (*Shad.*, 61)

Most of McKuen's poems describe the vicissitudes of sexual love affairs, intense but beautiful relationships which are momentarily meaningful but which never lead to marriage. Even if the lover is tempted toward permanence, he rejects the idea quickly, for when a commitment of love is made, it can't be taken back. Therefore, the lover is relieved on Sunday morning that he did not use words that tempted him on Saturday night: "tomorrow, together, love" ("Sunday," *The Earth*). The lover is afraid of permanence for another reason—it tends to destroy love. Love is transient—

> You can borrow but never own it
> after a while it says good-bye. . . .
> (L.W., pp. 101-102)

Profound change in the mores of the people: perhaps love and marriage do not, after all, as the old saying goes, "go together like a horse and carriage"?

McKuen's poems, in this vein, reflect what many young people feel—rootlessness, drifting, an alienation arising from a failure to find something to believe in. In "The Mud Kids," on the record album *The Earth*, the mud kids come one by one out of the "curious foraging rain," carrying their mud in buckets, sometimes hardening the mud into bricks, sometimes into Ken and Barbie dolls. They play with doll houses, sugar cubes, and each other instead of dolls; they grow up too fast and never enjoy the simple childhood pleasures. His poetry *reflects* the current uncertainty about the proper relationship between love and marriage, the current reexamination of Marriage and Home values.

Another longstanding American tradition notable for its absence in McKuen's poems is the belief that hard work is necessary for success as well as for inward joy and satisfaction. Gone are Mrs. Wilcox's exhortations to "never give up—you can do it if you try!" and Edgar Guest's philosophy that the challenge of hard work in "Life's Tests" builds the character of a man.[7] His poems reflect, instead, a tremendous shift in values, a reaction against Puritanical exhortations to obey God and work hard in order to do well on earth and in heaven. Instead, McKuen urges his readers to be attentive to beauty and to love, to be aware of life. We "must remain alive to every friendly sound" of seagulls and moles, for example; we must "learn to take it slow," not to "jostle the angels" ("A Walk with the Angels," *The Sky*). Lying on a beach, making love, we ought to notice how many different shades of lovely blue there are in the sky. And "we ought to make love well" so as not to disappoint "the something up above the sky watching us" ("How Many Shades of Blue," *The Sky*). This curious line represents the shift in viewpoint of modern youth in the late sixties who seemed to feel responsibility—not so much to work for certain future reward, but a responsibility to be aware of and to make the most of the *life* granted them for a brief, *present* moment. The poet praises "The Flower People" (*The Earth*) because they never cease trying "to fill their empty lives." They are always carrying flowers somewhere, to a church, a wedding, a graveyard.

The major sections of McKuen's books of poems consist of the histories of love affairs, celebrations of brief but intensely beautiful relationships between people. A smaller group of verses which I think of as the "end of the heyday poems" express a composed, regretful realization that youthful provisions of energy and vitality have been expended. The narrator is sometimes wistful but never entirely dejected by the loss of youth—he regards it as a proper part of the scheme of things—but he can accept age calmly because he has consciously and fully lived his youth.

Some poems, too, combine a gentle warning of approaching age with an invitation to make the most of youth. The image of America as defender of the world's freedom is now repalced by the "make love not war" philosophy reflected clearly in McKuen. In these poems, by quiet understatement, the ugliness of war is emphasized through contrast with what is beautiful and loved in life.

The rationale for killing in war has disappeared; McKuen, and the young people that he reflects, do not deal with ideologies or "hard facts" that make war inevitable, no matter how ugly. Another poem uses a series of gentle images from nature to accentuate the frequency and ease with which young lives are destroyed in war for reasons no one can understand. "Some of them fall like snowflakes," and "the blood from their cuts, / the life from their guts / spread over the silver sand."

Mrs. Sigourney's poems mirrored the common man's belief in dogma and hopes for a perfect life in heaven; in Mrs. Wilcox and Edgar Guest the importance of specific dogma was receding in favor of love, brotherhood, and a general faith in God's over-all Plan. By McKuen's day, Heaven has completely disappeared. It exists *only* in earthly joys.

References to God are rare and peripheral. A man in danger of death may think of God, but when security returns, "true-time" takes over and the man forgets Him. God is being redefined; in McKuen, God literally "is Love." LOVE is the message in McKuen's work. Sexual love is the subject in the majority of his poems, but he also writes about love as universal brotherhood. McKuen reflects younger people's reevaluations of middle class beliefs in home, work, country, religion. He works by speaking quietly; in soft, sometimes humorous, tones of understatement, McKuen presses young people to reexamine *their* values, habits, and tactics as well.

First, the attack on middle class materialism. Truth, beauty, love are all sacrificed for materialistic gain. Several poems invite the young to reexamine, reevaluate—their fads in clothes. And their drug experiments. The poet satirizes the excessive protesting with which much of the country has grown weary, including some interesting reverberations from Gertrude's speech in *Hamlet*: "Methinks Thou Doth Protest Too Much" (L. W., 107). Or a wry comment on student demonstrations.

McKuen, in his attempt to bridge the so-called "generation gap," cautions both young and old against excesses and tries to point out to each that each has something positive to offer the other. "The young can save the world," he remarked, "by growing older in a hurry." They "had better use their stones to build foundations, not to slice off roofs." The key to the proper relationships between generations is love—love and respect; without it life is war, and an empty one.

Love is McKuen's major theme—what sells his books and records is his constant reiteration of love and the need for love among human beings. People are lonely and miserable because they have lost the ability to communicate with each other.

What the world needs is love that encompasses all people—like Whitman's, perhaps—expressed succinctly as the poet looks down from a fourth floor hotel room into the street.

A large number of poems deal with sexual love—important because love is the only experience that can counteract long years of lonely isolation. The love affairs are brilliant, intense, but brief, "For love is only moments here and there / It comes and goes quietly I think." (S.S., 68) Love is like a dance—giving in, letting go, taking a chance: "Even the waltz ends." ("The Waltz") At the height of the relationship the lovers *believe* that their love will be permanent—but it never is. In *Lonesome Cities* a lover optimistically envisions a future in which the love endures: "Then we'll go gentle in the wood / and what we do for one another / will be warm and good. . . . I'll never be alone." But the next poem describes the pain of a dying love: "And where are we now? . . . Not even love enough to break each other's hearts." Needed and needful as it is, love is ephemeral—as the lover in *Lonesome Cities* who draws his sweetheart's face "on tablecloths across the country" but finds that "I draw your face a little fainter every day."

The major portion of most of McKuen's collections of poems chart the rise and fall of a love affair, which can be diagrammed like the action of a novel. This formula is most fully developed in the long narrative poem in *Listen to the Warm* and *In Someone's Shadow*, but some parts of the formula are developed in all the books.

I. Waiting for love
II. Discovery of love
III. Anticipation and perfect moment before the actual consummation of love
IV. Consummation of love

At the zenith of the affair the lovers are happy, fulfilled, grateful for the accident of having met each other.

V. Decline of love; satiety and uncertainty
VI. Attempt and failure to salvage the love
VII. Alone with only a memory

No poet of despair has ever been popular with the American people, and McKuen is no exception. In spite of the repeated emphasis upon the fact that even the most beautiful love will eventually die, McKuen ends every book with an optimistic note: Love *is* worth waiting for; it is the only experience that gives life meaning; and if one waits patiently it will come again.

Critics have been harsh with McKuen. Louis Coxe quips, "the poems make no demands. Ask no questions and you'll be told no truth." Only "people who ordinarily read scarcely at all" take time to look at McKuen's poetry; "they can fall in and out with no damage done and nothing taken away."[8] However, I've asked students to explain why they read McKuen, and their answers support the theory that popular art *protects* the audience from what may be a painful exploration of the nature of reality: his works are "calm and serene"; he can "sort of take you out of the world of conflict for an instant"; his poems "blank out sad thoughts"; his writings mirror "particular feelings I've had." To youth of both sexes, McKuen's verse is a stay against loneliness and alienation. This personal touch, the assumption that all his poems are private dialogues, lies at the base of his popularity—as the dust jacket of his best-selling record album puts it,

This voice belongs to a good friend. The name doesn't matter. It is more important that it is someone you might like to know, or someone you might like to have say to you the things that are being said here.

NOTES

[1]Carl Bode, *The Anatomy of American Popular Culture: 1840-1861* (University of California Press, 1959), 188.

[2]Royce Howes, *Edgar A. Guest* (Reilly and Lee Co., 1953).

[3]Poems are cited from the following books by Mrs. Wilcox:
Collected Poems. London: Leopold B. Hill, Woodbridge Press, Ltd., Guildford.
Maurine. Chicago: W. B. Conkey, 1901.
Poems of Passion. 1883 (Edition used had frontispiece torn out).
Poems of Pleasure. Chicago: W. B. Conkey, 1888.
Three Women. Chicago: W. B. Conkey, 1897.

[4]See Leslie Smith's study of sentimental novelists and Ellen Jarvis' study of women's magazine fiction, in this volume.

[5]It is interesting to note the similarity of this poem to a Rod McKuen verse three-quarters of a century later. Mrs. Wilcox writes:

> God measures souls by their capacity
> For entertaining His best Angel, Love . . .;

> What God wants of us
> Is that outreaching bigness that ignores
> All littleness of aims or loves or creeds,
> And clasps all Earth and Heaven in its embrace.

Compare McKuen:

> Each of us was made by God
> beautiful in His mind's eye.
>
> * * * * *
>
> It only takes an outstretched hand.

6 I have abbreviated citations to the books of poems.

Stanyan Street and Other Sorrows –– S.S.
Listen to the Warm ––––––––––– L.W.
Lonesome Cities–––––––––––– L.C.
In Someone's Shadow––––––––––Shad.

I have also cited three record albums on which McKuen poems are read: *The Earth, The Sea, The Sky.*

7 His biographers stress the fact, however, that McKuen does not follow this in his personal life, but works at a furious pace. "He has written songs in planes, buses, cars, and while walking. Rod's writing is compulsive. He once tried a six-week vacation, and returned with nineteen new poems." *Biography of Rod McKuen,* Jay Allen Public Relations, 170 N. Robertson Boulevard, Beverly Hills, California.

8 Louis Coxe, "Money in Art," *New Republic*, Jan. 3, 1970.

ROCK MUSIC, MEDIA, AND THE COUNTER CULTURE

David Wright

In March 1957 kids[1] were standing in record stores all over the country trying to decide whether they should buy "Young Love" by Tab Hunter or by Sonny James. They were wearing jeans, tennis shoes, and sweatshirts worn inside out, and they were not quite certain what "rock and roll" meant. Most of them had never heard of the East coast disc jockey, Allan Freed, who coined the phrase for the commercial world. What they did know was that the music did something for them, and they bought the records, which were usually performed and often written by people under twenty, by the million.

Today, in any record store in any reasonably large town, you see walls covered with black light posters that project the aura of the drug experience, exhort the young to revolution with slogans as "power to the people," and radiate the raw sexual presence of performers like Mick Jagger, the late Jimmy Hendrix, and the late Jim Morrison. But most important, you see young people who look as if they came from a totally different culture than their parents. Their hair is long and they are deliberately unneat; they emanate sexuality more shocking to their elders than that of center-city strip joints. With loud rock playing from four or five speakers, the kids are doing faint suggestions of dances as they look at record jackets, discussing what's going to be the next influence after the current country-western trend dies off, or the engineering on a new album, or a new amplified guitar sound.

The connection between the scenes of 1957 and 1971 is direct if not always obvious. It is essentially the same music, as evidenced by the number of prominent contemporary groups doing an occasional number from the mid-50's. The kids are the same as well. The people who were ten when Bill Haley altered their consciousness with "Rock Around the Clock" are now 24 or 25, but they're the same people. Most of the members of contemporary rock bands grew up playing Bill Haley, Little Richard, and Chuck Berry in high school gyms. They and the music coincided at a unique time in history. Rock is a medium—part reflector, part creator—of a new culture being built without system, master plan, or rules of order, by people under thirty.

Rock is symptomatic of radical changes in the total life style of people born after the Second World War. It is the public medium for the expression of value-systems which make up what is generally known as the counter culture. As such, rock reflects the conflict of two hostile cultures within our society. To understand the force and influence of rock is to understand the members of the counter culture.

This is the first generation to be raised by the Spock principles of permissiveness; it has been encouraged more than any other generation to explore its own potentialities and feelings. Equally important, it is the first television generation. At the age of eighteen, a recent survey shows, the average American youth has seen 15,000 hours of television. The oratory of politicians has been matched for the first time by continual images (visual, audio, and tactile) of contrasting reality. While two presidents have talked about the necessity of protecting the freedom-loving people and their freely elected government from communist aggression in Asia, the kids have seen, via television, burned peasants, burned villages, and dead American soldiers who are mostly under twenty-five and look a lot like them. This has had an effect on them, lending credence to Marshall McLuhan's claim that television has produced a generation gap which is not a matter of semantics, but a neurological fact. The media, especially television, have altered the perceptions of the younger generation in a way that makes them quite different from any of their forefathers in the post-Gutenberg era. If, as McLuhan proposes, print has stepped up the visual sense at the expense of his other senses, leading to a fragmentation of sensory unity, television and the electric media in general are reversing the trend. The contemporary media are returning the sensory ratios to their pre-print, pre-literate "tribal" balance. The auditory and tactile senses are returning, and today's kids are beginning to use all their senses again in a "seamless web," to use McLuhan's phrase, of experience. The rock generation is most assuredly a McLuhan generation.

A second and related explanation of the rock generation lies in the theories of Theodore Roszak, who believes that modern man has lost the unity and wonder of total experience because of his surrender to the scientific world view. Roszak sees modern society, dominated by industrialism, as the culmination of modern organizational integration, a technocracy. Emotional responses are eclipsed by rational responses; technical experts are the last court of resort in society; there is no appeal beyond the authority of science. Strong emotional drives of individuals and societies are then released in covert, irrational paths (like wars of intervention), which are then systematized as clearly and coldly rational.

McLuhan's and Roszak's theories are complementary. Today's counter culture originated in this new perception, that neurological rearrangement induced by the primacy of electric media as McLuhan claims, and gathered strength from the disillusionment with the lifestyle of the parent society that Roszak traces. Since society is seen as sterile and malevolent by larger and larger numbers of its youth, it should be clear that this much publicized "generation gap" is no semantic phenomenon but a deep national schism that takes on the proportions of a substantial struggle between two cultures.

This is a crucial point, for if in fact there is no such thing as a counter culture, then rock music cannot serve as its medium. There is a tendency to believe that this culture is not quite real, that it is a mutation in the otherwise healthy corpus of society, that it will either be reabsorbed into the super-culture or die of its own inability to deal with reality, and that the kids who make up this counter culture will probably graduate into very much the kind of life that their parents are living. This point of view rests on certain premises which are no longer valid.

First, it is very easy to see the future as a lineal extension of the present in much the same way that the present seems to be a logical extension of the past. Many scholars point out that every generation feels a generation gap, and that it is a matter of degree and not of kind. It is obviously true that history did not begin in 1945. Nor is it at all unreasonable to suggest that one can understand a lot about the present by understanding the cultural conditions that produced it. The error in the traditional academic approach to the present counter culture is that it does not relate to the fundamental forces that are making and have made it. The "things are always pretty much the same" theorem does not admit that radical changes in the environment produce radical changes in the order of reality. Yet, for the first time in history the inhabitants of one generation are hard pressed to understand the next. It is the acceleration of change that traditional social analysts of culture fail to appreciate.

The media are definitely changing social realities. "The Global Village" may not be a reality to many adults insulated from change by set roles, tasks and patterns of living, but it is to the young. Critics have often noted disdainfully that the children of the rich or at least the moderately rich are the ones most deeply involved in the current rebellion. It is because they are one of the few generations to grow up with the relative certainty that they would never suffer from material want, that they can engage in a drive for a new life style. They do not accept the traditional work ethic. They are, in short, the first children of technocracy, and they are different.

In the mid-1950's one of the first signs of friction between the parent culture and what was to become the youth counter culture appeared in popular music as "Rock and Roll." Significantly, Bill Haley's "Rock Around the Clock" was an unimportant record when it was first released in 1954. Yet a year later, reissued as the theme from the movie, *Blackboard Jungle*, it became the top selling single for eight straight weeks and was the number one 45 record of the year.

Rock originated from a merger of the styles of black rhythm and blues, country & western, be bop, and boogie woogie. But, of course, it was more than the sum of its parts. Almost immediately, it became clear that this was music entirely for and, in many instances controlled by, kids. And clearly, the message that rock sent out had a lot to do with sex. Parents recoiled. A Boston priest inveighed against the immorality of sensual, "black sweating bodies," and the ultimate corruption of white America's "young people." Disc jockeys apologized when they played rock on the air; but they had to, they said, because they had so many requests. Established music critics berated the absence of meaningful lyrics and the primitive rhythmic patterns and melodies. Mothers bombarded NBC with angry protests after Elvis

Presley's appearance on the Steve Allen show. Later Ed Sullivan would feature the pelvic contortionist only from the chest up. Usually the attacks on it suggested that rock and roll somehow mesmerized the kids and broke down their normal inhibitory mechanism, whereafter they easily accepted immorality. Had the charge been phrased in a positive rather than in a negative way, and had the kids achieved the awareness that they were later to attain, they certainly would have agreed. They loved it.

Among blacks the term "rock and roll" had specific sexual connotations. So when Little Richard said:

> Good golly, Miss Molly, you sure like to ball,
> When you're a rockin' and a rollin'
> I can't hear your mama call

or

> I got a gal named Sue, she knows just what to do:
> She knows how to love me, yes indeed
> You don't know what she's doin' to me,

he wasn't speaking the literal truth because the kids, especially black kids, knew exactly what she was doing to him. The men at the white record companies, who apparently had a pretty good idea as well, tried, with considerable temporary success, to suppress Little Richard and the others. They rewrote black rock and roll lyrics until they were totally inane, called in white singers with sexually neutral images like Gale Storm or Pat Boone, and retaped the tunes. Then they released them with financial backing that the small black companies didn't have. That was the phenomenon of the "cover record."

However, the attempt to control rock and roll failed dramatically. After Bill Haley's success, dozens of groups formed and recorded singles. It soon became obvious both from the number of new performers and the remarkable sales figures that no few industry executives were going to control this new phenomenon. In 1955, "Rock Around the Clock" was the only rock song on the year-end best seller list. In 1956 there were 16 in the top 50, in 1957, 30, and in 1958, 37 of the top 50 singles were rock and roll numbers. Small record labels appeared and disappeared along with groups that produced one big record and then vanished.

More important than the proliferation of the phenomenon in these early years, however, was the emerging content of the lyrics. Rock concerns itself exclusively with the young and their life style. Four major themes appeared quickly in the songs. The most obvious is the preoccupation with sexual freedom—the heart of rock and roll has always been its sex drive. In the words of Dennis Thompson of the MC5, Little Richard's songs are "all about getting laid." To a greater or lesser degree this is true of all early rock that was not part of the "cover record" movement.

The second major theme was the exploration of teenage love, with its inevitable disappointments and pathos. Often the conflict centered around what was described as a "teenage quarrel." The lyrics were adolescent situation-tragedies that every kid could relate to, either through direct experience or vicariously. Another theme that permeated these lyrics was a desperate need for security. The boy is usually assuring the girl that when they grow up everything will be the same:

> But when we grow up, some day I'll show up
> Just to prove I was telling the truth,
> I'll kiss you too, then I'll hand to you
> This rose and a Baby Ruth.

When these love songs did not concern themselves with teenage quarrels, bird dogs, or ruthless cheating, they examined parental pressures on young love:

> They're betting everything, that our love
>   won't survive
> They're hoping, hoping, in time we'll forget
> Each other lies . . .

But the parental pressure is not really resented. The teenagers understand and will forgive their parents because they love the older folks, who are "one in a million."

> They're one in a million,
> A million to one.

Of interest is the clear and consistent protestation of innocence in these ballads, coexisting with the hard sexual innuendo of the up-tempo songs. It was a conflict working itself out in favor of the latter on the kids' own private, national medium, the record player.

By 1958, rock lyrics began to examine another enemy of the teenage culture, the parental work ethic, the first instance of rock's explicit criticism of the parental life style. "Yakety-Yak" was a classic confrontation between teenager and parent. The song is laced with parental threats. The youth is ordered to do menial tasks such as taking out papers and trash, and scrubbing the floor. The threat is withholding "spending cash," the youth "ain't goin' a rock and roll no more." The youth is further enjoined from resenting his treatment because his father is hip and knows the teenager's "hoodlum friend outside."

> Don't give me no dirty looks
> Your father's hip, he knows what cooks
> Just tell your hoodlum friend outside
> You ain't got time to take a ride.

Other songs like "Summertime" contained such immortal lines as "I'm sorry teacher but zip your lip because it's summerti-i-ime," and

> Well, we'll go swimmin' every day
> No time to work just time to play
> If your folks complain, just say
> It's summerti-i-ime.

These songs are seemingly insignificant until you consider that these same young people moved from this to going to Canada, to massive marches to protest American foreign policy, to fighting police in Chicago, even to burning the Bank of America in Santa Barbara.

That kind of change, of course, could not have been foreseen in the late 50's, but the rather remarkable songs of self-examination that comprise the fourth major theme in early rock give evidence that more than a mere subgenre of music is involved. Rock had become much too identified with the emerging life style of the young to be merely music to them. Parents and adults in general who so vigorously condemned rock, and wistfully predicted its imminent demise, were really attacking a new and alien system of values that rock projected and that the young happily endorsed.

Sociologically speaking, early rock and roll was an outlaw phenomenon. Its heroes shocked the sensibilities of parents. Elvis Presley appeared with the exact style of haircut that mothers had warned their children was the sure sign of a budding criminal mentality, and only confirmed hoods wore their collars that way. Consider Little

Richard. Parents may never have heard "Good Golly Miss Molly, you sure like to ball," but they got the general idea from his appearance. Chuck Berry was, of course, one of the kids' favorite sex symbols, widely believed to have committed any number of statutory rapes. Jerry Lee Lewis was the last straw. He married his thirteen-year-old cousin. He was from the deep South and when attacked, he answered, with genuine surprise at the uproar, that a lot of people did that. But not in suburban America. What Lewis had done, in effect, was to marry vicariously several million pubescent girls in front of their parents, which caused a national scandal. Lewis' reservations were refused at the better hotels, and contracts for personal appearances were cancelled. (Recently he has been making a comeback, with Little Richard and others.) These and other rock and roll luminaries were outlaw heroes to the kids, and outlaws to their parents.

Under attack, both devotees and performers attempted to defend themselves. They began to try to define what they were, and what their music—which had wide non-musical connotation— did for them. Rock was "movin' and groovin' " and therefore "forever will stand."

Many musical groups dealt with this attempted definition of style and values, and the drive for self-analysis has remained constant in the music to the present. Recently, lyrics have improved and are much more explicit about the function of rock within the counter culture. Rock is magic and touches the magical in a youngster's heart:

> Do you believe in magic in a young girl's heart?
> How the music can free her whenever it starts . . ,

The magic in rock and roll can "free [the] soul" of anyone, but it is difficult to explain it to a "stranger." But for the young the magic communicates:

> I'll meet you tomorrow sort a late at night
> And we'll go dancin' baby, then you'll see
> How the magic's in the music and the music's
> in me.

It took until 1965 for this rather remarkable document to be produced, but it is nonetheless an astute, self-validating analysis. On the other hand, it may mean nothing to an adult; "it's like trying to tell a stranger about a rock and roll." This, among other things, suggests the power of a medium that can only be understood by the people it is intended for—a nearly ineluctable cultural code.

In the midst of a highly rationalistic, emotionally repressive society, then, a medium exists that is experience-oriented, that has to be understood primarily on its own, and very different level. Furthermore, rock and roll is more than just a medium in the traditional sense of the word; it is an environmental envelope as well as a means of communication. The entire social pattern of the counter culture from the record hop, to parking, to drug happenings, to peace marches, to Woodstock and Goose Lake, is rock and roll-centered. The average kid knows the lyrics to several hundred rock and roll songs and partially remembers several hundred more. (According to one expert, Jon Citron, the complete rock and roll library contains well over 30,000 tunes.) So the message, whatever it happens to be, is not only heard, but may very well be memorized.

In the sixties this music became much more issue-oriented, but there are several aspects of the "message" which have remained constant. Rock is not (especially recently) unintelligent, but it is anti-rational. It emphasizes the importance of experience, often sexual experience. (Experience, in this context does not mean pure flights of emotional ecstasy. It has more to do with the kind of integrated perception that McLuhan speaks of.) Rock is idealistic, but not always optimistic. Inhibition, either in the form of behavior modification or censorship is thoroughly condemned. While the entire rock phenomenon is made possible by advancing technology, the message is anti-materialistic and anti-technological. (When I pointed this seeming contradiction out to several of the kids I interviewed in a survey on rock, as well as the corollary that big rock musicians make a great deal of money, they all said, "So what," and that's the answer.)

Another important point about rock music concerns the relationship of the audience to the performers and their music. The primary allegiance is to the music, and once it leaves the distributor, it belongs to the kids and not to the musicians. There is, to be sure, a personality cult surrounding many of the top bands, but it remains always separate from the music. Many kids were disgusted with the Rolling Stones after their Hell's Angels-assisted performance in California which left one dead and several injured, but they still bought their records.

Many popular cultural forms merely reinforce value systems. Rock does that, but it does much more as well. Acting in a capacity that fulfills the traditional definition of a news medium, rock presents both sides of several current issues of great interest to kids. Furthermore, it is frequently the only medium they can turn to for uncensored treatment of topics that are controversial to *them,* as, for example, drugs. What Art Linkletter and others do not realize when they advocate censorship of drug material in the popular music industry, is that the vast majority of kids are not interested in destroying themselves with drugs. The government, via the regular news media, tells them that all drugs are harmful; what they hear on their own medium is that there are distinctions between safe drugs and unsafe drugs. To be sure, many of these facts have been learned by someone's unhappy experience. It is possible, in addition, that some of the information they get from the songs is erroneous, but at least the information is freely exchanged. The effectiveness of the medium in this area is demonstrated by the fact that the government has hired even such rebellious rock musicians as Frank Zappa & the Mothers to do anti-"speed" spots on radio.

As many different points of view as there are within the cultural community, are likely to show up in rock music. The medium is completely open; nobody tells the musicians to restrain their vocabulary because they might offend the sensibilities of the community. Rock musicians don't hesitate to take sides on issues because it's an election year. One of the unmistakably clear things I learned from interviewing students from four different universities was that none of them trusts the regular news media very much. Basically, they believe that the government manages the news that it releases for its own political purposes; so rock serves, in part, as a substitute for untrustworthy news media. But this is only part of a much larger integrated cultural function, for politics in the counter culture is part of the larger life style.

Once having realized how this cultural medium operates and how directly it affects its audience, it is relatively easy to see how and why rock changed as it did from the fifties to the latter sixties and early seventies. In the early sixties, it looked like rock might die altogether. East coast promoters, mostly in Philadelphia and New York, seemed to be trying to systematize a commercial market; singers like Frankie Avalon, Neil Sedaka, Paul Anka, Freddie Cannon, Bobby Rydell, and Fabian produced records from the same commercial mold and sang recipe songs like "Wild One," "Puppy Love," "It's Time to Cry," and "Calendar Girl." There seemed to be no technical or musical innovations about to appear to provide relief. Teenagers, during the 50's, were accustomed for the first time to seeing themselves as heroes or anti-heroes in movies or on stage. Now they were seeing themselves as characters in perverted death rituals: after his girl friend is killed by a train because she returned to the stalled car on the tracks, a bereaved boy ponders,

> What was it you were looking for
> That took your life that night . . ?

These songs, and there were many in the same vein, are interesting for several reasons. First, the strong automobile theme appeared at the time when the first of technocracy's children were getting their drivers' licenses, which suggests how closely rock reflects the life style of the young. Second, these songs probably suggest something about the kids' reaction when first confronted directly with the parental culture's obsession with speed and power. But most important, these songs reflected the same kind of internal sickness in the medium as can be seen in any traditional genre of art when it starts to run out of vitality. This period lasted from about 1960 until early 1964.

Then the Beatles arrived, playing early Little Richard and Chuck Berry. Along with reinvigoration, of course, the Beatles added musical and technical genius and stimulated all kinds of innovation throughout the rock world. But once the changes had started, even the Beatles themselves were challenged to keep up, and they in turn became more and more innovative.

Then, on July 25, 1965, at the Newport Folk Festival, Bob Dylan came on stage with a rock band, to the disapproval of the folk purists. But Dylan, in his inimitable way, knew something and folk rock was born. Besides providing a tremendous new musical stimulus, the infusion of the folk idiom into rock music added a tradition of well-written, topically oriented lyrics. So, during the last half of the sixties the cultural medium was still fulfilling the same function for its audience as before, but with new vigor and a new-found ability to articulate its message. It was now geared to handle the acute conflicts the counter culture would face in the years ahead.

The war in Vietnam accelerated the confrontation between generations that would no doubt have taken place eventually. To the kids the war was not a matter of national principle, but an ulcer that drew attention to what they saw as a diseased body politic. Repulsed, their life style became more and more visibly different from that of the super culture: long hair, freaky clothes, communal living, and drugs. All of these things were immediately reflected in rock, beginning in late 1966, when the first strong youth opposition to the war began to crystalize.

Of the new material treated in the music, the drug theme was, of course, the most controversial. Yet, it might easily have been predicted. Drugs provide experience, and non-rational experience had always been one of the major drives in the counter culture and had always been reflected in the music. Rock picked up the new involvement with drugs and presented a mixed message. Marijuana was uniformly endorsed. (On the other hand, nowhere is there a more terrifying account of the effects of heroin than in "Heroine" by the Velvet Underground.) Songs about drugs, true to the medium, attempted to present the experience, not a rational treatise. "Strawberry Fields Forever" or "Lucy in the Sky with Diamonds" (LSD), or "Yellow Submarine" meant something to kids in much the same way other rock songs mean something to them. Drugs were a central theme as long as people were experimenting. There are relatively few drug numbers now, not because kids are not using them, but because they feel they now know what they need to know about them.

Beginning at the same time, in late 1966 and early 1967, increasingly angry political songs began to appear. Since that time all the varying political stances of the counter culture have been reflected in the music. Rock became a debate of a new sort, mostly between the advocates of non-violence and the advocates of "ripping off the establishment." The theme emerged in disdainful satires of the war and the super culture. Others in the movement replied that it was

more important for the kids to get together than it was to attack
the super culture, and they sang, "Come on people, now, smile on
your brother, everybody get together now, try to love one another."
And the Beatles chided the ideological, communist left, "If you're
carryin' pictures of Chairman Mao,/You ain't gonna make it with
anyone anyhow." But gradually as the war escalated and it became
increasingly clear to the kids that few paid attention to their peaceful protests, the tone grew angrier:

> They got the guns, but we got the numbers
> Gonna win, yeah, we're takin' over . . ,

Some of the original Hippies moved to the country and began
new rural communes, believing that the bitterness generated by the
confrontation was destroying them. Bob Dylan was, in his own
private way, one of them. From songs like "Masters of War" from
his "finger pointing era," he moved to his lyrical, apolitical, rural
album, *Nashville Skyline*.

But over and above the polemic differences between the Jefferson Airplane's

> We are all outlaws in the eyes of America . . .

> We are forces of chaos and anarchy . . .

and Bob Dylan's claim in *New Morning* that "buildin' me a cabin in
Utah . . . is what it's all about," there is a more fundamental
similarity. Both sides of this dialogue cohere to the notion of an
irreversible cultural revolution. And, uniquely, conflicts within the
counter culture as to how best to get there appear first and most
clearly in its primary medium, the music.

NOTES

[1]The use of the word "kids" is deliberate, to indicate a particular segment
of the youthful public who consider themselves, as adults do, a cultural unit.
"Young people," "youth," and similar terms do not always carry the proper
connotation. This paper is also supported by a number of taped interviews,
and with musical illustrations of many of the points discussed.

FOLK MUSIC'S AFFAIR WITH POPULAR CULTURE:
A REDEFINITION OF THE "REVIVAL"

Joseph Janeti

Prologue

The seven years from 1958 to 1965 witnessed a movement which
has been variously termed a "revival," "arrival," "fad," or "boom,"
but which may be more practically seen as the popularization of folk
music in America. In one sense it would be a grand oversimplification
to view this phenomenon as merely a "fad." Indeed, the various socio-
cultural indices which marked this material's growth from an antiquarian
oddity to a commercially viable commodity suggest that there was much
more at work than merely the manipulations of Madison Avenue. On the
other hand, by the early 1960's, it was evident that the current "boom"
was not merely the work of the academicians, political activists, and
musicians who had helped bring it about.

The problem is further compounded, moreover, by the refusal of
many academicians and musicians to take either the movement or each
other seriously. Degree-in-hand scholars in the field of folklore are somewhat reluctant to focus their attention on the guitar-strumming undergraduate performing for a few friends in the campus lounge. Surely this
is not genuine folk music! At the same time, this very guitar-strumming
undergraduate is not willing to admit to any antecedents prior to Bob
Dylan, and in some more extreme cases, Joni Mitchell. Thus the whole
problem of continuity is acutely distorted.

Furthermore, when academics approach the topic, they often
severely limit the aspects of it which they will consider. Folklorists
generally exclude revival material, claiming it is not genuine folklore

and is really a matter for the sociologists. Sociologists, on the other hand, often ignore the musicians, whom the musicologists refuse to consider as musicians at all. Thus, this always bastard, sometimes prodigal son of many, is generally accepted, and for that matter, acknowledged, by few.

It is our purpose here to survey those elements in twentieth century American civilization which seem to have most directly brought about this "revival," this popular interest in folk music. The three elements considered—the role of academics; the role of progressive social movements; and the role of musicians—were relatively diverse. Often they operated with little concern for each other. What is clear is that each, on its own, brought folk music before wide audiences. As each approached the late 1950's, interaction between them became more and more frequent. At last, when the genre became a popular culture item, the boundaries between each became difficult to discern and, in fact, often irrelevant. The "revival" itself is briefly treated, since it is characterized by many more elements than those here described, and is not within the scope of this study.

The Role of Academics

One of the most important forces which helped bring about the popular interest in American folk music was one which had been at work, almost silently, for over seventy years. The *Literary History of the United States* notes that a "stirring of the historic sense," in the latter part of the nineteenth century, which turned attention to various aspects of Americal culture, also served to "stimulate exploration of the riches of American folksong and folklore."[1] Yet, practically every study of the folk revival excludes a survey of the growth of academic interest in folksong. The two exceptions are the *Literary History*, and the more systematic *American Folklore*, by Richard Dorson.[2] Taken together, these studies indicate the important landmarks in the involvement of academics with folksong. Neither, however, uses such a study as a prelude to understanding the folk revival as a movement within the realm of popular culture.

America's academic concern with folklore might be said to have begun with Joel Chandler Harris's *Uncle Remus: His Songs and His Singing* (1880). More properly, however, the credit of being first should go to that group which, in 1888, founded the *American Folklore Society*. Although interest in the society flagged in its early years, the concurrent interest of anthropologists in the North American Indian kept the society alive until the first International Folk-Lore Congress in Chicago in 1893. The American Folksong Society, the first body devoted to folk song *per se*, was founded in 1898.

The first decade of the twentieth century brought several important developments in the study of American folksong. N. Howard Thorp published *Songs of the Cowboys* in 1908, the first true collection of American folksongs. The Texas Folklore Society, the first of the regional societies, was founded a year later, while at the same time, John Lomax, whose story is told in great detail by Oscar Brand in *The Ballad Mongers*,[3] was busy compiling his *Cowboy Songs and Other Frontier Ballads* (1910), which included an introduction by President Theodore Roosevelt. This fact in itself gave the collection a kind of popular appeal which it otherwise would never have had.

After *Cowboy Songs*, developments came more quickly. In 1916 Cecil Sharp began collecting old English ballads in the Southern Appalachians. The collection appeared in 1918 as *English Folksongs from the Southern Appalachians*, at the time probably the most important collection available.

The twenties found Louise Pound producing the impressive *American Ballads and Songs*, and Carl Sandburg his *American Songbag* (1927). Not only was Sandburg's volume a substantial collection of songs, but, what is perhaps even more important, it brought folksong before a segment of the public which might never have considered it save via Sandburg and his reputation as poet. Of foremost importance in this decade was the creation of the archive of folksong in the music division of the Library of Congress (1928). Not only has its printed material served scholars writing treatises of various sorts, but its almost limitless recorded resources have been made available to interested collectors and musicians.

The 1930's witnessed the appearance of a number of studies in folklore, marked in many ways by greater depth and complexity than their predecessors. In part, this was a result of what Harvey Swados described as an "upsurge of self-awareness" on the part of Americans;[4] another scholar has pointed out that this "heightened social awareness renewed interest in national values and traditions" and set researchers off looking for things uniquely American.[5] Under the sponsorship of the Works Progress Administration, a number of them discovered a good deal of America's traditions and "usable past" in the collection of what might be termed "folk materials." The Lomaxes, John and Alan, already well versed in methods of collecting, began scouring the South and West with a portable recording device. The material they collected not only considerably enlarged the Library of Congress folksong archives, but also provided the basis for another outstanding collection, *American Ballads and Folksong* (1934). The most important academic work of the period, however, was Stith Thompson, *Motif Index of Folk Literature* (1936). This monumental work was a dictionary, encyclopedia, and bibliography of folk literature all in one; moreover, it identified various traditions in folklore, studied them comparatively, and brought together all that had been done in the various fields of folklore up to that time.

The period from 1942 to 1951 witnessed the appearance of three periodicals which were to be important for the study of American folksong, the *California Folklore Quarterly* (1942) (changed to *Western Folklore Quarterly* in 1957), the *New York Folklore Quarterly* (1945), and the *Midwest Folklore Quarterly* (1951). These three journals, with the *American Folklore Quarterly*, were the only scholarly publications of the period to present regular reviews of folksong materials. 1942 also witnessed the foundation, at Indiana University, of the first Folklore Institute in America.

The 1950's saw the publication of an increasing number of folksong studies and collections,[6] notable for their depth and scholarly methodology (the lack of which had generated frequent criticism of the Lomax works). Moreover, the first folk-museum (at Cooperstown, New York), and the first record company devoted exclusively to folk materials (Ethnic Folkways) were founded in this decade.

As the 1950's came to a close, the "revival" hit. Publications and research projects increased, multiplied, and increased again. The "academic" aspect of folklore attracted professionally trained scholars, and large numbers of amateurs as well. The collectors and professional folklorists had done their part to preserve a body of cultural material, and to nourish buds of interest which, for seventy years, had sprung up along the way. Both of these functions were now to fall into other hands.

The Role of Musicians

If sheer numbers of articles are any indication, the chapter of American folk music's history which has been best written is that chapter concerned with the musicians themselves. In this sense, historians, both professional and amateur, have remembered well those "ballad-makers . . . fiddlers in buckskin . . . banjo-pickers and lonesome harmonica blowers . . ." who carved the music "out of the rock of their lives."[7] Indeed, it would be conservative to estimate that ninety percent of the existing surveys of the folk revival find its origins in the work of particular musicians. These surveys, moreover, take every form—from haphazard liner-notes to full-length books, from enlightened essays to biased prefaces. It would be pointless to attempt, in one essay, to consolidate this almost limitless fund of material. For present purposes, the story may be told by indicating the major landmarks; on these, save for instances of obvious prejudice, most of the writers agree.

It might be reasonably asserted that an audience for folksong did not exist in the United States before the 1920's. That decade, however, witnessed several developments which at least suggested that a change was about to take place. In 1925 there began, on radio station WSM in Nashville, Tennessee, a broadcast known as the "Grand Ole Opry," which featured what might be loosely termed "country music." The following year, the Okeh record company decided to initiate a country music catalogue. John Jacob Niles, who had traveled extensively in the Appalachians, began touring college campuses singing the ballads he had collected, soon joined by Carl Sandburg, who had already achieved a reputation as poet, and whose *American Songbag*, published in 1927, had given him a following among the folklore enthusiasts beginning to congregate on university campuses. The first of the many annual folk festivals which were to appear over the next thirty-five years, was founded by Bascom Lunsford in Asheville, North Carolina, in 1928. Most impressive, however, was the promising note on which the decade ended. Josh White, who was destined to reach an ever-widening public for the next forty years of his professional life, received one hundred dollars to do a series of recordings for a company which would eventually become Columbia Records.

The 1930's brought, with the depression, a series of develop-ments which were to prove of great importance in the popularization of folk music. As many commentators on the period have noted, the 1930's were marked by a pervasive cultural introspection. While the novelists were asking where they had come from, American artists were striving to paint the American scene, and musicians, under the auspices of the Federal Music Project, were trying to create a distinct American music.[8]

In short, the decade was characterized culturally by the push toward national expression, similar to that called for a century earlier by the Knickerbocker men of letters and the Hudson River School of painters. The movement, pervasive as it was, sent researchers to study the most fundamental aspects of the national experience. Under the auspices of the Federal Writer's Project, guidebooks of the various states were compiled, filled with material which glorified the American landscape and catalogued local beliefs and customs. Journalists and photographers combed the American countryside attempting to find the character of the real American—the hard-working, home-loving individual, beset with the troubles of the depression, but possessed of a stubborn will to survive.

All of this cultural introspection, this interest in the American, the land, the humble farmer and worker, quite naturally did a great deal to create an audience for the folk and their music. Consequently, when, in 1934, the Lomaxes brought to New York one Huddie Lead-better (better known as Leadbelly), to whom they had been introduced in a Texas prison on one of their collecting trips, they found an audience eager to hear this huge dynamic man sing. Leadbelly became a kind of symbol, a man embodying a folk art. As a cultural item, he was a significant attraction; as a musician he served to underscore the vitality of an almost unknown tradition. Other developments in the '30's which served as an index of the growing popularity of folk music, were the establishment, in 1934, of the first national folk festival (held in St. Louis), and the initiation by CBS of *The Wayfaring Stranger*, a weekly radio broadcast by Burl Ives, a young singer of folk songs beginning to attain national popularity.

It could well be argued that the single event which did more to foster the "arrival" of folk music was Woodrow Wilson (Woody) Guthrie's appearance in New York City in 1939. Guthrie at once embodied all the folk symbols. He was the depression man, the representative Okie, the prototypical down-on-luck, up-on-will-to-endure American. What's more, he was articulate, productive, and willing, and he became, to his audience, both the summation of the nostalgic agrarian mythology so basic to American culture, and the people's spokesman for the New Deal. At that moment he seemed to represent where America had been and where it was going. The thousand-plus songs that he wrote mirrored every folk vision; he became such a charismatic leader that even today his influence on American folk music still remains strong.

While Guthrie provided a symbol and an inexhaustable fund of material for the folk revival, it needed one last catalyst to burst into flame. This catalyst was added when Pete Seeger met Woody Guthrie in March of 1940. What Leadbelly and Guthrie contributed to the folk music revival in symbol, direction, and tone, Seeger contributed in energy, dynamism, and synthesis. He was sufficiently removed in upbringing and education from the "folk" and their music to evaluate them objectively. Once convinced of the value of the "folk ethic," and the vitality and cultural relevance of folk music, he immediately initiated a process of exploration and assimilation.

This accomplished, he set out on a "rainbow quest" to introduce Americans to the dynamics of the "folk life," and to weave it all into a "rainbow design," his own personal symbol for an American Utopia, which, he implied, could be done through the language of folk song; Seeger perhaps did more to bring about the popularization of American folk music than any other individual. In Seeger's case, it must suffice merely to suggest various projects in which he played a vital role. Foremost among these were *People's Songs Bulletin*, a magazine which he hoped would serve as catalyst for a national folk song revival; *Sing Out!*, which would become the national folksong magazine—official organ of the revival; and the Newport Folk Festival— by far the largest and most popularly successful annual happening of its kind. Lastly, Seeger himself cut over one hundred record albums— a number surpassed not even by Frank Sinatra.

The 1940's brought a number of important developments in the swiftly expanding realm of folk music. Seeger, Guthrie and several others formed a singing group called the Almanac Singers, which performed in many parts of the United States at union meetings, rallies, etc. A considerable number of people were introduced to folk music and its topical derivative—"people's music," through the singing of this group. After the World War, a conscious attempt at bringing about a "revival" was instituted. One of the organs of this attempt was the nationally distributed *People's Songs*, a monthly folksong bulletin which contained a great deal of topical material. To help meet the expenses of the bulletin, "hootenanies" were held at Union Local 65 at Astor Place. After three years the periodical folded due to lack of funds, but not before a national audience for folk music had been created. Moreover, the basis for numberless

future concerts had been laid by means of the *People's Songs* hooten-
annies. A series of small hootenanies, held in Seeger's basement apart-
ment in Greenwich Village's McDougal Street, inspired Lee Hays to
try to get a singing quartet formed. The resulting group—the Weavers—
made the breakthrough which finally catapulted folk music into the
world of popular culture. The Weavers—Ronnie Gilbert, Lee Hays,
Fred Hellerman, and Pete Seeger—got their first booking through the
efforts of Seeger's wife, Toshi, at New York's *Village Vanguard*. Their
popularity was immediate and unexpected. They soon had a recording
contract with Decca, and, in 1950, brought folk music into popular
culture with their recording of Leadbelly's "Goodnight Irene," which
sold over 1,000,000 copies and put at least one folksong into the
mouths of millions of Americans.

Folk music's popularity started to increase geometrically. Coffee
houses began featuring folk entertainers; *Sing Out!*'s subscription list
expanded from 500 in 1951 to 25,000 in 1965; other popularly successful vocal groups followed the Weavers—The Tarriers, the Gateway
Singers and, of course, the group that really made the "big time"—
the Kingston Trio. The appearance of television's *Hootenany* symbolized
folk music's long-in-the-making arrival as a really hot commercial commodity.

But at this point, the folk-revival movement was no longer in the
hands of the musicians. Rather, it was now a huge, sprawling phenomenon whose existence was intimately woven into the world of promoters,
agents, and Madison Avenue. The main thrust of the folk musician's
role in the historical development of a cultural phenomenon was over.

The Role of Progressive Social Movements

For several reasons, the part played by progressive social movements in bringing about a popular interest in folk music is most
difficult to assess. For one thing, when a particular political goal
is attained, the goal itself, as well as the topical songs it generated,
often have an antiquated quality about them. Workers today need
little prodding to join a labor union; and rarely, if ever, in the process,
do they sing union songs. Yet the labor movement, and other progressive or liberal social and political movements of the thirties and forties,
had much to do with the persistence of the folksong and the folk movement.

The contributions of various progressive ventures to the popularization of American folk music may be said to have begun at the turn of the century with the "one big union" movement.[9] In 1905, The Industrial Workers of the World (IWW) was founded. The Wobblies, as they were sometimes called, were never really successful, attaining a maximum membership of only 100,000 in 1910,[10] but in terms of a people's music (contemporary, topical folk music), the I.W.W. proved to be highly significant. In 1906, during a Seattle membership campaign, the Wobblies decided to become a singing labor movement.[11] They soon published one of the most interesting songbooks of the century, *Songs of the Workers*, subtitled *To Fan the Flames of Discontent*. (As of April, 1968, the book was in its thirty-second edition.) It contained a variety of songs to be used at union meetings, rallies, and the like. Singing meetings became characteristic of the Wobblies, who besides introducing many workers to "people's music," set a significant precedent for future usage of such material by other socially progressive groups.

A second period may be defined as covering the mid-1930's to World War II. Basically, contemporary political and economic issues revolved around the organized labor question; and it was at this time that the Congress of Industrial Organizations (CIO) was formed by John L. Lewis. The CIO was, in part, a reaction by liberal and radical labor leaders against the more staid AFL. As Irving Howe and Lester Coser suggest, organizing for the CIO was a dangerous business, and one of the few groups willing to carry out the risk was the socially progressive American Communist Party.[12] At this point in American history, many were claiming that Communism was "twentieth century Americanism." Indeed, it was a curious twist of the cultural introspection of the 1930's, that many of those who voiced the greatest concern for political principles which were avowedly American, looked at the nation, as Harvey Swados suggests, through red-tinted glasses.[13]

At any rate, whatever the political background, the outlook for labor was militantly progressive. The virtues of folksong for labor organizing and political ends were expounded; union men went back to the Wobblies for inspiration; and the Party men updated Worker's Music League Theory.[14] The movement was not fully convinced, however, until the "premature anti-Fascists," who had gone off to fight in the Spanish Civil War, returned from the conflict with their collection of topical songs. These new-found heroes of the American left made the use of folk song fully respectable.

As R. Serge Denisoff points out, the progressive labor movement swelled and enlisted the talents of members of the folk community (Aunt Molly Jackson, Leadbelly, Woody Guthrie) and "ideological" folk as well (Pete Seeger, Burl Ives, and the Lomaxes).[15] Led by the Almanac Singers, the movement used folk song for ideological purposes, and introduced it to millions of Americans at union meetings, rallies, and picket lines.

From 1945 to the early fifties, the folk music revival was led by many of the same individuals and groups who had been active in the pre-war period. It was their hope that a singing labor movement would help set off a national folksong revival. They banded together and formed a group called People's Artists, and published the monthly *People's Songs Bulletin*. People's Artists supplied songs for every important liberal movement in the country including civil rights, union organization, and the 1948 Wallace-For-President Movement. The pages of *People's Songs*, which was published from 1946 to 1948, and of *Sing Out!*, which began in 1950 and was a People's Artists publication for several years, abound in notices of the appearance of musicians at various types of progressive political and social gatherings.

Through People's Artists, larger audiences were introduced to folk and folk-type music than would ever otherwise have heard it. This process, in fact, is indicative of the part played by all progressive movements in the popularization of folk music. In general, these movements provided situations, audiences, and capital for the expanding idiom. As Charles C. Alexander has pointed out, "it is easy to exaggerate the importance of political radicalism" in cultural expression.[16] What is important for folk music's *popularization* is not so much the ideology of the particular organization which used it, but rather, that through their resources and sponsorship, thousands of people heard it who never had before. Ultimately, it was this vast new audience that would support the New York concerts of the late 1940's, and who would buy the commercial folk recordings which were to be released by the millions after 1950.

Epilogue

During the "revival" years the popularity of folk materials expanded phenomenally, folklore departments opened in colleges and universities, new folksong publications appeared, and musicians found themselves in demand for performances. Untapped sources of materials were uncovered, new technical devices tested and adopted, and progressive movements began to use folk materials in new and expansive ways.

The revival introduced folk music into new areas and to new audiences, so many that a whole set of studies are needed to survey the field adequately. Needed are surveys of the role of technological improvements in recording methods and their contributions to the revival, of the relationship of photographic studies to folk music, of the growth of folk festivals, of the influence of the folk music revival on the handicrafts revival, of the expansion of the musical instrument manufacturing industry, and of countless other aspects of the period are not only possible, but available to interested scholars, professional and non-professional. In one very real sense, what happens depends, as Jan Brunvand has suggested, on the favorable attitude of the popular culture researcher and the academic market.[17] Studies of the folk revival thus far have been few. Whether more are done—by folklorists of musicologists, or by social, cultural, and intellectual historians, or by the new researchers in popular culture—the folk revival must be studied and assessed while it and its materials are still fresh in our minds. It is already five years since it began to wane; the phenomena of popular culture, always ephemeral in nature, have a way of getting lost in history. It would be unfortunate if the scholars of the twenty-first century, in reconstructing the facts and meaning of this late twentieth-century cultural movement, would find it an antiquarian project like nineteenth century hymn metrics or New York Pinkster holidays.

NOTES

[1] Robert Spiller, *et al.*, ed., *Literary History of the United States: History*, New York, 1963, 703.

[2] Richard Dorson, *American Folklore*, Chicago, 1959.

[3] Oscar Brand, *The Ballad Mongers*, New York, 1962, especially chapter 5, "Setting the Stage."

4Harvey Swados, *The American Writer and the Great Depression*, New York, 1966, xv.

5Charles C. Alexander, *Nationalism in American Thought 1930-1945*, Chicago, 1969, xi. For an extended discussion of this point see Swados, xv-xxxiv, and Harold Stearns, *America Now*, New York, 1938, vii-x.

6Chief among these were Tristram P. Coffin, *The British Traditional Ballad in North America* (1950); G. Malcolm Laws, *Native American Balladry* (1950), and *American Balladry from British Broadsides* (1957); and Donald K. Wilgus, *Anglo-American Folksong Scholarship Since 1898* (1959).

7John A. and Alan Lomax, *Folk Song U.S.A.*, New York, 1947, v.

8See Swados, xxix. For a discussion of art and architecture in this period, see Alexander, 60-75. Note especially the compiling of the *Index of American Design* which contained 20,000 plates of American art, crafts and architecture.

9The period demarcation here utilized is basically that suggested in the sociological analysis of propaganda songs, R. Serge Denisoff, "Protest Movements: Class Consciousness and the Propaganda Song," *Sociological Quarterly* (1968), see especially 231-233.

10Denisoff, 231.

11For particulars, see John Greenway, *American Folksongs of Protest*, New York, 1960, 174.

12Irving Howe and Lester Coser, *The American Communist Party: A Critical History*, Boston, 1957, 371.

13Swados, xxxi.

14For a discussion of the Communist Party's use of music see R. Serge Denisoff, "Urban Folk 'Movement' Research: Value Free?" *Western Folklore*, vol. xxviii, no. 3 (July, 1969), especially 192-193.

15*Ibid.*, 194.

16Alexander, 49.

17Jan Harold Brunvand, *The Study of American Folklore*, New York, 1968, 144.

TRAVIS McGEE: THE THINKING MAN'S ROBIN HOOD

Etta C. Abrahams

If one were to evaluate popularity by number of copies sold and number of pages written, John D. MacDonald would certainly be considered a popular writer. His first story, "Interlude in India," appeared in *Story Magazine* in 1946. Since that time twenty-five years ago, he has written and published nearly a thousand short stories. He has been a frequent contributor to a wide range of magazines, including *Argosy, Astounding Science Fiction, Black Mask, Collier's, Cosmopolitan, Detective Story Magazine, Detective Fiction, Detective Book, Dime Detective, Detective Tales, Ellery Queen's Mystery Magazine, Esquire* and even *Good Housekeeping.*

In addition to the stories, MacDonald has written at least fifty-eight novels, eleven of which are in the Travis McGee series.[1] These novels have been translated into Danish, Norwegian, Swedish, Dutch, French, German, Hebrew, Italian, Spanish, Portuguese, and Japanese. They have also been reprinted in Great Britain. Fawcett Publications, the publishers of the Travis McGee Series, estimates MacDonald's McGee sales alone at over seven million in the United States, and predicts that these sales will increase to ten million within the next two years.

What are the reasons for the popularity of Travis McGee, aside from the obvious fact that MacDonald is a prolific writer? What is there about McGee that has produced at least two fan magazines (one in France) and an extensive, forty-one page bibliography? And what is there about the character of Travis McGee that has attracted so many millions of readers?

A partial answer to these questions can be found in Fawcett's

marketing approach. Each novel in the series contains a color in the
title, and the color is represented on the jacket. Thus, in *Dress Her in
Indigo*, the main color is, indeed, indigo, and so is the middle initial of
the author's name ("D" is in indigo), as well as the borders surrounding
both the title and the sketch of McGee. Furthermore, there is an indigo-
clad (although only partially clad) female on the cover. There is *always*
a sexy woman on the cover.

The titles and cover designs of the novels have virtually little to do
with the novels themselves. For example, the cover of *The Girl in the
Plain Brown Wrapper* depicts a raven-haired sexpot clad only in a brown
paper bag; in the text of the novel, however, the plain brown wrapper
refers to the wrapping in which McGee hides the mangled corpse of
a twenty-four year old blonde victim. Yet these covers do serve their
purpose. They are, first of all, a means of identification for the buyer,
who knows that he may have read "orange" but has not yet read "gray";
the partially-disrobed female obviously serves another purpose in attracting readers to the novel. And once the novel is read, it is indeed fulfilling to note that MacDonald matches a line in the novel with the title:
"And I watched the gray appear. Gray for fright. Gray for guilt. Gray
for despair." (p. 183, *Pale Gray for Guilt*)

However, McGee himself is the main reason for MacDonald's
success with the series; the reader wants to learn more about him, and
keeps reading the next novel to learn. Although there are many ways
to explore Travis McGee (for example, McGee as the Hemingway tough
guy, or as Hemingway man; McGee as descendant of Hammet's "hard-
boiled dick"), I have chosen to focus on MacDonald's concept of McGee
in the context of the series itself, dealing with (1) McGee as hero; (2)
McGee as lay philosopher and social critic; (3) the villain in the Travis
McGee series; (4) McGee's women; and (5) McGee and violence.

Unlike earlier detectives, McGee is not a detective in the "hard-
boiled" sense. His profession is not that of the aging, nameless, gun-
slinging hero of Dashiel Hammet's *Red Harvest*; nor is he sex-driven
Shell Scott, the hard-boiled dick in Richard S. Prather's series; nor is
he Mickey Spillane's animal-reflex Mike Hammer or Tiger Mann;
nor the cynical, hard-nosed professional, ex-G.I. Lew Archer, Ross Mac-
Donald's private eye. He is, rather, a composite of these, and more. He
is, first of all, quite human; his philosophy is more complex than that of
any of the others, although his escapes are similar—gin, women, music,
his boat, his car. Like the others, he is basically a loner, but unlike them,

he is a subjective commentator on modern society, a social critic of the times. What makes Travis McGee a hard-boiled detective are the strengths he shares with the other heroes—what makes him popular are the weaknesses he shares with Everyman. He is, for example, capable of making mistakes and of feeling guilty, of feeling pity for weaker men and women, of falling in love and losing, of getting hurt and living with pain, of going flabby and having to get into shape. These are things everyone can identify with: you too can slay dragons.

The plot of a McGee novel is relatively standardized. It opens with McGee, a wreck-salvager by vocation, relaxing on board his 52 foot barge-type houseboat, "The Busted Flush" (which he won in a poker game), moored at Bahia Pier in Fort Lauderdale. An old friend, or a friend of a friend, or a friend who has a friend, seeks his help to rectify a crime already committed. Often the crime is not one that could be called illegal; it is generally legal swindling involving large sums of money, or jewels, or an inheritance. McGee agrees to help; he's a sucker and can't refuse—yet he always makes a deal to collect for himself fifty percent of whatever is recovered.

The rest of the novel is concerned with getting back the money, through an elaborate swindling scheme similar to the one originally committed, except in reverse. During the recovery, several sadistic murders occur, or are uncovered; at least one brutal rape is performed and avenged; and the major villain (the one who has usually committed the brutal rape) meets justice.

In the process of righting wrongs, McGee is a keen observer of modern society, and he often takes time to give the reader his opinions —opinions which the reader must trust and believe in as valid because (1) Travis McGee is a man of experience, he thinks usually more or less what the reader is likely to think, and (2) in expressing this McGee offends nobody except the wrongdoer. Thus, McGee on modern music:

Of course it is music, styled to accompany teen-age fertility rites, and thus is as far out of my range as "Rockabye Baby." FM radio was a great product when it was servicing a fringe area of the great American market. But it has turned into a commercial success, so they have denigrated the sound, and they have mickey-moused the stereo and you really have to search that dial to find something that isn't either folk hoke, rickiticky rock, or the saccharine they pump into elevators, bus stations and Howard Johnsons. (6, *Pale Gray for Guilt*)

On automobile manufacturers:

We hate our cars, Detroit. Those of us who can possibly get along without them do so very happily. For those of us who can't, if there were an alternative, they'd grab it in a minute. We buy them reluctantly and try to make them last, and they are not friendly machines anymore. They are expensive, murderous junk, and they manage to look glassily contemptuous of the people who own them. (15, *Pale Gray for Guilt*)

On a computerized society:

They yearn for security, but all they can have is what they make for themselves, chittering little flocks of them in the restaurants and stores, talking of style and adornment. . . . They have been taught that if you are sunny, cheery, sincere, group-adjusted, popular, the world is yours, including barbecue pits, charge plates, diaper service, percale sheets, friends for dinner, washer-dryer combinations, color slides of the kiddies on the home projector, and eternal whimsical romance—with crinkly smiles and Rock Hudson dialogue. (101-2, *The Deep Blue Good-By*)

On race relations:

And if the black man demands that Big Uncle take care of him in the style the hucksters render so desirable, then it's a sideways return to slavery. Whitey wants law and order, meaning a head-knocker like Alabama George. No black is going to grieve about some nice sweet dedicated unprejudiced liberal being yanked out of his Buick and beaten to death, because there have been a great many hard-working blacks beaten to death too. . . . And so, Mrs. Lorette Walker, no solutions for me or thee, not from your leaders be they passive or militant, nor from the politicians or the liberals or the head-knockers or the educators. No answer but time. (*The Girl in the Plain Brown Wrapper*, 153)

In addition to the above quotations, McGee is likely to comment on education, hippies, pollution, the System, or anything else that strikes him. In each of his comments there is an implicit, almost wistful longing for a better time that, perhaps, never existed—a time when man was not entangled in his society; a time before machines and computers and gray flannel suits and commuters; a time when you were on a first-name basis with everyone in town; a time when you could choose your friends and trust your fellow man.

McGee is the wish-fulfillment of all those who would wish to escape the problems, pains, and complexities of modern life. Because he has escaped. He can loaf on the Busted Flush, fish and keep her in trim, drive his vintage Rolls Royce, "Miss Agnes," when and where he wishes. He has neither family nor bills. He is attractive (six foot four and rangy, somewhere in his early thirties) and has all the voluptuous women he wants. He reads a lot (and often advises the reader what to read), likes to play chess, chooses his friends as he wishes.

Yet he also functions effectively in society when he needs to. He has money, enjoys traveling, knows how to dress for all occasions. He knows what wine goes with what course (although he prefers Plymouth Gin), and while he likes a good steak, he enjoys any good food. He has the best of both worlds and can operate well in each. His personal philosophy, implicit in every novel in the series, is best expressed in *Pale Gray for Guilt*:

> "What's wrong with folks lately, McGee?"
> "It's a mass movement against head-knocking, Sheriff."
> "What kind of a joke is that?"
> "All kinds of head-knocking. Commercial, artistic and religious. They're trying to say people should love people. It's never been a very popular product. Get too persistent and they nail you up on the timbers on a hill."
> He stared at me with indignation. "Are *you* one of *those*?"
> "I recognize the problem. That's all. But the hippies solve it by stopping the world and getting off. No solution, Sheriff. I don't seek solutions. That takes group effort. And every group effort in the world requiring more than two people is a foul-up, inevitably. So I just stand back of the foul lines and when something happens that doesn't get called by the referees, I sometimes get into the game for a couple of minutes." (M, 157)

When McGee enters the game, the villain has apparently already won; it is up to McGee to reverse the decision, and to replace things as they were. He faces, generally, three villains: the powerful mastermind, a weak sub-villain (a corrupt lawyer, for instance) and an animal. Before it's over McGee must defeat all three, by different but suitable methods. The mastermind (with one or two notable exceptions like Tom Pike in *The Girl in the Plain Brown Wrapper*, who serves as both master-mind and demented goon), usually socially well-placed, admired by his friends, is often, like McGee, a loner, a drop-out who lives the clean life of crime. He is clever and brilliant and earns McGee's grudging respect. McGee bargains with him and cajoles him; He cannot swindle him, but he can outwit him. The master-mind may end up a little poorer, but it doesn't really affect him or his life style. Both he and McGee adhere to the same code: Never give a sucker an even break. But his sucker is the man or woman who is McGee's client; McGee's sucker is the failed, weakling lawyer, who drinks a lot, sweats a lot, is nervous, inept, may have an unhappy marriage—the master-mind's tool, he is also the chink in the master-mind's armor. It is he McGee swindles and sometimes ruins; if he isn't too far gone he may recover, a sadder but wiser man. In *The Deep Blue Good-By*, for instance, there is an indication suggested that the man McGee has tortured by alternate scalding and freezing to get information may, after it is all over, change his ways and straighten out his messy life. More often than not, it is too late for salvation; in *Bright Orange for the Shroud* the weakling lawyer sleeps in a drunken stupor while his wife is raped, and then, while he still sleeps, is murdered by her. Not many of McGee's villain-pawns ever escape retribution.

The goon, or third villain, presents the only real physical danger McGee must confront—psychological games and swindles don't work with him, for he is too stupid, too brutal, or too insane. He must be dealt with physically, just as he has dealt physically with his victims. The goon-villain is easily identified by his sexual brutality, his insane laughter and/or grin, his animal-like physique, his senseless cruelty. His end is violent, and the way in which he meets it often coincides with the atrocities he has committed. In *Pale Gray for Guilt*, the villain has his head crushed by the wife of the man whose head he smashed in. In *The Girl in the Plain Brown Wrapper* Tom Pike dies a death of slow strangulation while McGee and the police watch; he has murdered his wife by slowly destroying her mind, and has mur-dered a girl McGee loved by stabbing her in the neck. In *The Deep Blue Good-By*, the grinning rapist-murderer meets death, caught in a ship's anchor:

I could not move or think or speak. The known world was gone, and in night-mare I fought something that could never be whipped. I could not take the light off him. He rolled again, and then I saw what it was. His throat was wedged in that space between the flukes of the Danforth, and the edges of the points were angled up behind the corners of his jaw, the tension spreading his jowls into that grin. (137)

In *Bright Orange for the Shroud* the man who has raped three women, murdered one, and caused the suicide of another jumps off the Busted Flush into shallow waters; quite fittingly he "burst himself and impaled himself" through the groin on a piece of rotting driftwood. *Dress Her in Indigo* contains the brutally-conceived "justifiable" death of all. Walter Rockland, the animal, has destroyed the daughter of a friend of McGee's sometime companion, Meyer. Not only has he sexually dehumanized her, but through the use of LSD and other drugs, he has both demented and addicted her. Furthermore, there is some evidence (although this is disproven in *her* case) that he murdered her. What better death then, for such an animal as Rockland than the following:

"Was he shot, or what?" Meyer asked.
"I don't think the question is material. I do not know everything that was done to him [Rockland]. But I think he was tapped on the head and then stripped, spread and wired in place and gagged. Then various things were done to him. The most impressive, perhaps, being a knife line drawn across the belly, then down the tops of the thighs, then across the thighs about six inches above the knees. Then the entire area thus outlined was carefully flayed, skinned like a grouper. I would guess that he was not blinded until a bit later on." (182)

If the animal-villain's punishment is terrifyingly barbaric, the reader also notes it is mild in comparison to the way he has treated his victims—generally women. The women in the Travis McGee series fall into four categories, although the types may overlap: variations on the whore with a heart of gold; the neurotic-intellectual, or sexually frustrated wealthy, cultured woman; the wholesome, stable, sometimes mysterious female capable of being loved and loving, whom McGee loses; the bitch-woman, nymphomaniac, or golddigger who delights in psychological emasculation. Each of these women appears in one form or another in every Travis McGee novel.

The first type is best exemplified by Chookie McCall, lithe, dark voluptuous night club dancer in love with the wrong man. In *Bright Orange for the Shroud* she begins by practicing sex for therapy and winds up falling in love with her patient and marrying him. She can cook, is passionate, enjoys life in general; McGee may sleep with her occasionally, but more frequently, although he wants her, he rejects her gently:

"If it's pure recreation, dear, without claims or agreements or deathless vows, I'm at your service. I like you. I like you a lot. I like you enough to keep from trying to fake you into anything, even though, at the moment, it's one hell of a temptation. But I think you would have to get too deeply involved in your own justifications because, as I said, you are a complex woman. And a strong woman. And I am no part of your future, not in any emotional way." (15)

When Chookie emerges from the bathtub some fifteen minutes later (where the above lecture had taken place) she thanks McGee "for being smarter about me than I am." (15)

Like this big-hearted whore, McGee may also use his body therapeutically, usually as a prelude to a cure for those women who, directly, or indirectly, have fallen prey to the animal-villain. Lois, for instance, of *The Deep Blue Good-By*, has been repeatedly raped and held prisoner by him; a wealthy New England gentlewoman by birth, she turns into a hysterical alcoholic. McGee, in nursing her back to health, sleeps with her and even falls in love with her. In the same novel, Cathy Kerr, who has put all her faith in "the illusion of love, magically changed to a memory of shame," (17) becomes Lois' replacement at the end of the novel. As a matter of fact, she becomes the "big-hearted whore" to McGee who is grief-stricken at Lois' death, and ends up as *his* physical therapist. And in *The Girl in the Plain Brown Wrapper*, the final scene shows McGee in bed with the wife of the lawyer-dupe, a woman who had given up on men and needs McGee to restore her respect for sex and masculinity.

But sometimes McGee comes too late for these women, as he does for Vivian Watts in *Bright Orange for the Shroud*, the wife of the dupe in the swindling scheme. She is an aristocrat, plays a perfect game of tennis, and is, on the surface, coldly aloof. Perfectly groomed and austerely polite, she calls up in men, comments McGee, the cry "I'd like to show her what it's really like—if only she would —and if only I could." The brute of the novel, Boone Waxwell, can and does, by raping her in her bedroom while her husband is sleeping. Shamed by her aroused response, she can only commit suicide. In the McGee series the women who are most often brutalized are, like her, austere, beautiful, intelligent and doomed. They are the seeming untouchables, and are often cruelly taken down a peg—or two— or more.

Amid all this frustration in the series, a good woman does exist —good, that is, by McGee's standards—and he can fall in love with red-headed Puss, in *Pale Gray for Guilt*. A girl of mysterious past and frequent disappearances, she suffers fits of depression and bursts of affection, but she will help McGee any way she can. What might have happened between them is lost, however, for at the end of the novel she reveals that she will soon die from cancer of the brain. Another is Helena Pearson who dies early in *The Girl in the Plain Brown Wrapper* (also of cancer), and a third is Lois of *The Deep Blue Good-By* who

McGee rehabilitates only to see her killed in the end by the grinning villain. Travis sheds tears to show that he is human, gets drunk, or goes on a long cruise, but the pain is always there, to be lived with, never really forgotten. They die to keep McGee free, and they reaffirm the reader's faith that even though there are too many "bad" women in the world, good ones (although perhaps not many) do exist.

Then there are the bitch women, the ones who wield the shears, often nymphomaniacs—sex without love, sex for money, empty sex. McGee either tricks them (for instance, he leaves a note for one of them who has pre-sexually passed out from alcohol, saying, "It was great."), cynically pairs them with someone else who is their equal, or rejects them bluntly, as in *Bright Orange for the Shroud*:

"Sweetie," I said, "You are a penny from heaven. And you probably know lots and lots of tricks. But every one would remind me that you are a pro, from Wilma's old stable of club fighters. Call me a sentimentalist. The bloom is too far off the rose, sweetie. I'd probably keep leaving money on the bureau. You'd better peddle it. Thanks, but no thanks." (190)

In *Dress Her in Indigo,* the most recent of the series, strays somewhat from the standard plot-line and characters of the preceding McGee novels, particularly in the women. There are the party type, cuddly one-nighters usually present at McGee's boat parties, but the girl McGee must find and rehabilitate is not a wealthy, cold, potentially passionate woman but a hippie in her late teens. His therapy is not sex, but a lecture, a bath, and two plane tickets home for herself and girlfriend. Nor is the nymphomaniac in the novel a bitch. True, she uses her men (including McGee) to their fullest capacity, but she wants nothing from them; although they suffer the wounds of the bed, they carry them like a red badge of courage for the rest of their lives. This woman is ageless (much like the heroine of Gertrude Atherton's *Black Oxen*) by reason of an operation that has kept her young. (An ironic note is her name: Lady Rebecca Divin-Harrison, reminiscent of Lady Brett Ashley, who also enters the scene in the company of homosexuals. One can only wonder how aware MacDonald was of Hemingway in creating the character.) Finally, the master-mind villain in this novel is a woman, and a lesbian to boot. She is very attractive, however, and of course, very frigid, so McGee deals with her by gagging her and wrapping her naked in a wet sheet.

Just as women and sex are essential to a Travis McGee novel, so is violence, deliberately and often frighteningly sadistic. It is not the bullet-through-the-heart type of violence found in the usual "hard boiled dick" novel, but rather a slow, torturing kind of violence. Both victims and villains die this way, and so do those innocents—cancer is not an easy out. Villains are strangled, are impaled on rotting wood, are slowly hanged, or have their genitals flayed while they still live. Victims are buried in swamps with a description of what they'd look like after the crocodiles got to them; they may also have their heads smashed, or are stabbed in the neck, or pushed out a window. The tortures in MacDonald's novels, too, although often psychological, hint at underlying sadism and violence. McGee, though reluctant, leans towards the uses of torture and in a way he too is a sadist. He admits to this streak in himself in *The Deep Blue Good-By*: "Maybe I was despising that part of myself that was labeled Junior Allen. . . . But pity, indignation and guilt are the things best left hidden from all the gay companions." (17) But McGee's violence and sadism is "justified." First of all, he is paying off someone more violent than himself. Second, violence and torture are ways to track down the villain. In *Bright Orange for the Shroud*, McGee ruins Vivian's carefully executed suicide. He carries her from her bathtub to her bed, smears the lipstick on her carefully made-up lips, destroys her beautifully written suicide note in which she confesses to murdering her husband, and rips her orange bathrobe, her "shroud," from her body. But all this is a plan to frame the real villain, Boone Waxwell, for her rape, her "murder," and her husband's murder. MacDonald makes it clear, over and over, however, that McGee does not like brutality and sadism; sometimes he vomits, and never does he enjoy it.

And, as MacDonald reminds the reader, the violence of his novels reflects, unfortunately, the fact America is a violent society, to be dealt with in kind. Even teenagers are shown to have violent sexual tendencies; the cars Americans drive are death-mobiles; the music of America is loud and violent. We are a country, McGee implies, that breeds violence, that breeds the Boone Waxwells, the Junior Allens, the Tom Pikes, the Walter Rocklands and—one must add—the Travis McGees.

Violence, sex, social commentary, the thinking observer and righter of wrongs, these form the essence of the Travis McGee series. The reasons for the popularity of John D. MacDonald's Robin Hood-detective may be inferred from this evidence. McGee gives his readers something to think about; he gives them opinions which reaffirm their own; he gives them sex in all its forms, natural and depraved; and he makes possible a temporary realization of the fantasies of those who wish they too could sleep with good-hearted Chookie or red-headed Puss, could beat up the ape-like Boone Waxwell, or get away from it all on his boat. MacDonald has something for Everyman and Every-woman in the Travis McGee series, and the success of his formula is reflected in its popular appeal.

NOTES

[1] These novels are *The Deep Blue Good-By* (1964); *Nightmare in Pink* (1964); *A Purple Place for Dying* (1964); *The Quick Red Fox* (1964); *A Deadly Shade of Gold* (1965); *Bright Orange for the Shroud* (1965); *Darker Than Amber* (1966); *One Fearful Yellow Eye* (1967); *Pale Gray for Guilt* (1968); *The Girl in the Plain Brown Wrapper* (1969); and *Dress Her in Indigo* (1969), all published by Fawcett Publications. Page numbers in parentheses refer to these editions.